# PORTRAIT OF THE NORTHERN ISLES

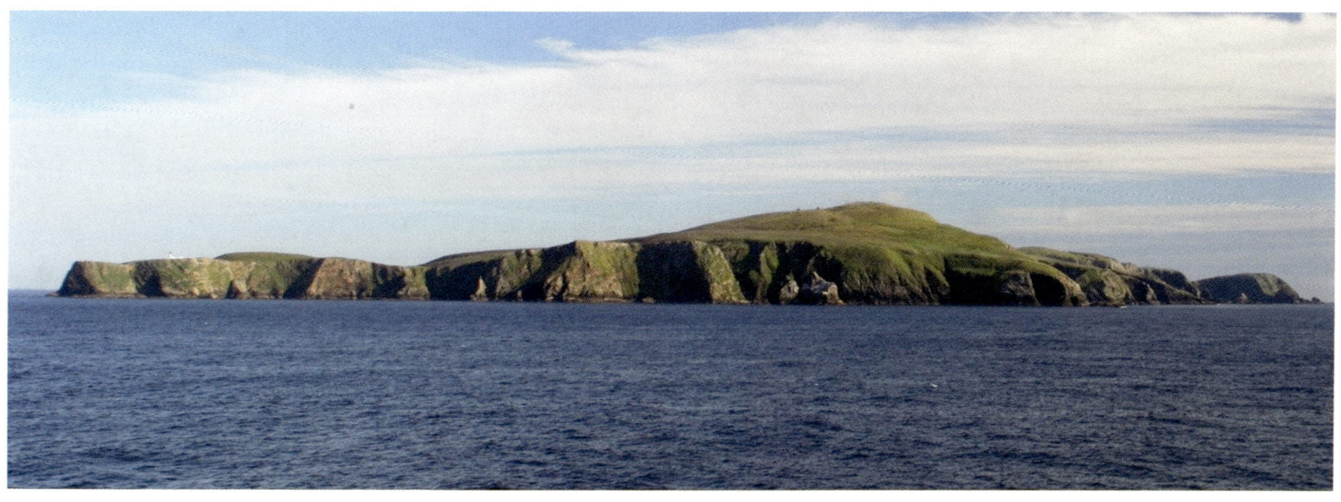

GRAHAM UNEY

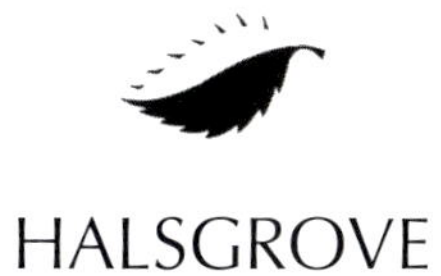

HALSGROVE

To Olivia, for being there on Orkney during my first visit,
and for making Shetland even more wonderful.

First published in Great Britain in 2009



Title page: Fair Isle, lying mid-way between Orkney and Shetland.



British Library Cataloguing-in-Publication Data
A CIP record for this title is available from the British Library

ISBN 978 1 84114 881 6

**HALSGROVE**
Halsgrove House,
Ryelands Industrial Estate,
Bagley Road, Wellington, Somerset TA21 9PZ
Tel: 01823 653777 Fax: 01823 216796
email: sales@halsgrove.com

Part of the Halsgrove group of companies
Information on all Halsgrove titles is available at: www.halsgrove.com

Printed and bound by Grafiche Flaminia, Italy

# INTRODUCTION

Scores of rough-edged islands dot the wild seas, like a careless scattering of beautiful jewels, far to the north of mainland Britain. Here, in Orkney and Shetland, a vividly diverse and brazenly stunning landscape awaits.

This, the Northern Isles, is where the adventurous traveller will discover some of Britain's most charismatic wildlife, or come to explore hidden secrets from our ancient past, all set in a broad landscape of magnificent coastal crags and voes, rolling moors of heather and bilberry, small-scale farmlands of rich flower-filled meadows, and Scandinavian-style towns and villages thronging the steep-sided fjords of countless sea-lochs.

Each isle within the Northern Isles is unique – each is very different from its neighbours both in terms of physical geography, and in character. Every single island within the Northern Isles group has something to offer, and this book hopes to introduce you to the magic of these beautiful yet harsh places.

There are obvious as well as subtle differences between the two main groups of islands here. Shetland lends itself to wild savagery, remote headlands, enormous sea cliffs teeming with birds, and barren moors of breathtaking beauty, while Orkney, at first glance at least, is more tamed, and gentler. Orkney's landscape rolls from out of the sea, over the traditionally farmed agricultural fields, and soft curves of the hill farmer's land. Both groups are essentially Viking lands, and the people from both feel culturally independent from Scotland. They are proud of their origins, and this is reflected in the many Old Norse names that dot the maps and road signs. There are few Gaelic names here, and most of those that have evolved into part of the mother tongue are to be found on Orkney.

Orkney lies just off the north coast of Scotland. Drive up through the Caithness Flows to John o' Groats, or to the rocky promontories of Durness Head and Duncansby Head and gaze northwards over the tumultuous waters of the Pentland Firth and you'll see Hoy, Swona, Stroma, and South Ronaldsay spread over the blue horizon. Mainland Orkney lies at the centre of the group of islands, and here, as on Shetland, when locals talk of Mainland, they mean the biggest island in their own group, rather than Scotland! Similarly, you should never call the people from these islands 'Scottish'. Those from Orkney are Orcadians, while those from Shetland are Shetlanders, and they don't mind telling you that either!

North of Orkney Mainland are yet more stunning islands. Westray and Papa Westray lie close together just beyond Rousay, Egilsay and Wyre, while eastwards the isles of Eday, Stronsay, and North Ronaldsay stud the sea.

Shetland is remote by anyone's reckoning. Way out north, far beyond Orkney, lies a little rocky bump, known as Fair Isle. This is the most southerly island of the Shetland group, then across the seas, and still to the north, a voyage will bring you to Mainland Shetland at Sumburgh Head. Mainland Shetland runs roughly north–south, and is elongated, with many fjords and inlets cutting into the coastline. Countless islands and skerries cluster around Mainland, from the most southerly at Fair Isle to the most northerly at Muckle Flugga beneath the Hermaness cliffs on Unst, and all are uniquely special places. Perhaps even more remote than Fair Isle is the lonely outpost of Foula, set way out in the North Atlantic west of Shetland. This book will introduce you to these fabulous places and more.

These islands have their own capitals too. Kirkwall is very much the main town of Orkney, while Lerwick is at the centre of life in Shetland. Stand in the streets of Lerwick and the next nearest city is Bergen in Norway! This gives you some idea of just how far north of Scotland Shetland is.

*Portrait of the Northern Isles* is a beautiful collection of photographs taken in all seasons within these wild island groups, introducing you to the savage landscape, the wildlife, and the proud but gentle people of Orkney and Shetland. Whether you intend to pay a visit to the Northern Isles yourself, or would rather long for the cold wind in your hair and the salt spray in your face from the comfort of your own armchair, this collection of images will help to inspire you.

# LOCATION MAP – Northern Isles

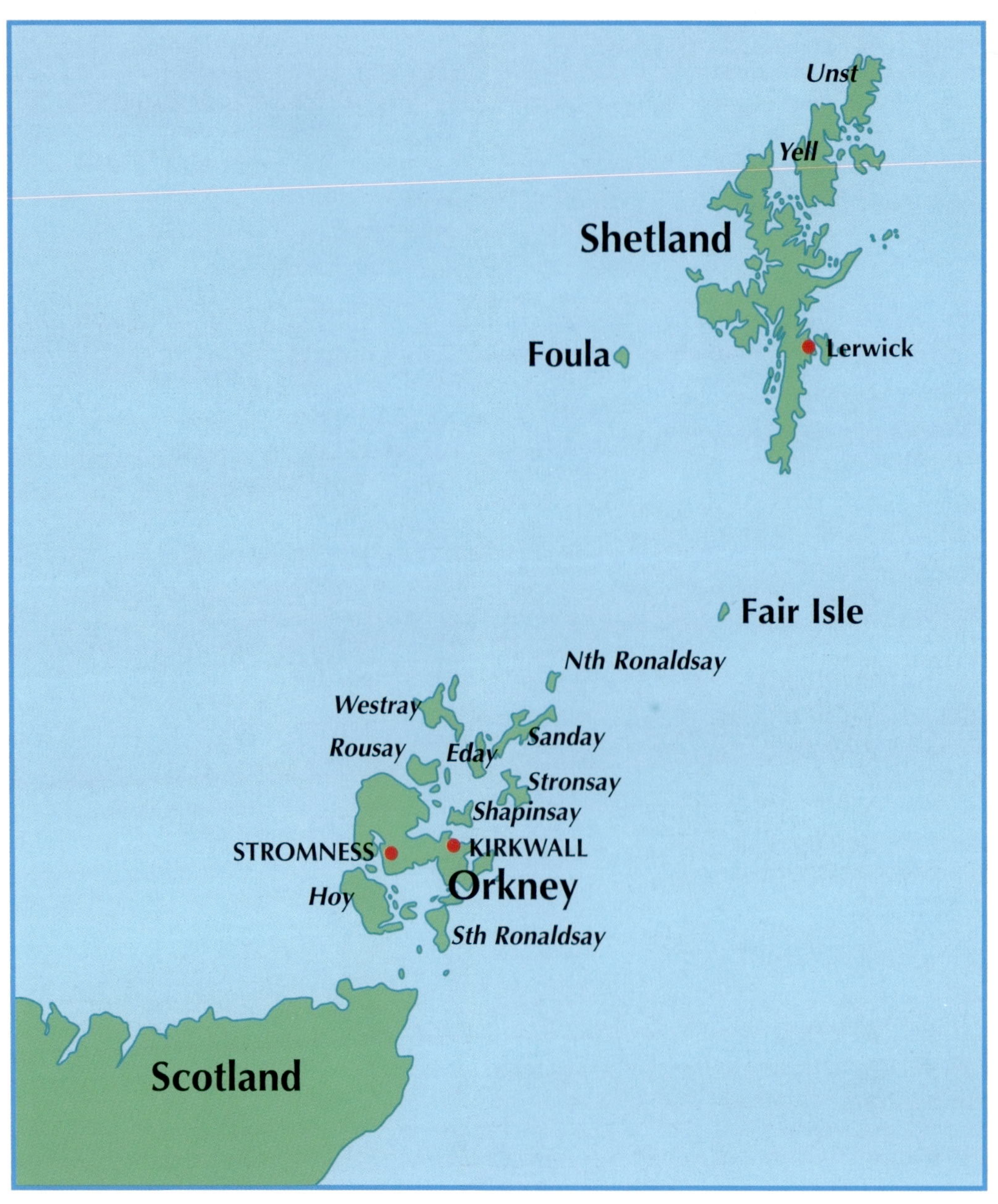

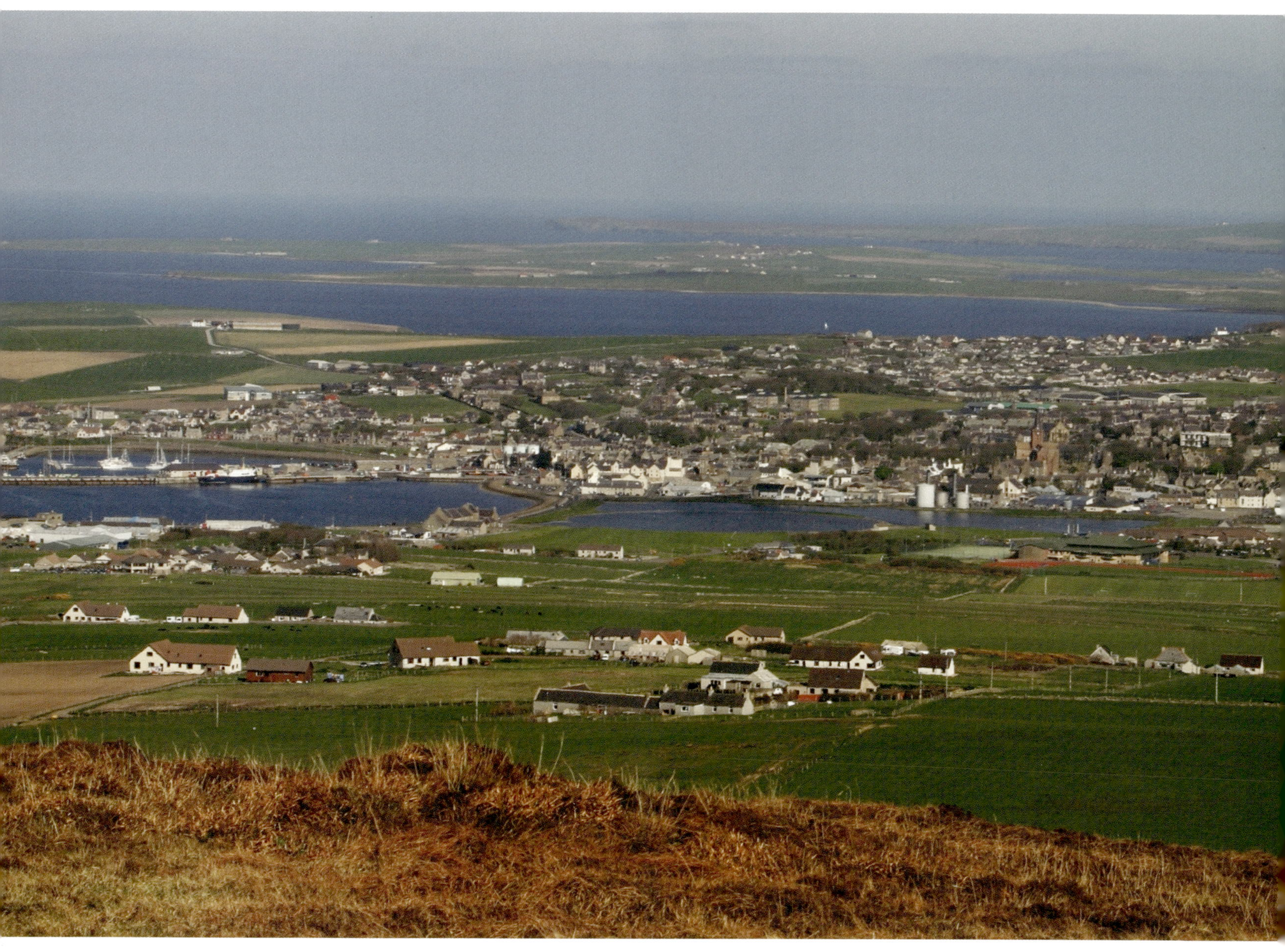

From the summit of Wideford Hill on Orkney, Kirkwall spreads out below, filling the shores around the bay.

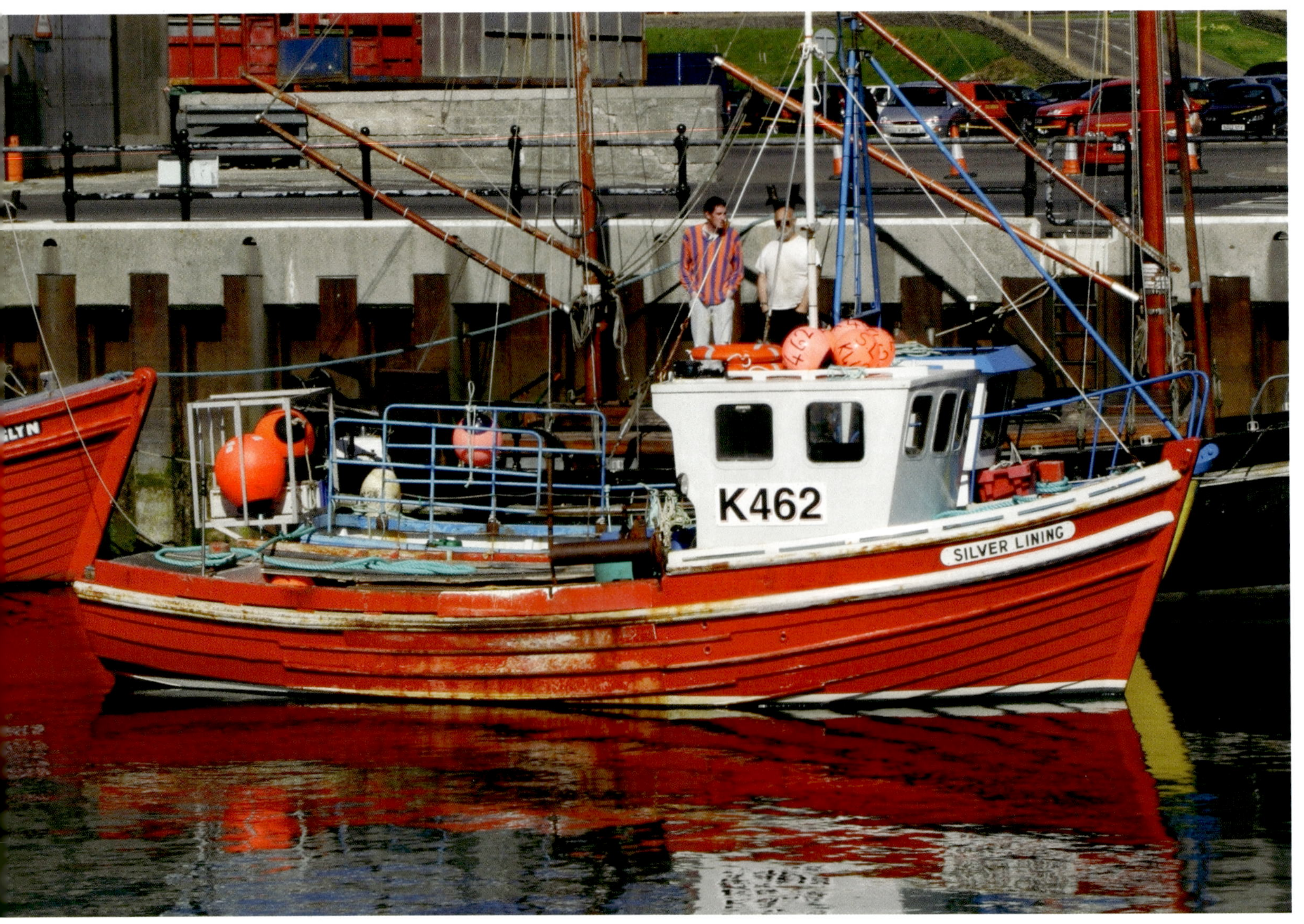


Fishing is still one of the chief industries on both Orkney and Shetland. Here the crew of a small boat prepare to head out to sea from Kirkwall. Kirkwall harbour is relatively busy with such boats, but Stromness, the second town of Orkney has the main fishing fleet.

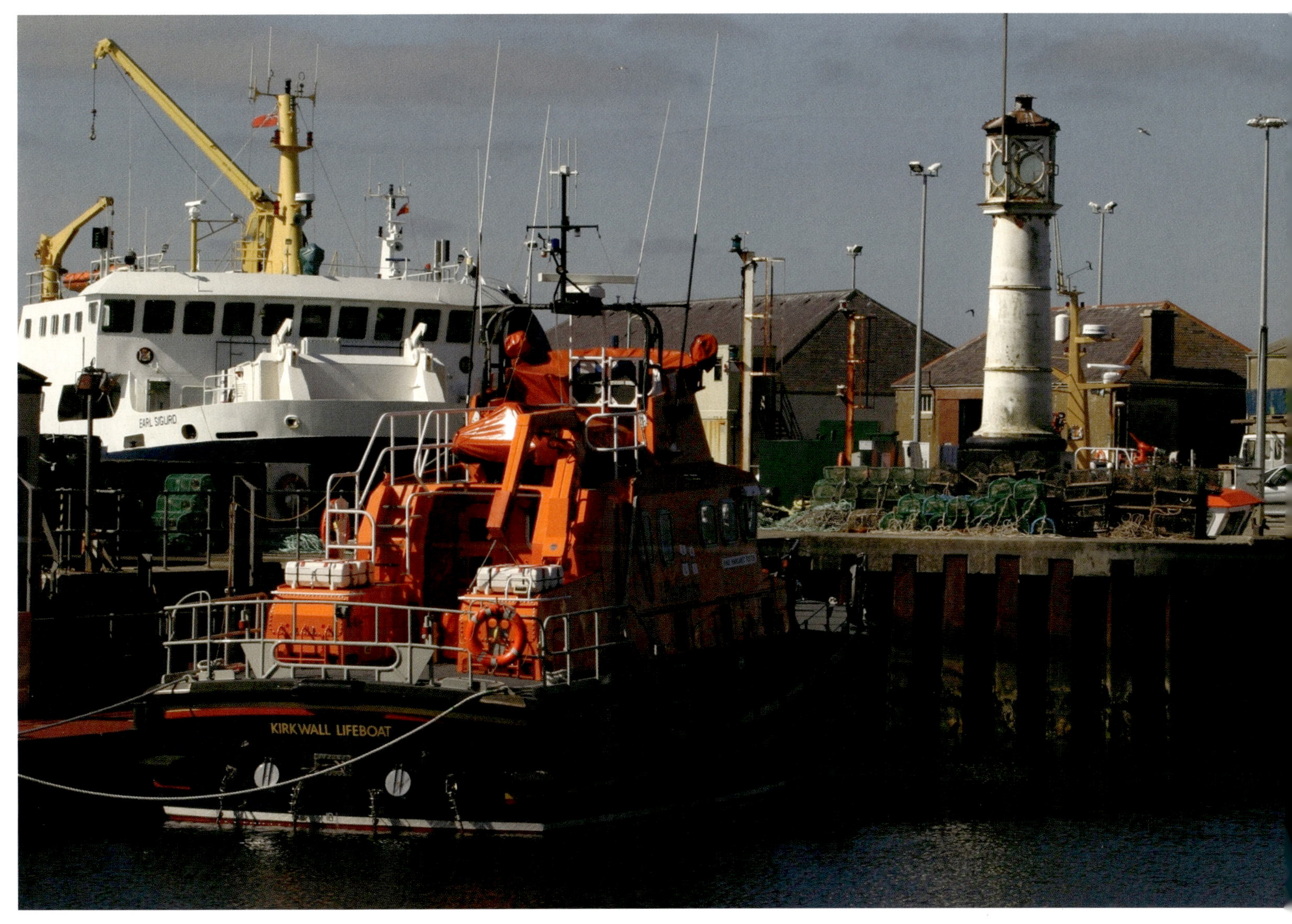


The Kirkwall Lifeboat at its moorings in the harbour.

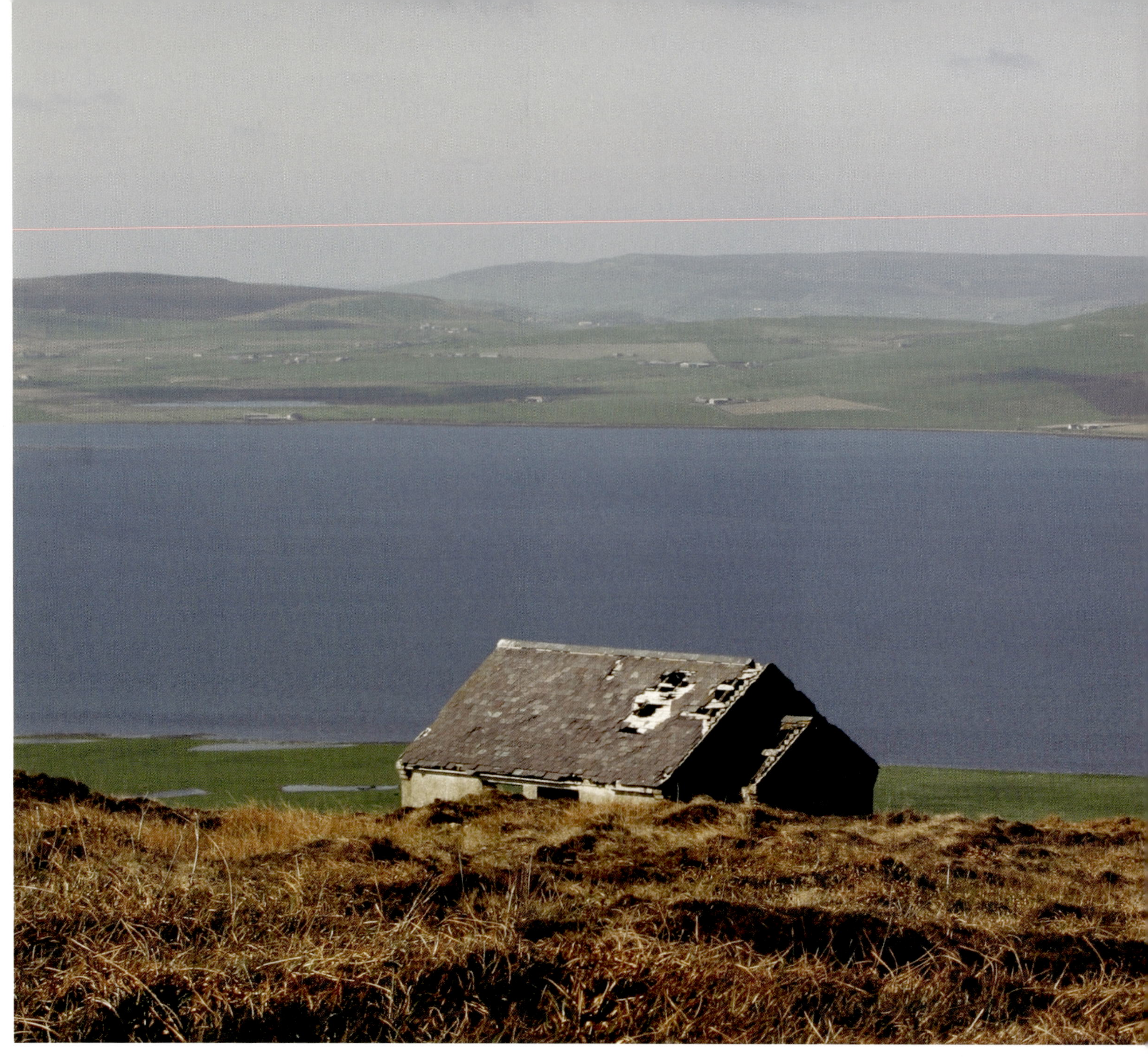

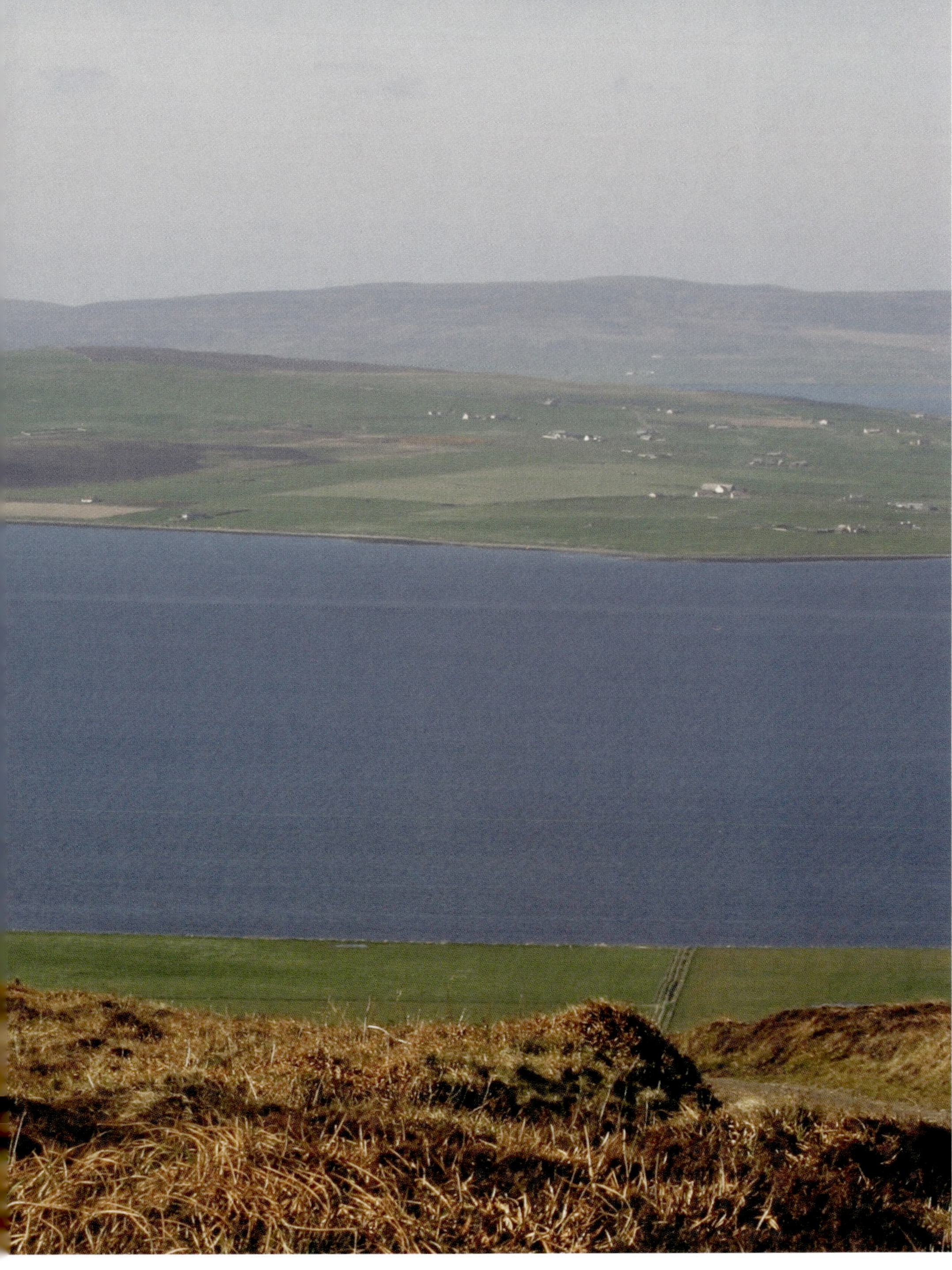

Wideford Hill is a prominent natural feature on Mainland Orkney. From its top the views northwards to the islands of Egilsay, Wyre, and Rousay are superb.

Scapa Flow lies to the south of Mainland Orkney. The British Home Fleet was based in Scapa Flow during the Second World War, from where it helped to protect the Arctic Convoys to Murmansk. On the night of 13 October 1939, the German U-Boat U-47 slipped between Mainland and Lamb Holm, squeezing by the sunken blockships that had been placed there during the Great War. Just after midnight the U-Boat commander, Lieutenant Gunther Prien sighted the HMS *Royal Oak*, and ordered torpedoes to be fired at the huge ship. Of the crew of 1400 men, 833 lost their lives that night. Following this event Churchill gave orders to have permanent concrete blocks put across the gaps between the islands around Scapa Flow, and these, the Churchill Barriers can still be seen today.

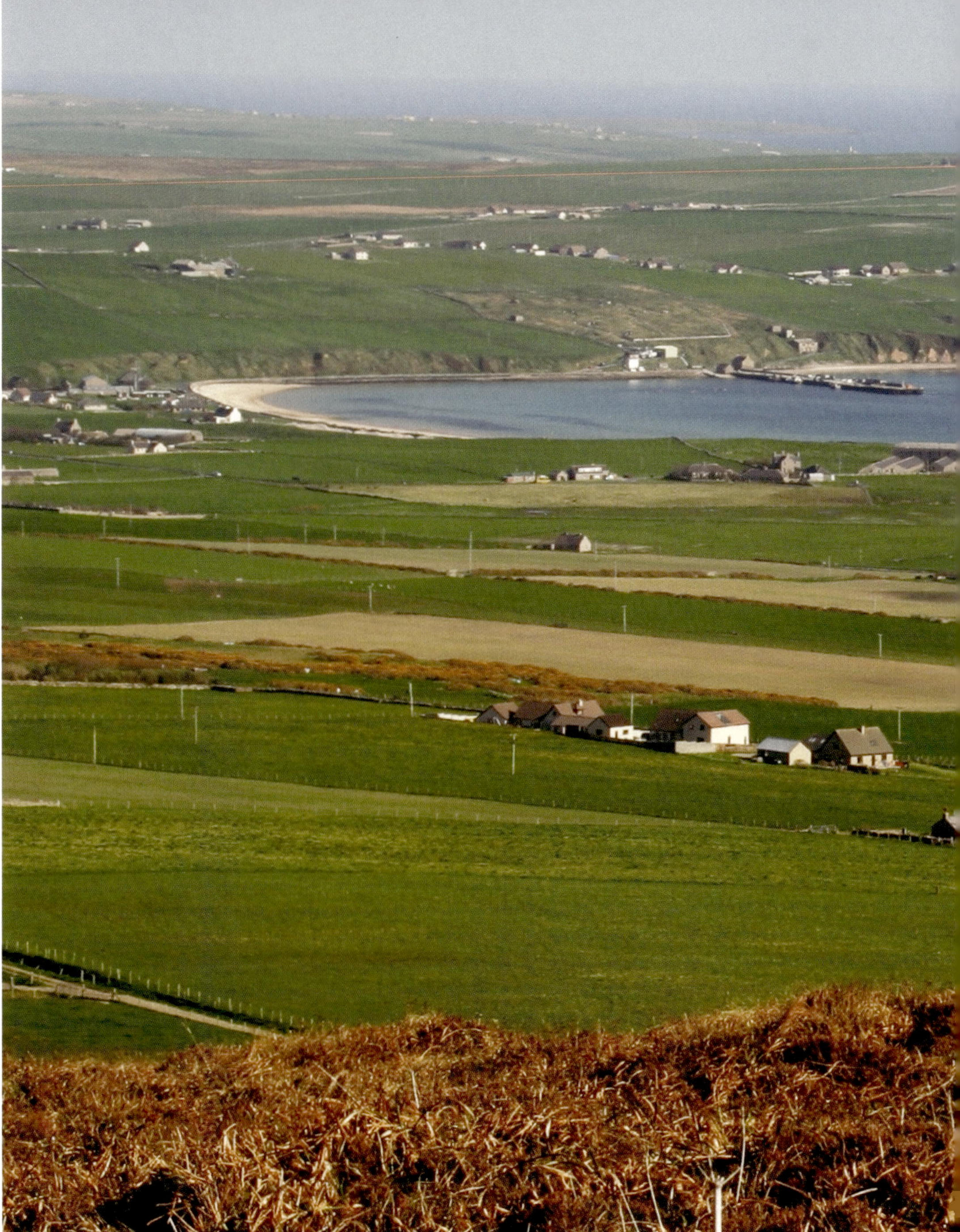

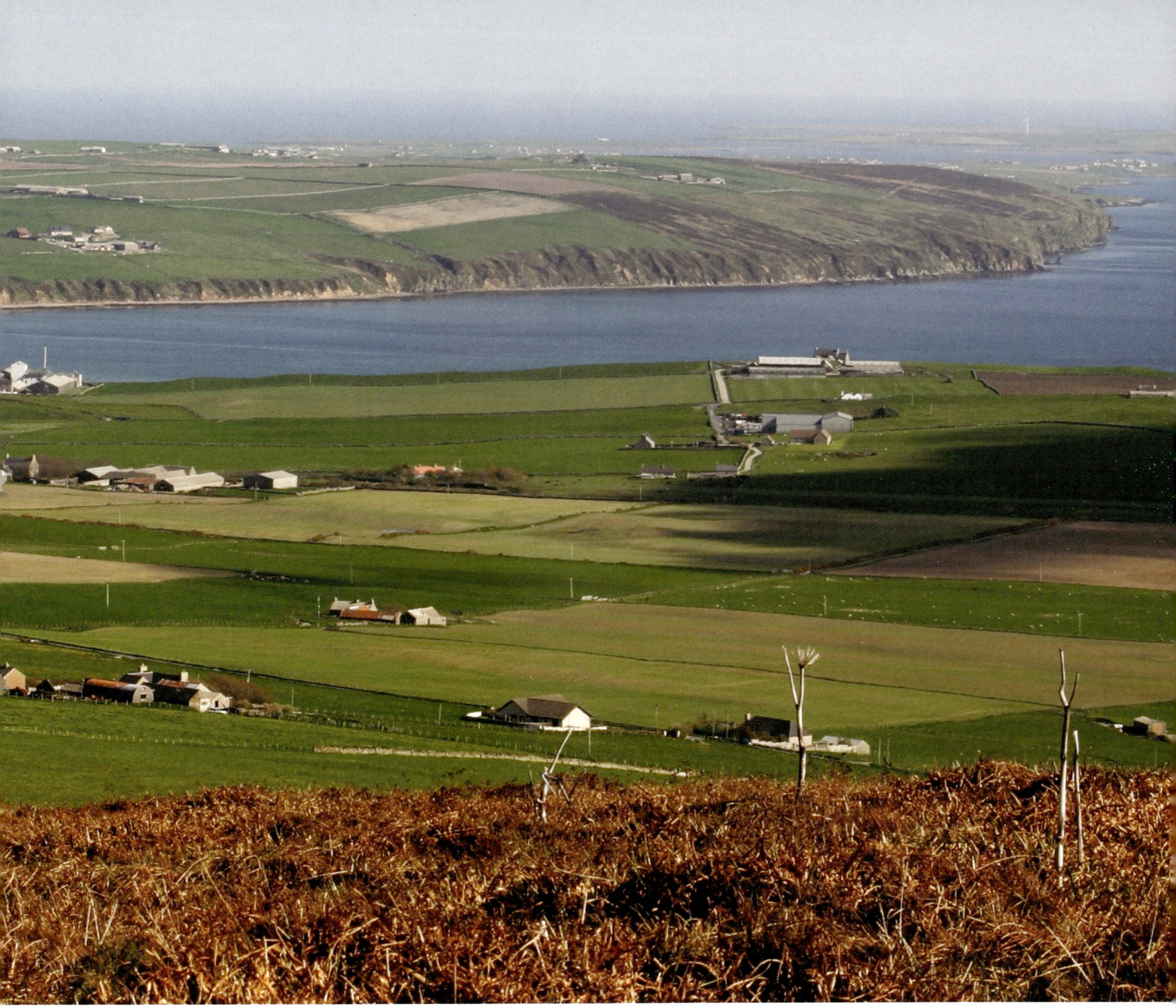

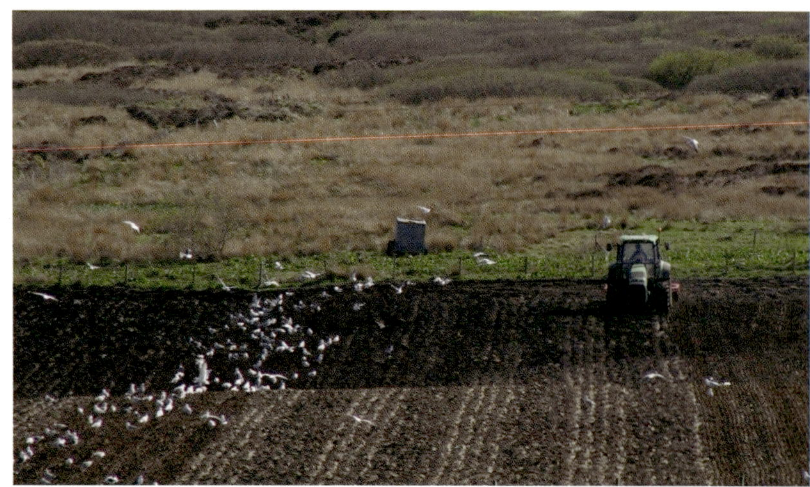

Farming on Orkney is still very much a part of the economy, and despite the harsh climate arable crops do well.

On Burger Hill there are a number of small wind turbines, providing power for the scattered villages of Birsay and further afield. Nestled in the woodlands below, themselves a rare thing on Orkney, lies the turreted house at Woodwick, now a superb country hotel and restaurant.

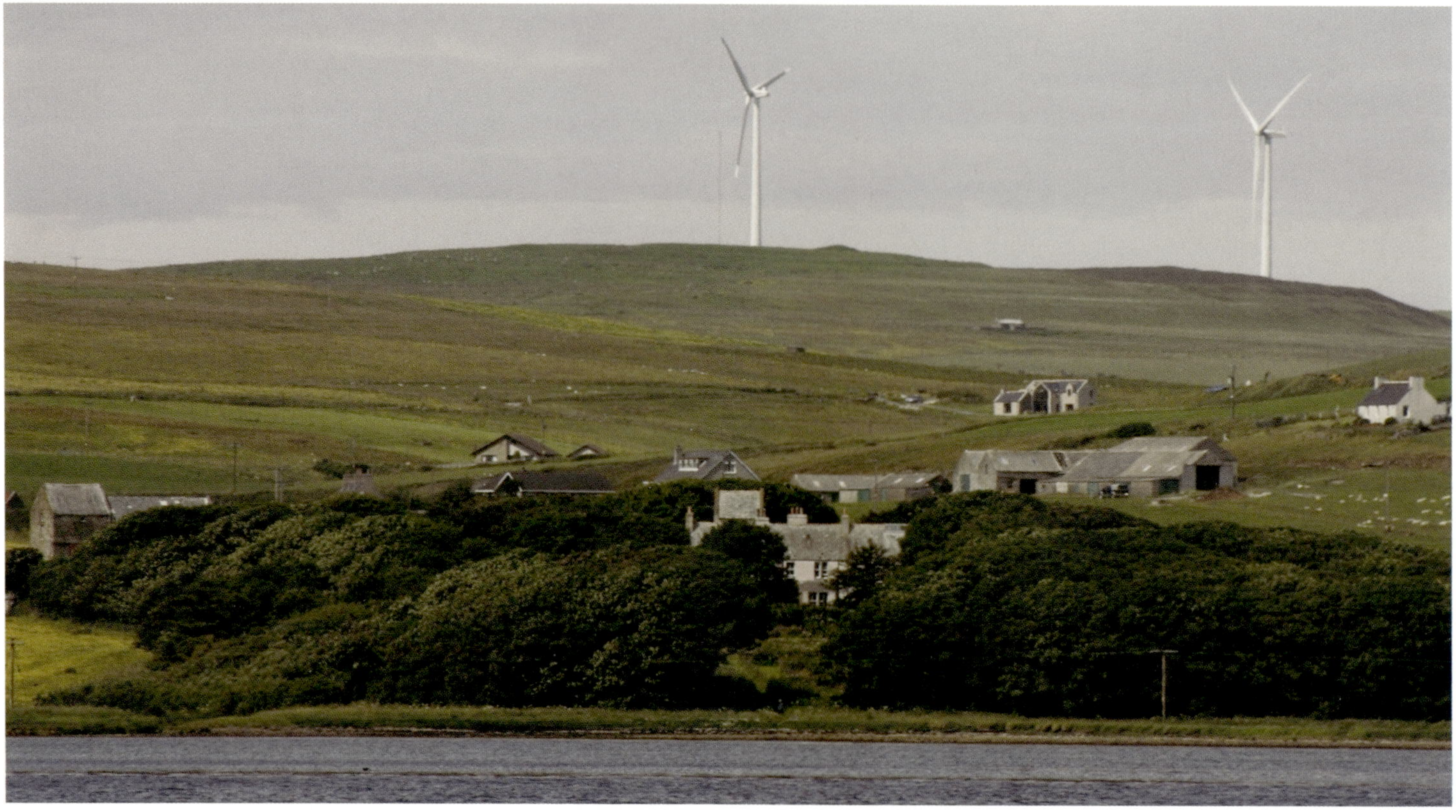

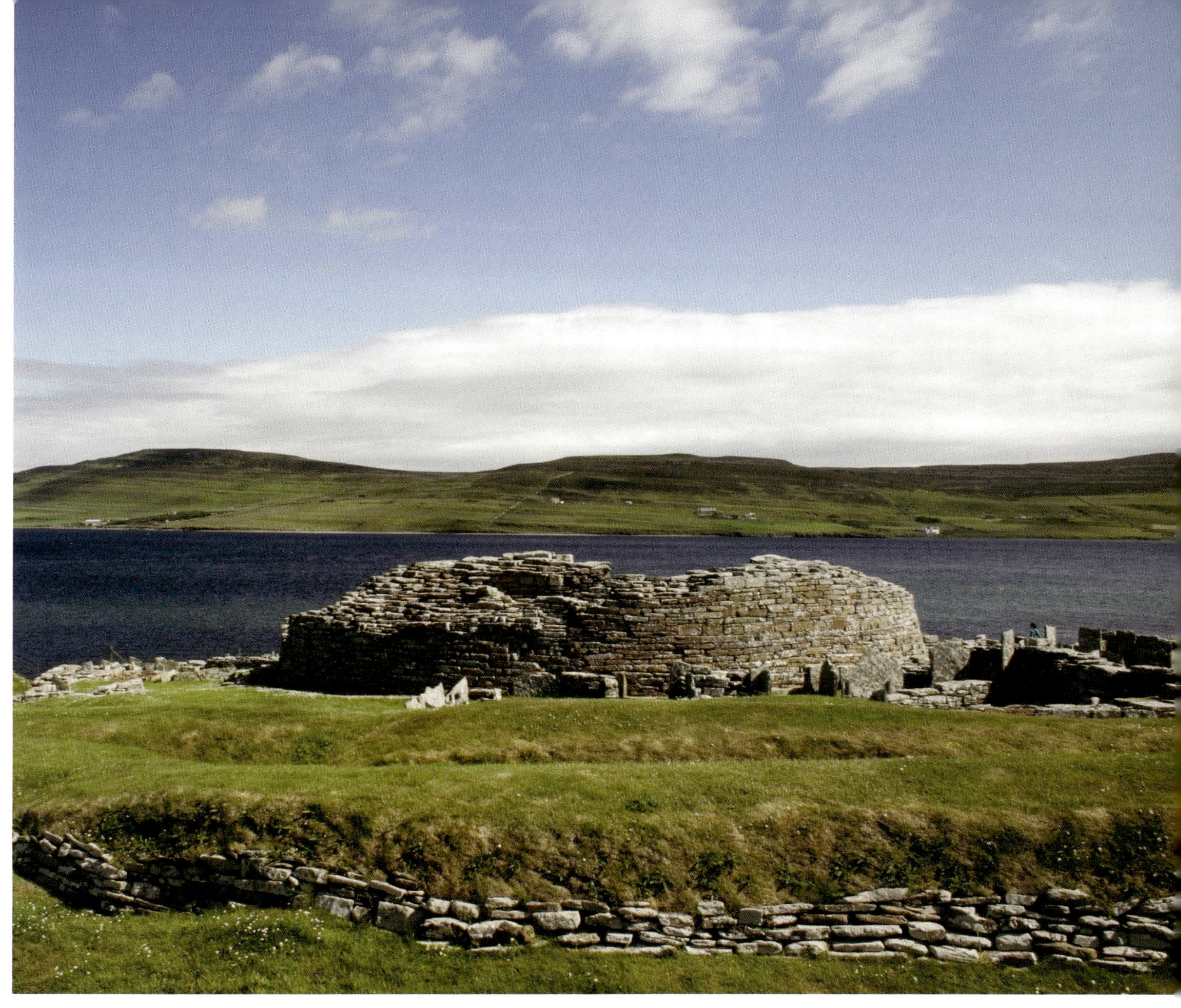

The Broch of Gurness is without a doubt one of the most outstanding Iron Age villages to be found in Scotland. The village here began around 500BC and is surrounded by impressive ditches and ramparts.

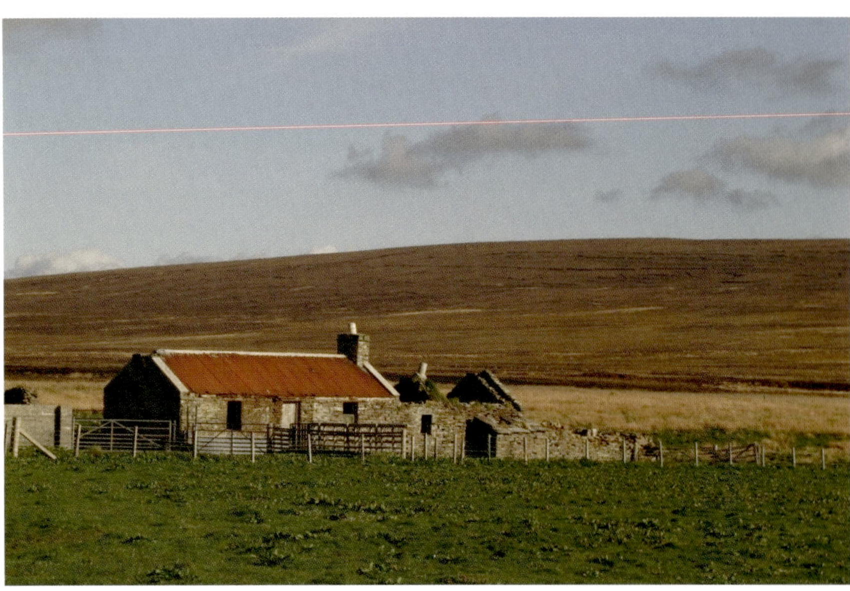

Further inland on the Birsay Moors, a lonely cottage at Millgeo stands on the edge of Little Billia Fiold.

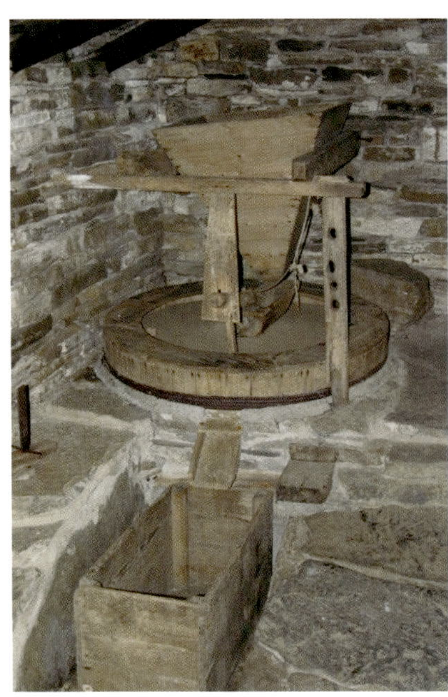

Beside Millgeo is the superb Click Mill. Click Mills were used throughout Orkney and Shetland, and also on Lewis in the Outer Hebrides. They are of Scandinavian origin, and are unusual in that the wheel is horizontal. This one near Dounby is in full working order.

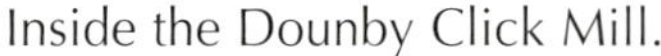

Inside the Dounby Click Mill.

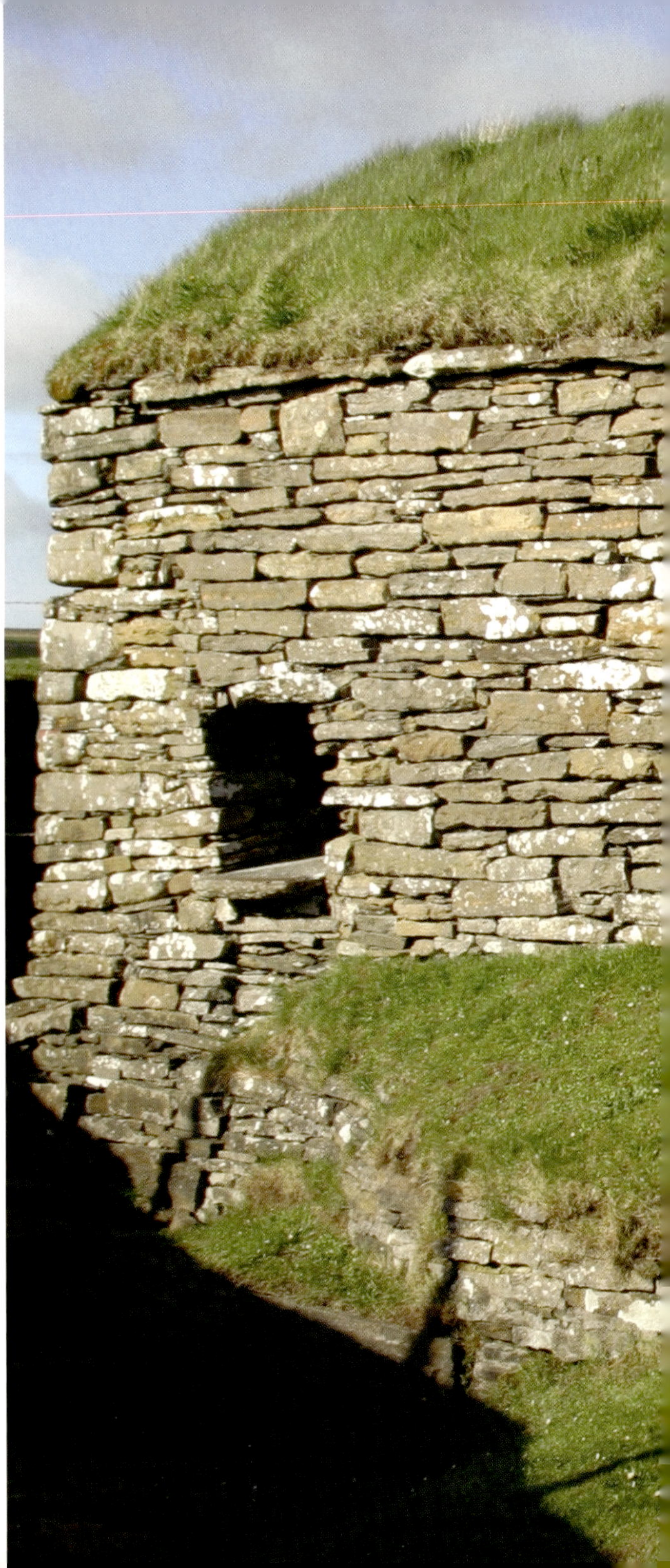

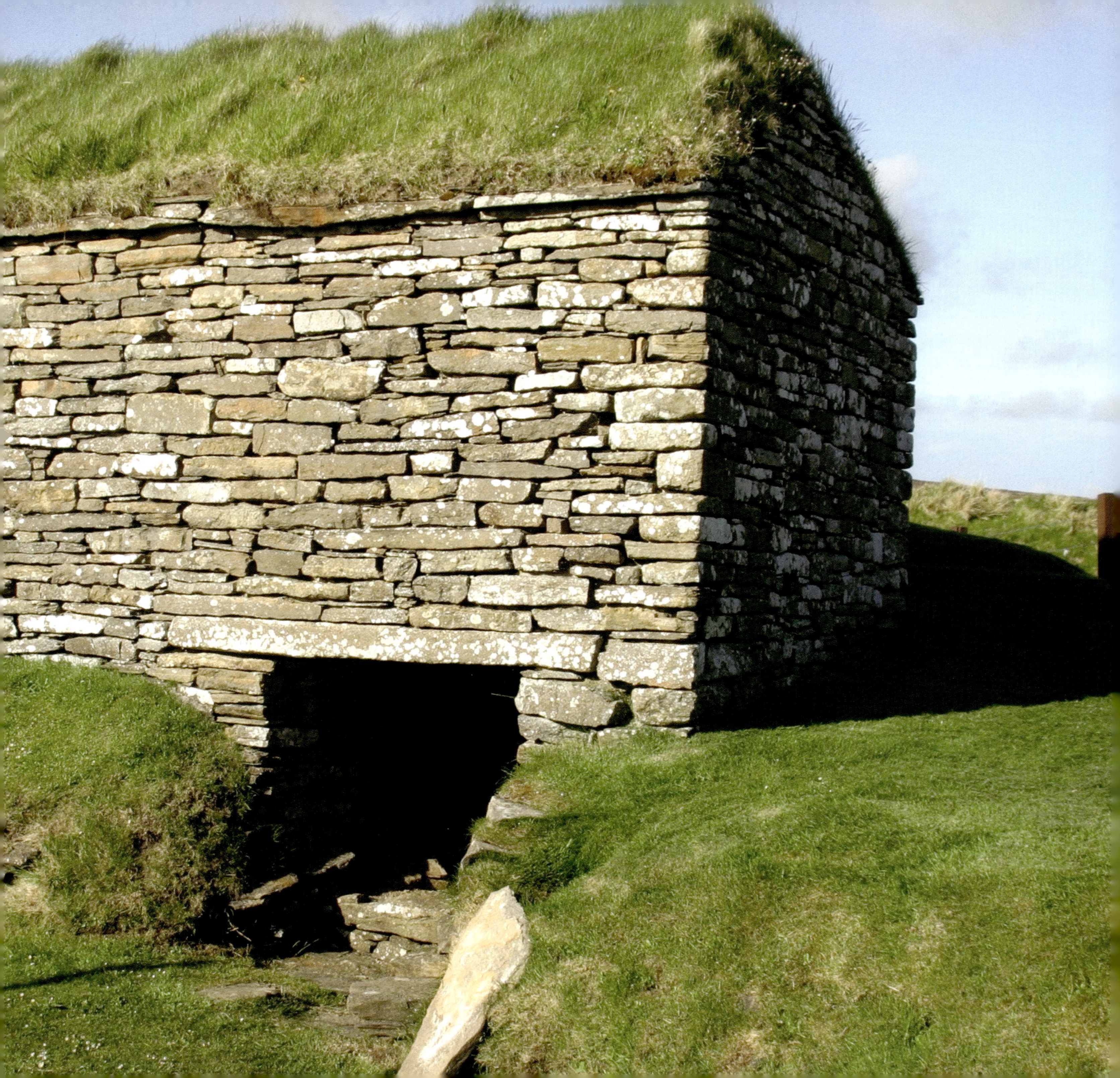

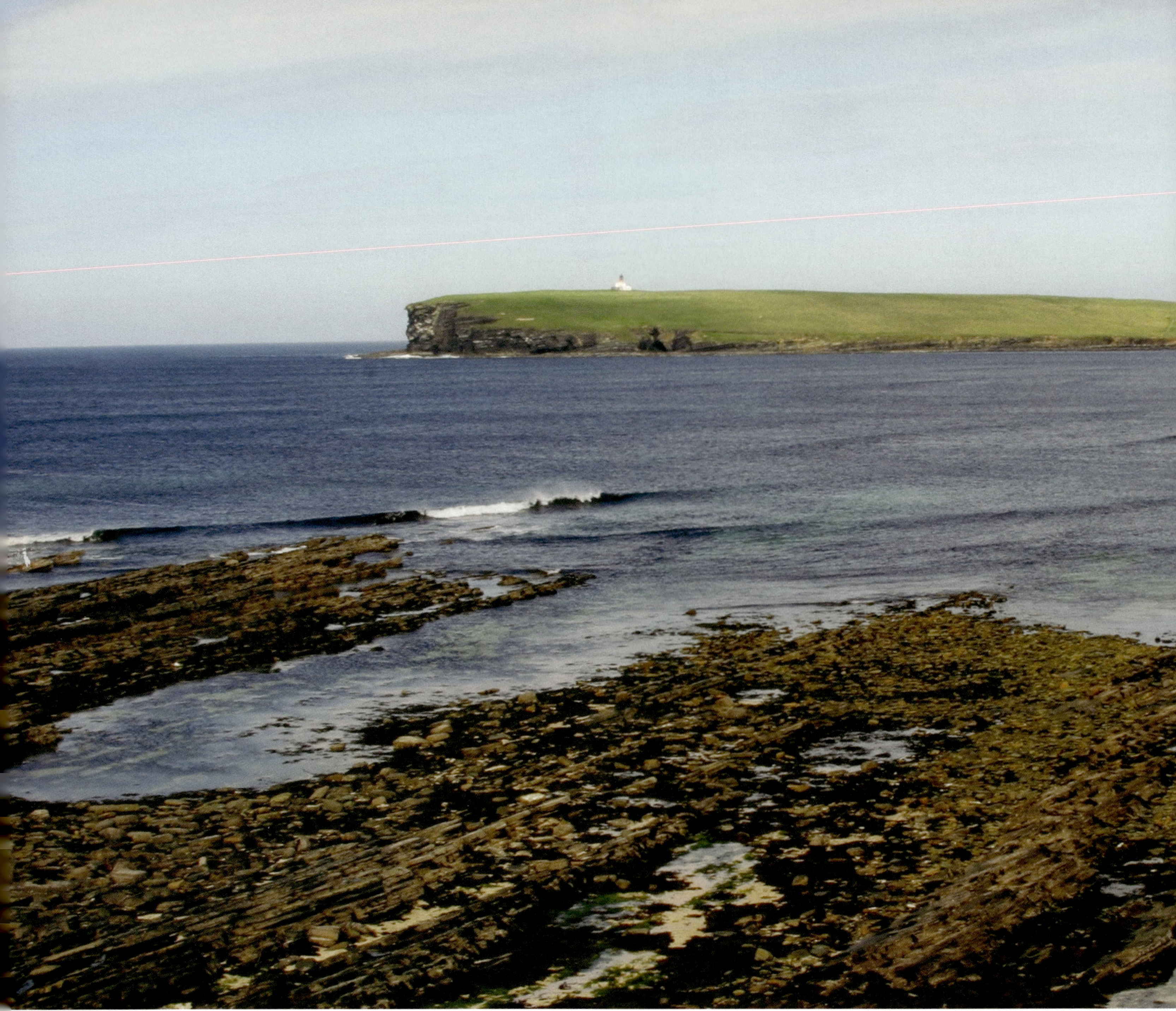

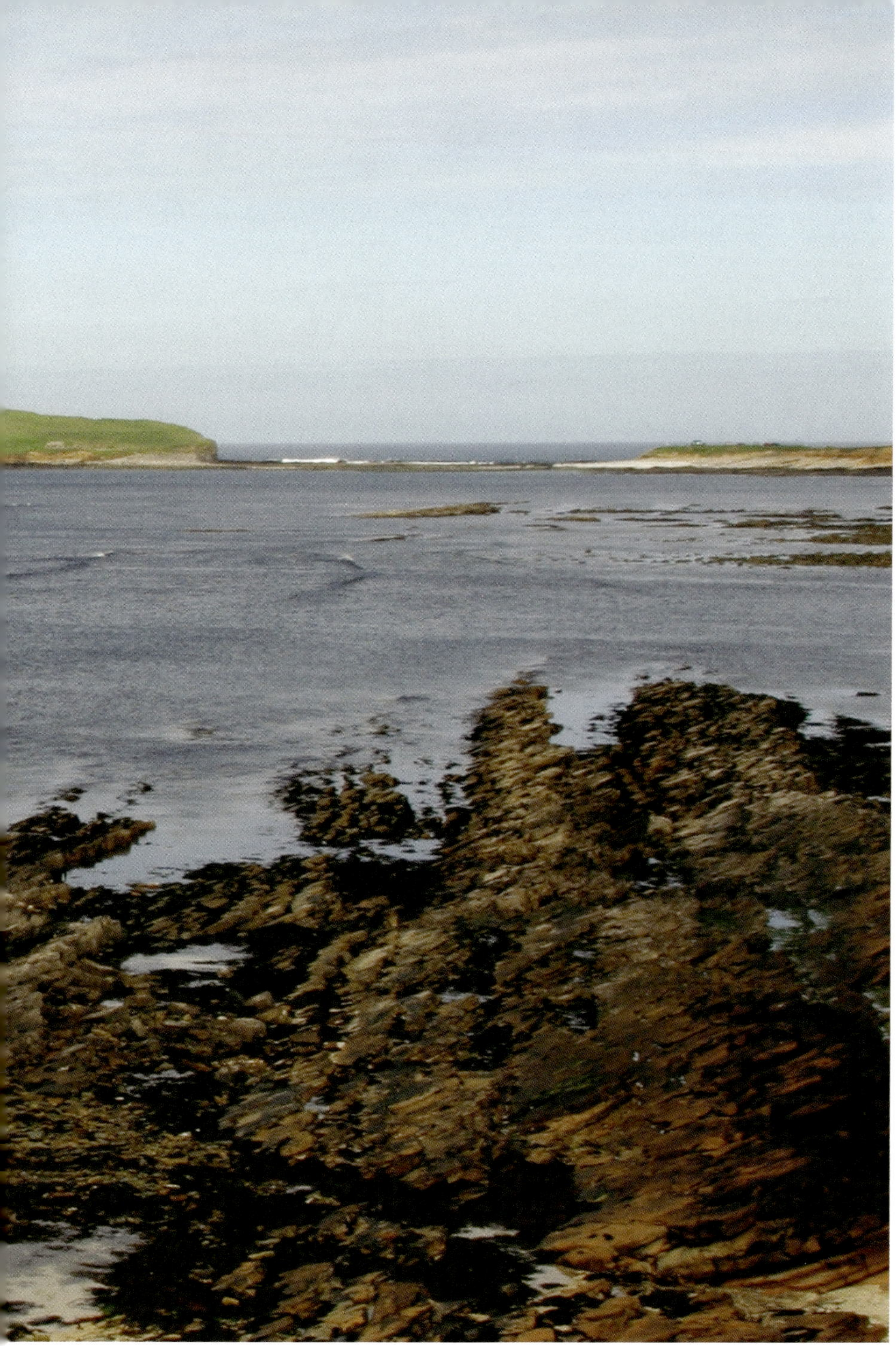

The Brough of Birsay is an island connected to Mainland Orkney by a causeway at low tide. The island was an important Pictish stronghold from around the sixth century and many interesting archaeological remains have been found here from this period

The lighthouse on the Brough of Birsay. The cliffs here hold nesting shags, fulmars, and a few puffins, razorbills and guillemots during the busy summer season.

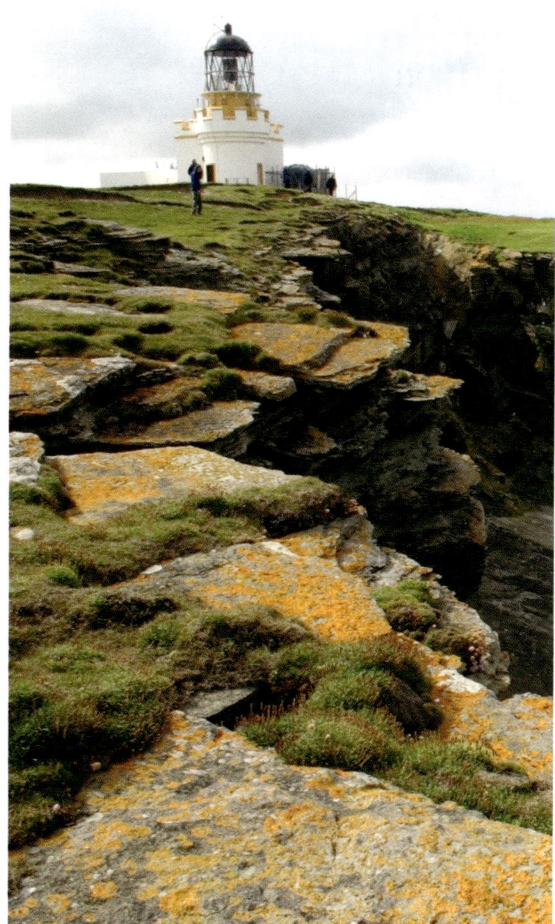

The Earl's Palace at Birsay was once the most important settlement on Orkney. Robert Stewart, illegitimate son of King James V of Scotland, was given the Earldom of Orkney in 1568. The following year he began building this impressive palace, and held it as the capital of the islands until his son, Patrick, began constructing the new Earl's Palace at Kirkwall in 1607

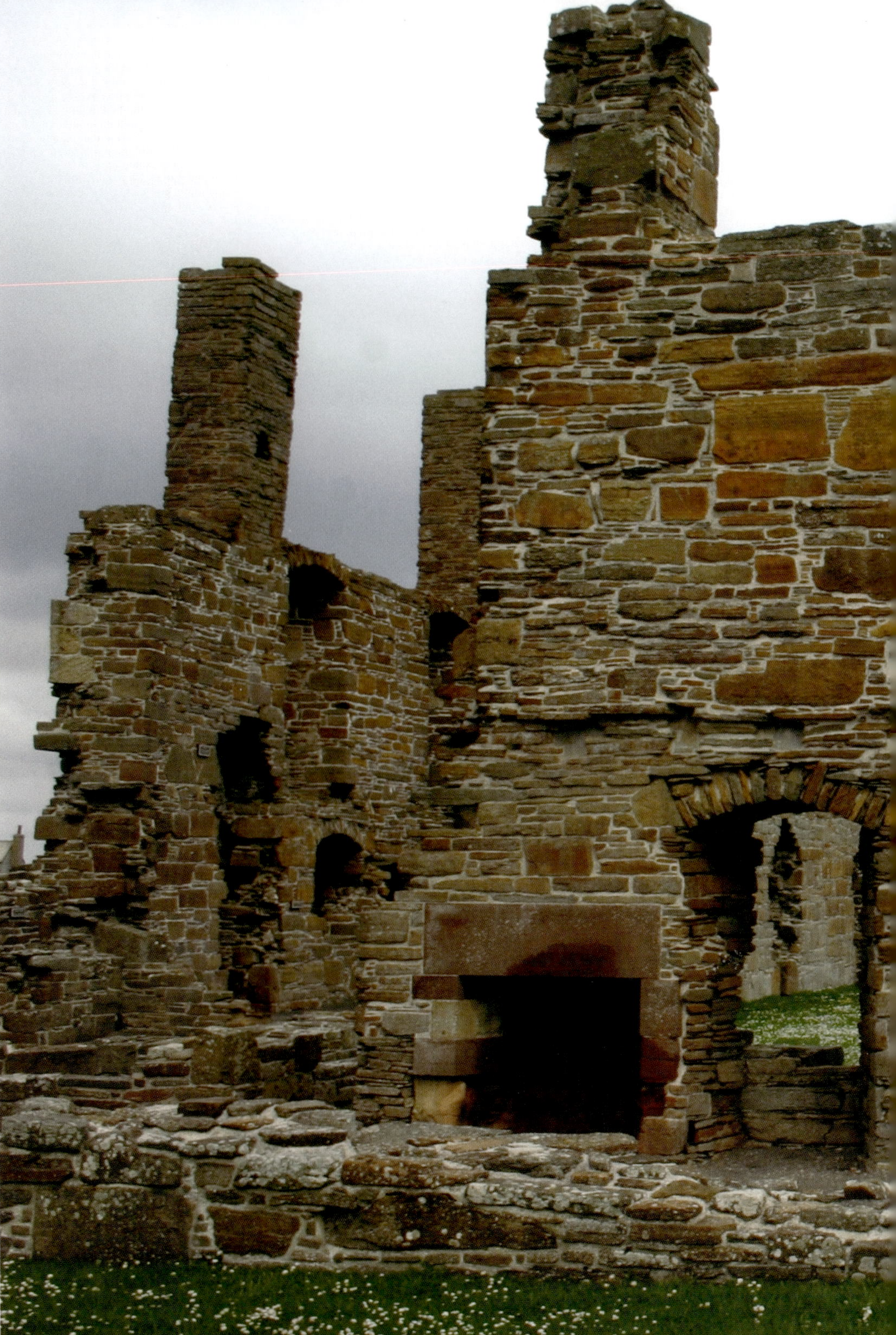

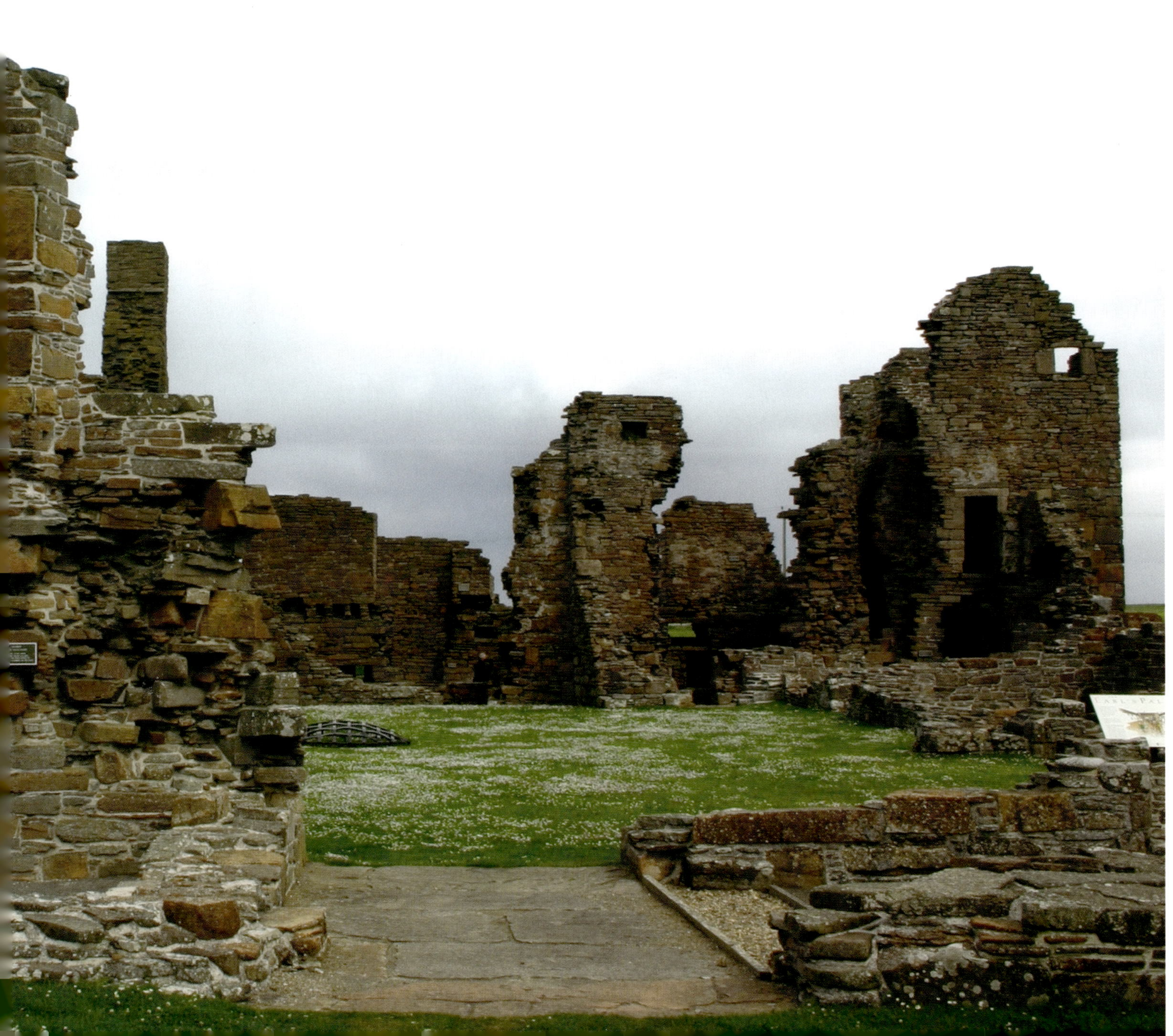

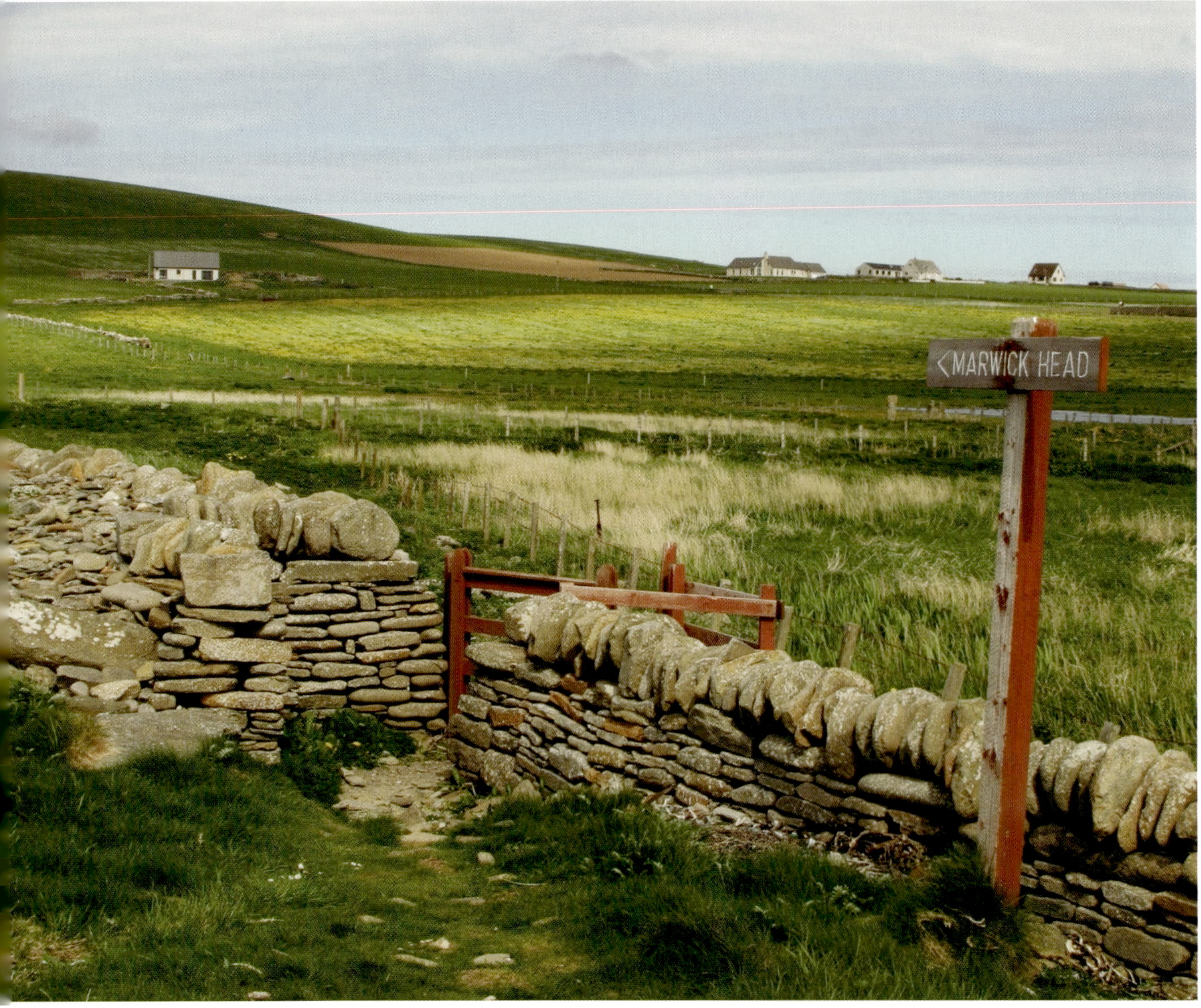

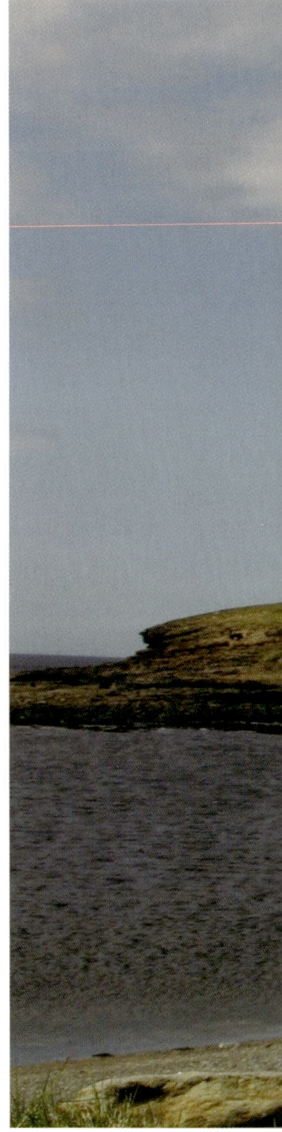

Typical views across wildflower meadows at Mar Wick. In the summer months these fields are ablaze with colour, and the grating churr of corncrakes carries over on the calm air.

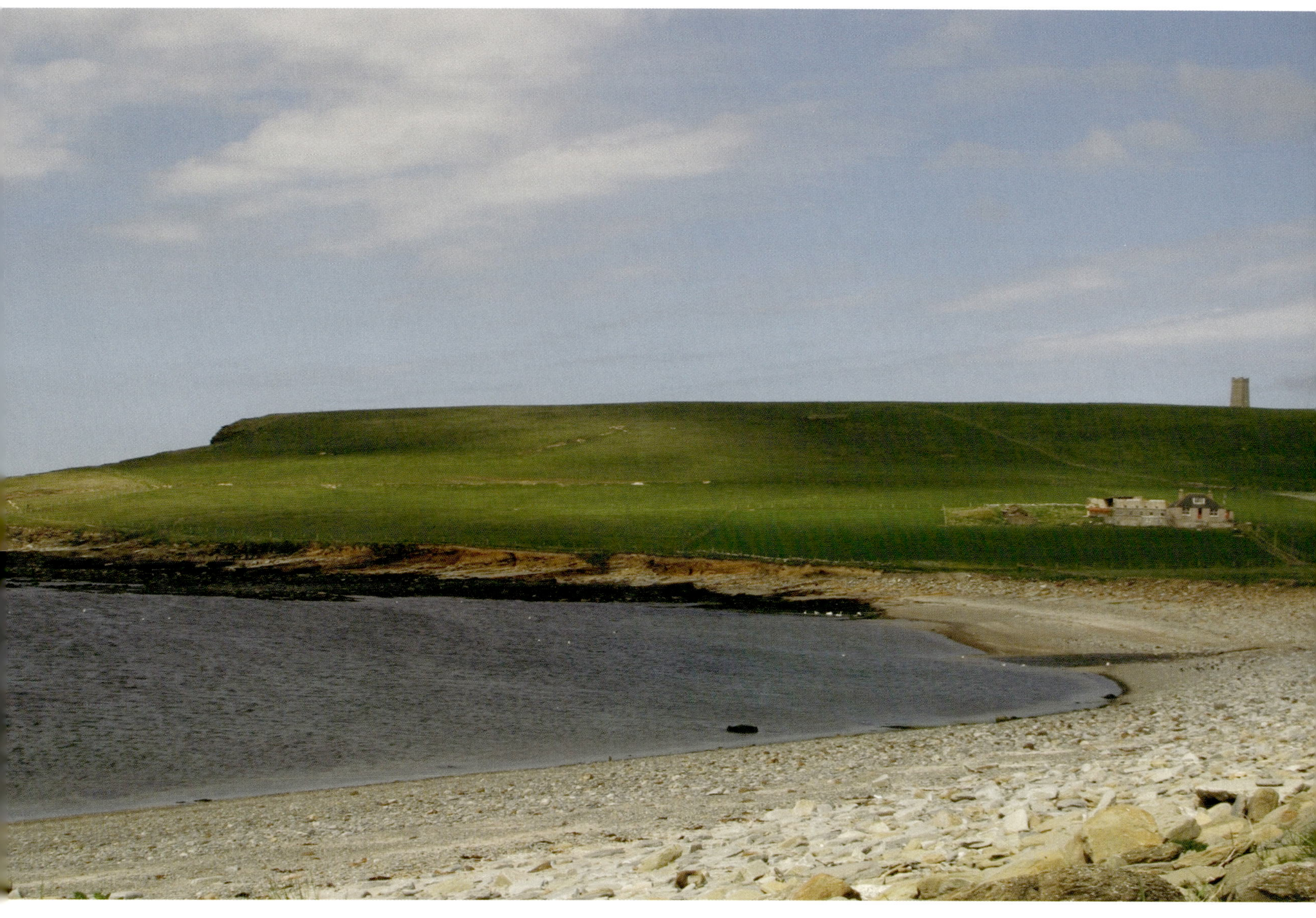

The huge cliffs of Marwick Head as seen from the bay of Mar Wick. Wick is the Old Norse name for a bay or cove.

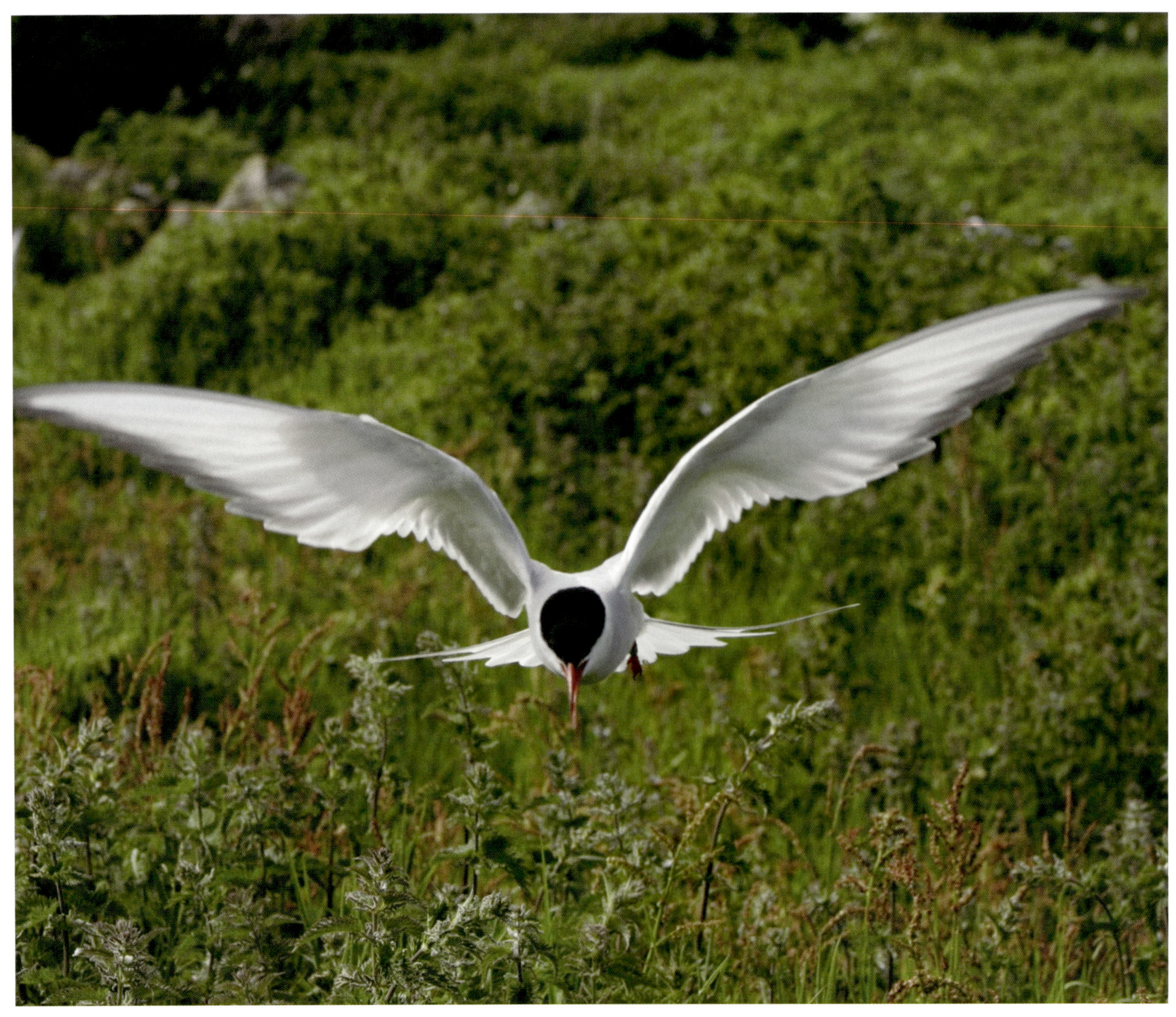

Above the high tide line in Mar Wick Arctic terns nest amongst low vegetation in the summer months.

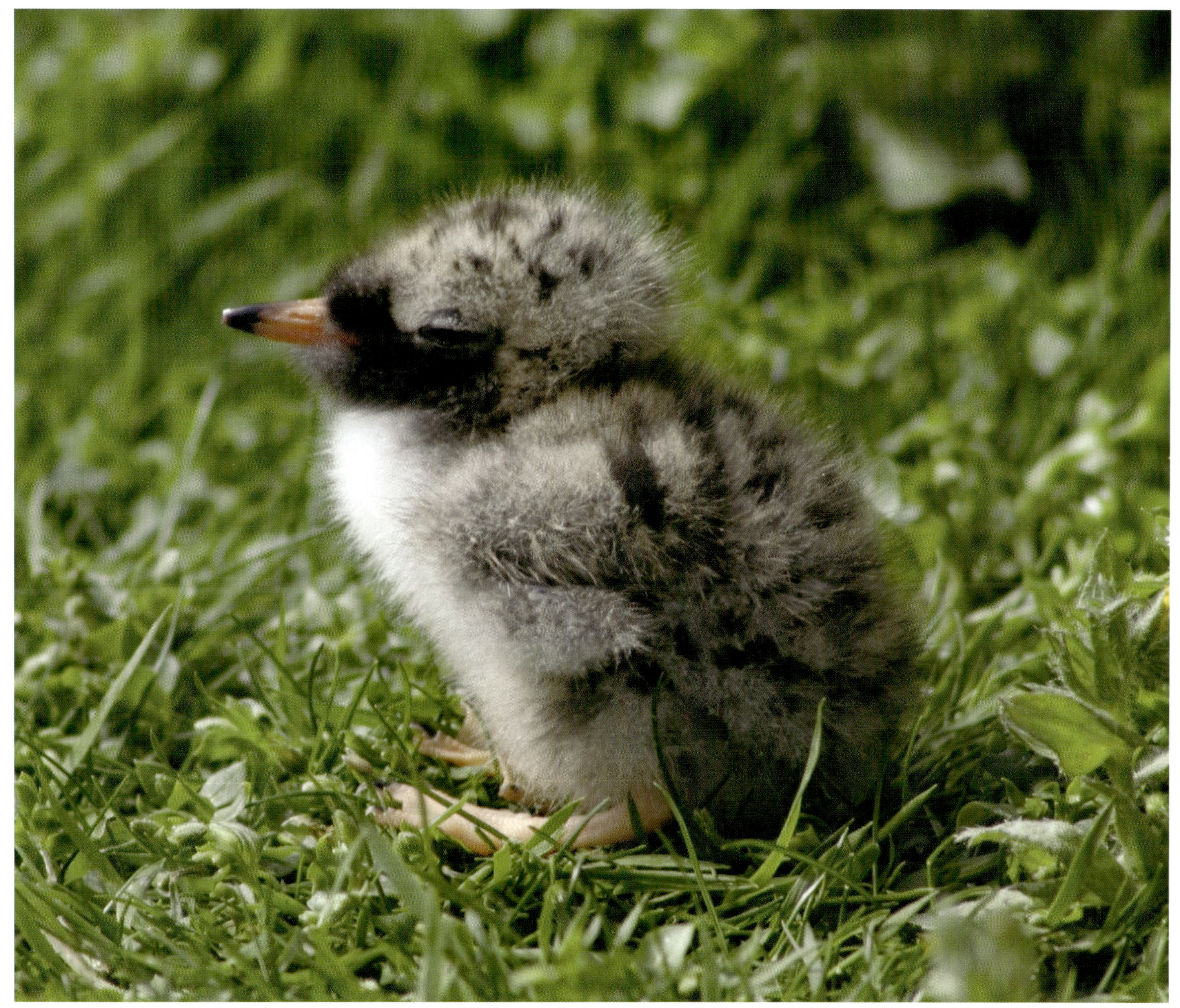

An Arctic tern chick, fresh from the nest.

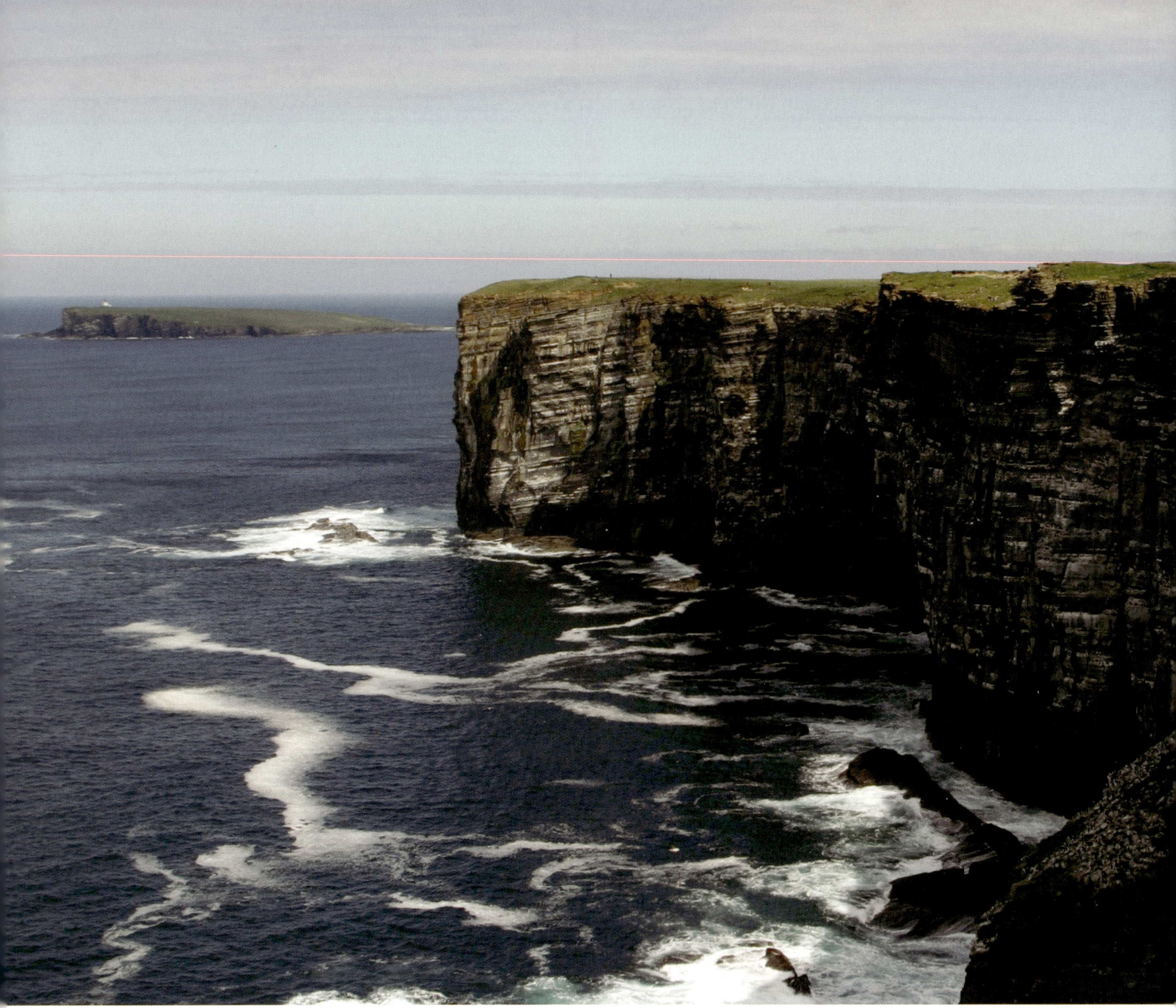

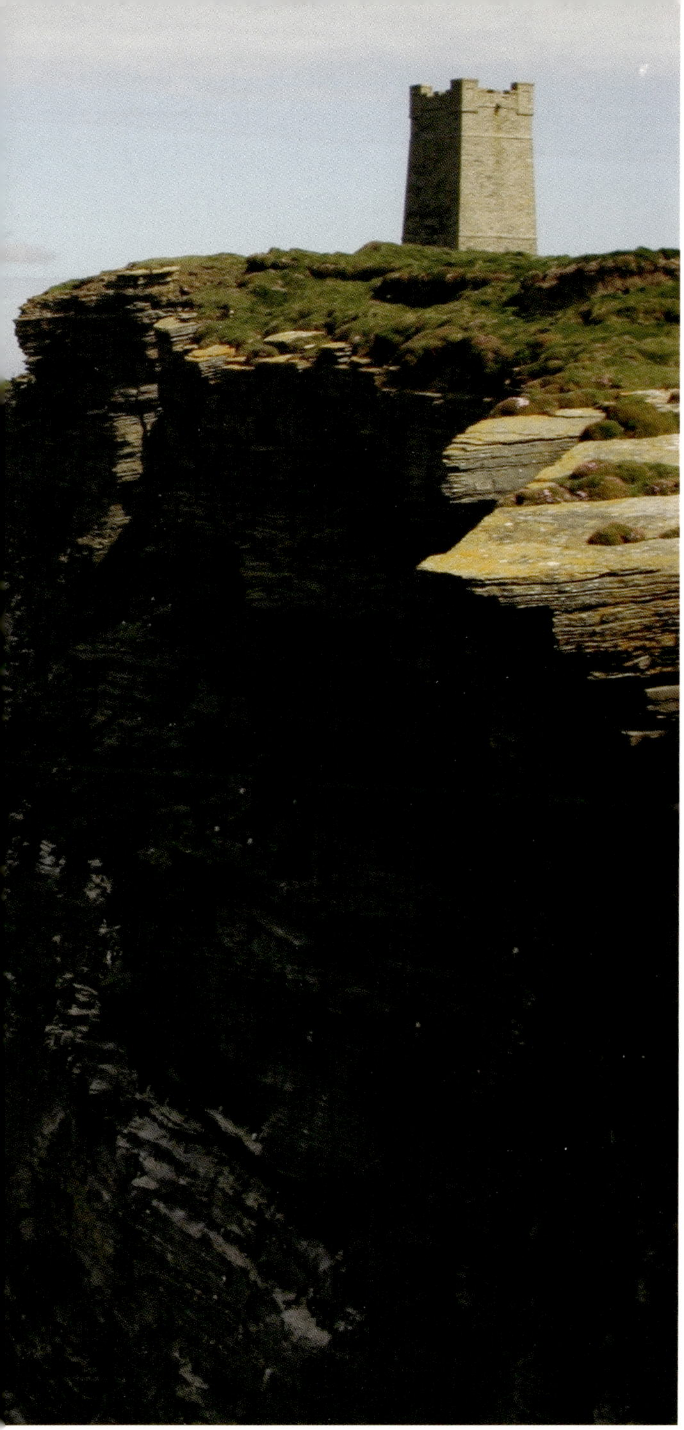

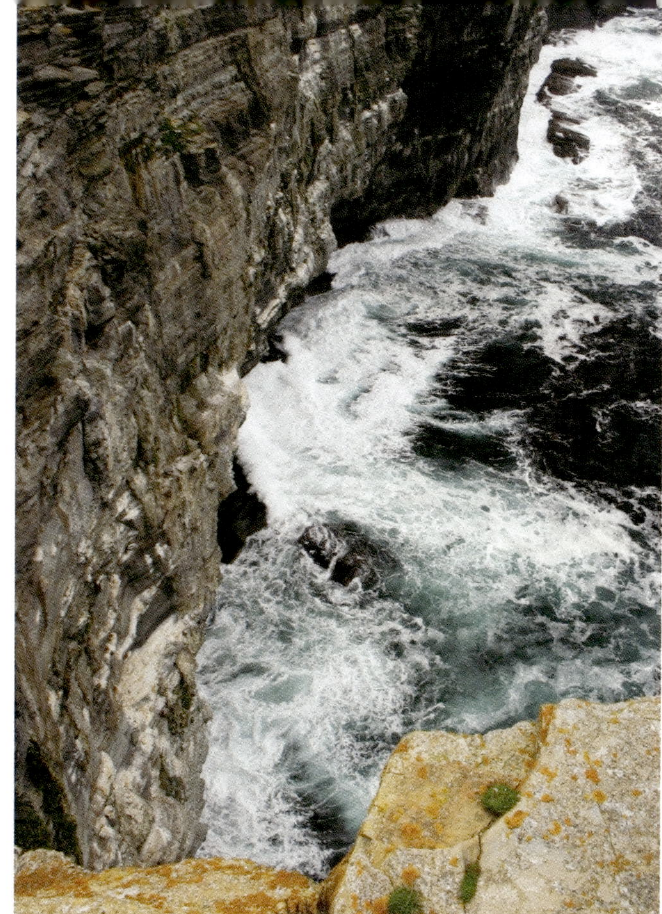

Looking down into the broiling seas beneath Marwick Head. Today the cliffs are part of an important seabird nesting site, with thousands of guillemots, razorbills, puffins, kittiwakes, shags, fulmars, rock doves, and ravens breeding here. The RSPB now own and manage the headland as a nature reserve.

On Marwick Head stands the Kitchener Memorial. This was erected in 1926, to commemorate Lord Kitchener and the crew of the HMS *Hampshire* which was sunk off this coast in 1916 by a German mine. Only 12 of her crew survived. Kitchener was then Minister of War, and in June that year he had arrived in Scapa Flow to visit Admiral Jellicoe to discuss his account of the Battle of Jutland.

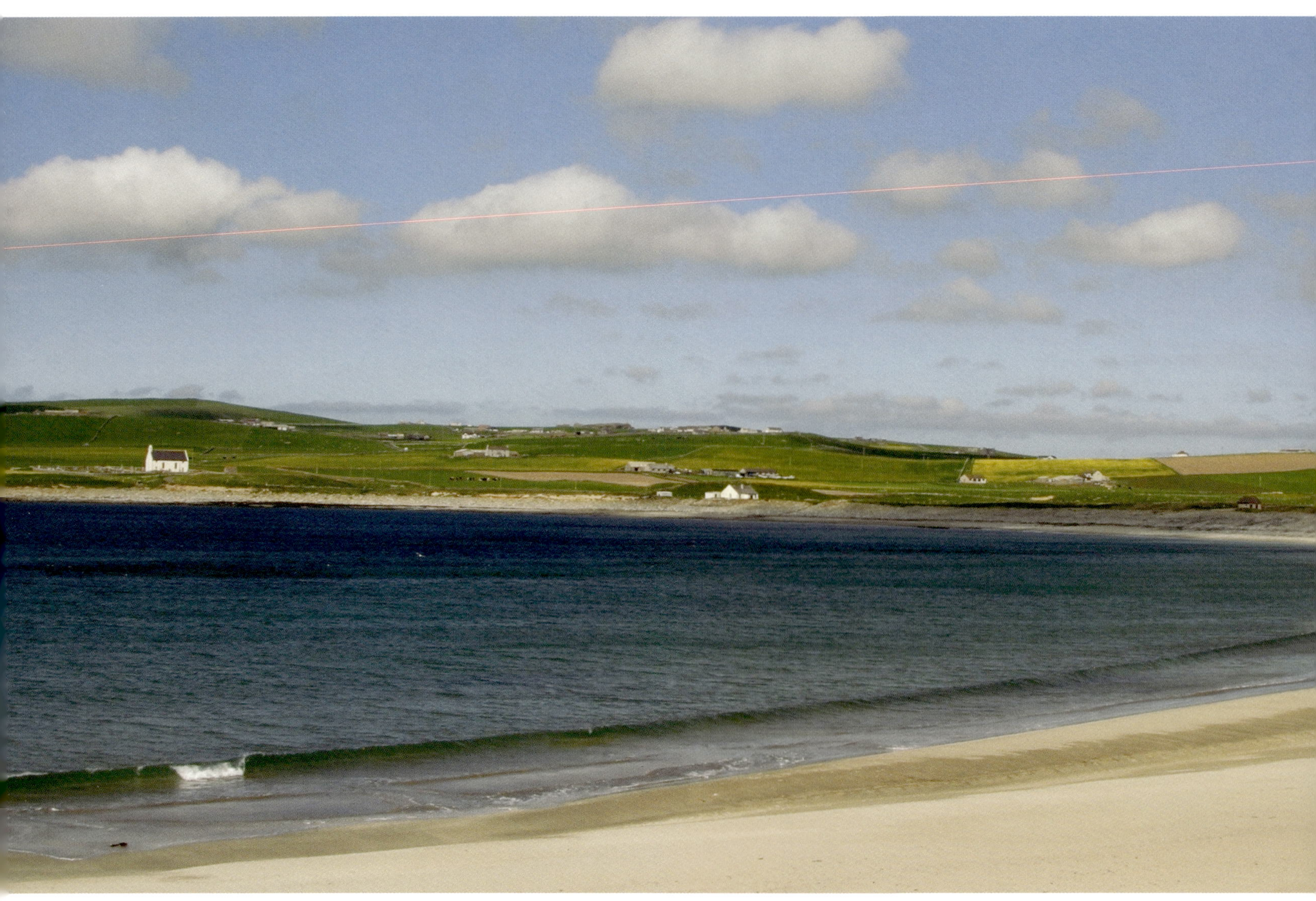

The tranquil waters of Skaill Bay, not always so peaceful and serene however!

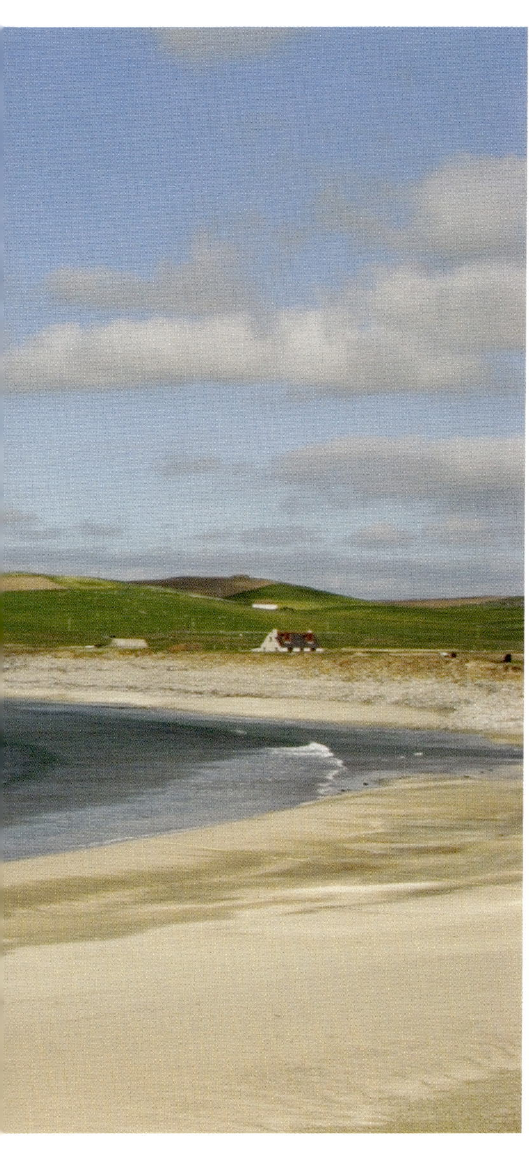

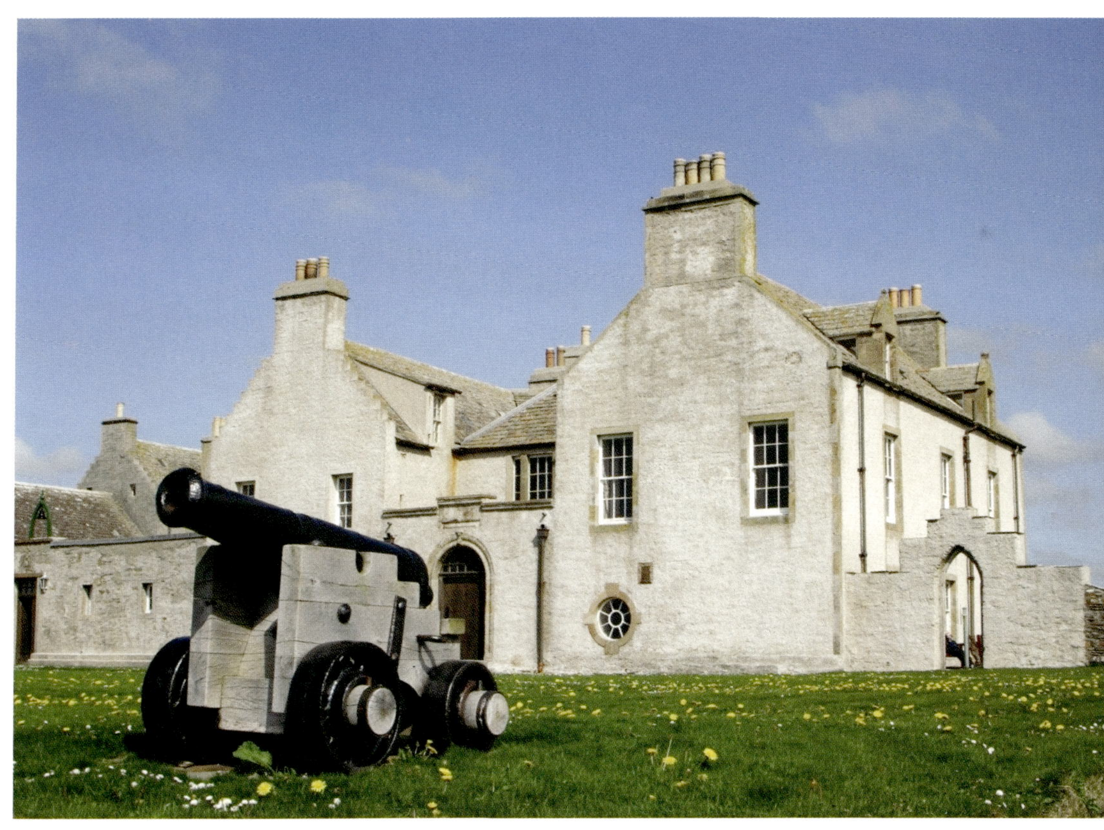

Skaill House is an early seventeenth-century mansion containing lots of interesting artefacts, including the dinner service from Captain Cook's *Resolution*. It stands guard over Skaill Bay on the west side of Mainland Orkney, on the same site as the famous Skara Brae.

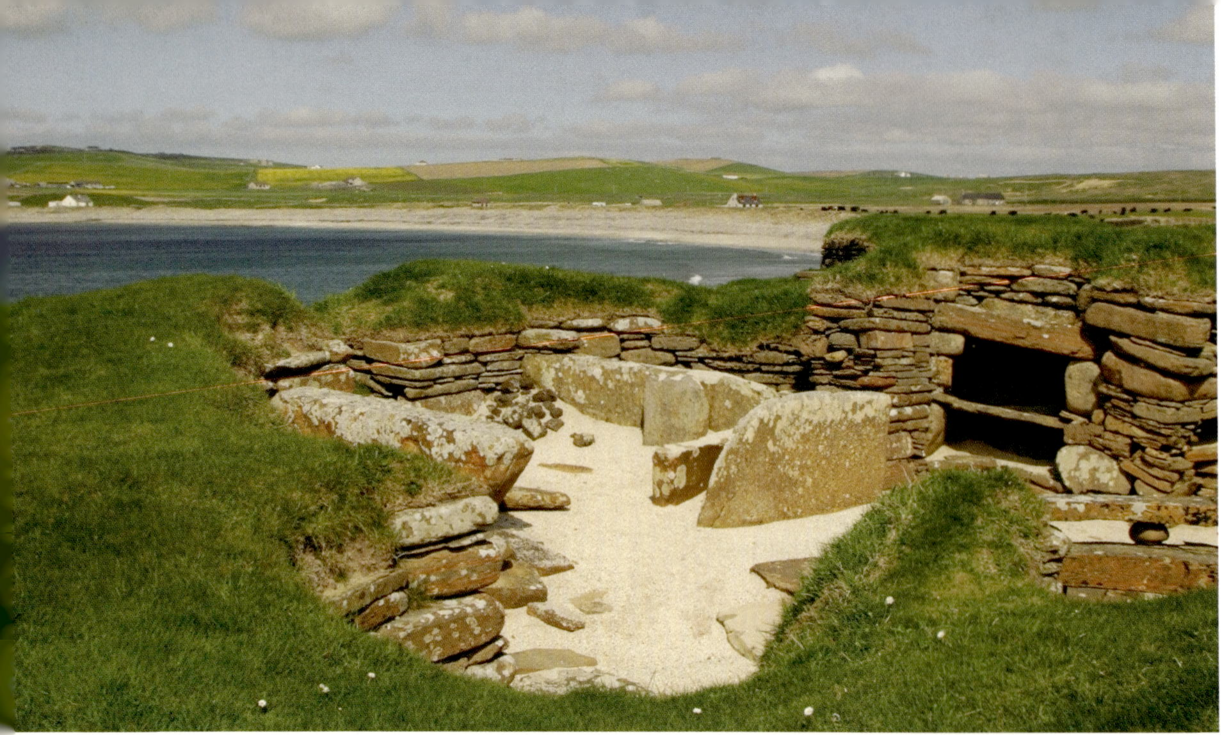

Skara Brae is arguably the most important Stone Age site in Britain. This 5000 year old village site was buried under a huge sand dune, and nobody knew of its existence. Then in 1850, a terrible storm blew in off the Atlantic, tearing across Skaill Bay. The sand was blown off the dunes, revealing what is undoubtedly the best preserved Stone Age village in Northern Europe.

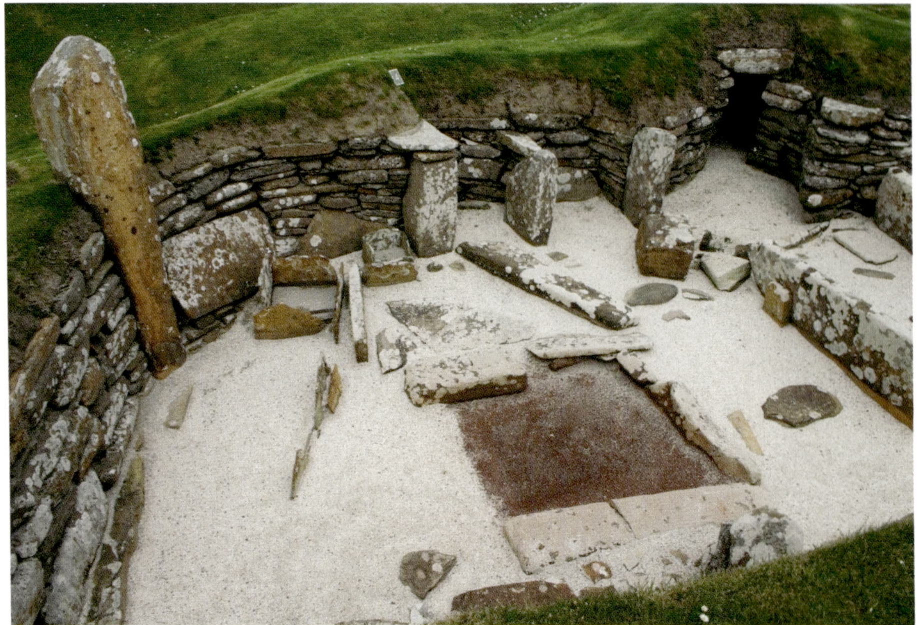

Left: It is known that Skara Brae was occupied for around 600 years from about 3000BC, and you can still see the stone furniture, fireplaces, drains and even damp-proof coursing in the foundations!

Right: Skara Brae however, is not that far from the shore today, and many people worry that with rising sea levels, this superb ancient village could be lost beneath the waves.

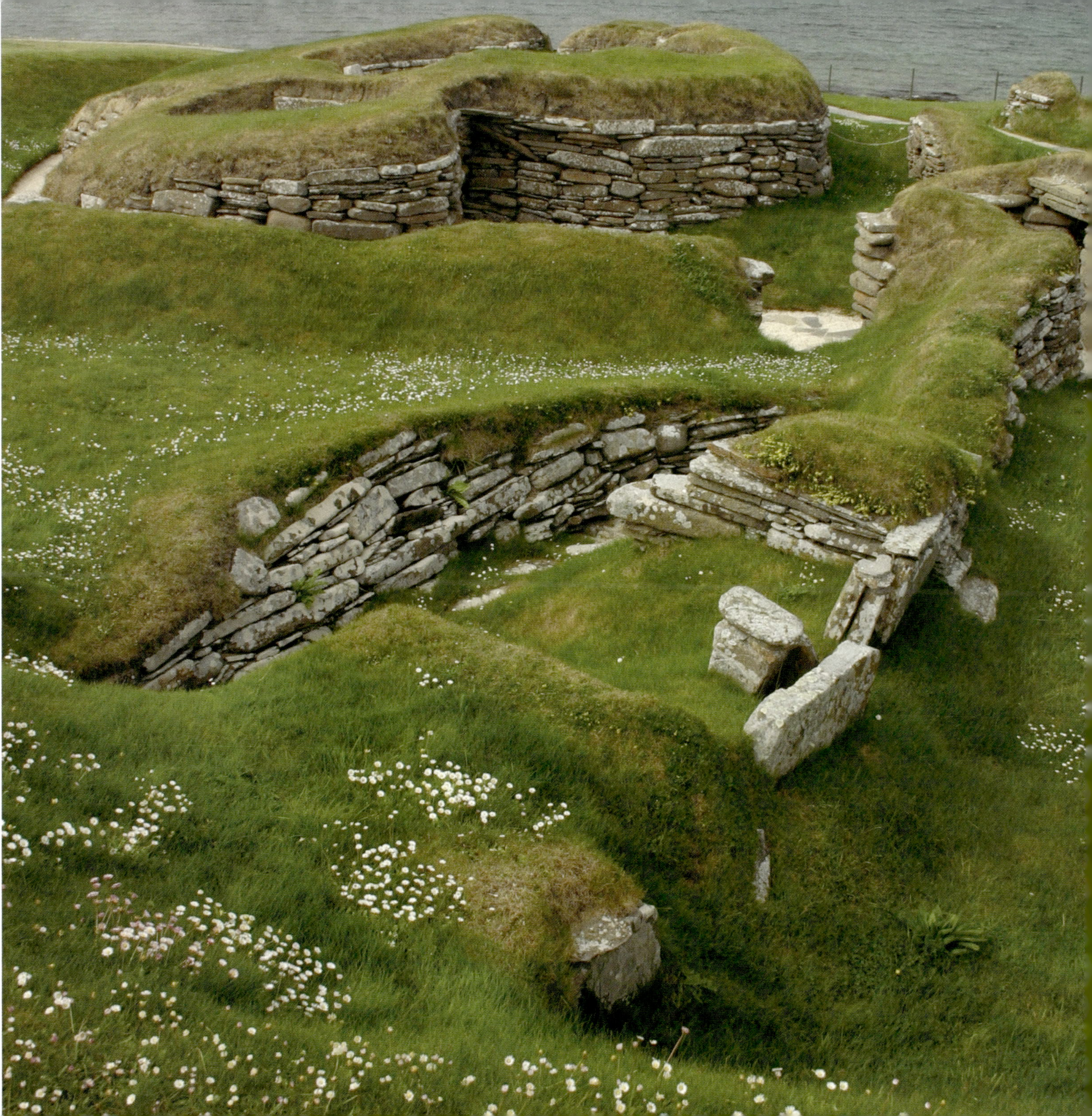

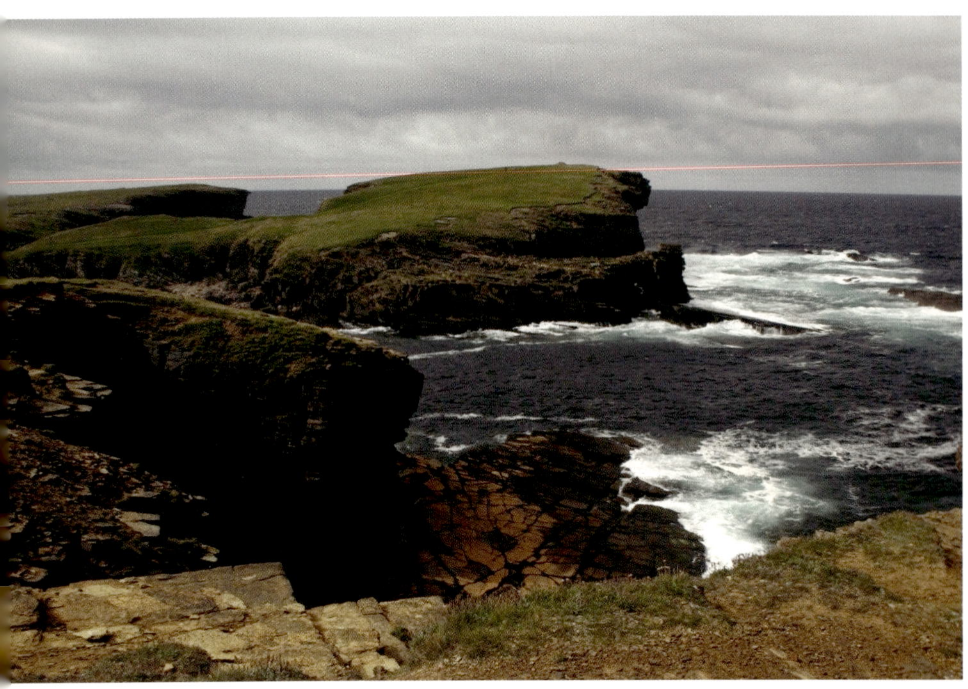

A little further south along the coast from Skara Brae
the cliffs rise again at Yesnaby.

There is some superb seacliff scenery along the coast at Yesnaby, and a walk here should be at the top of everyone's list of ways to get the wind in your hair!

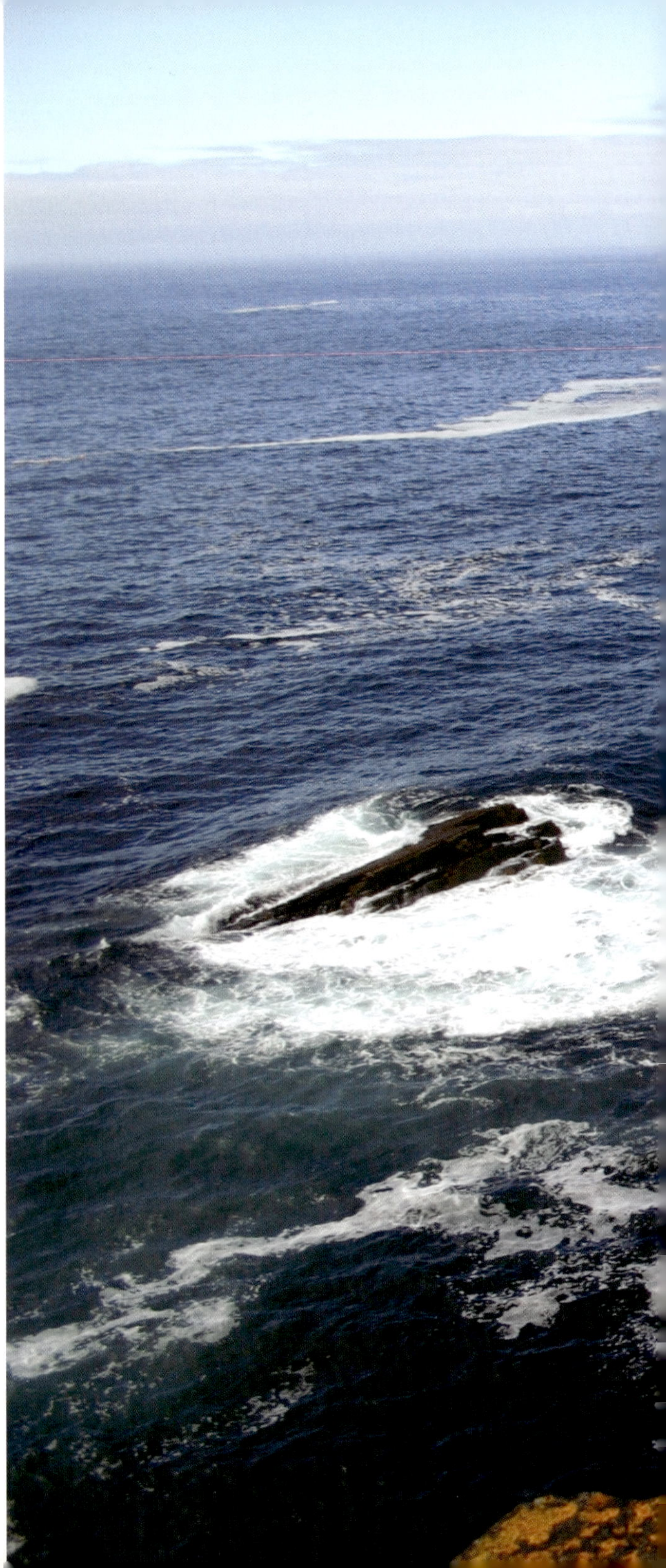

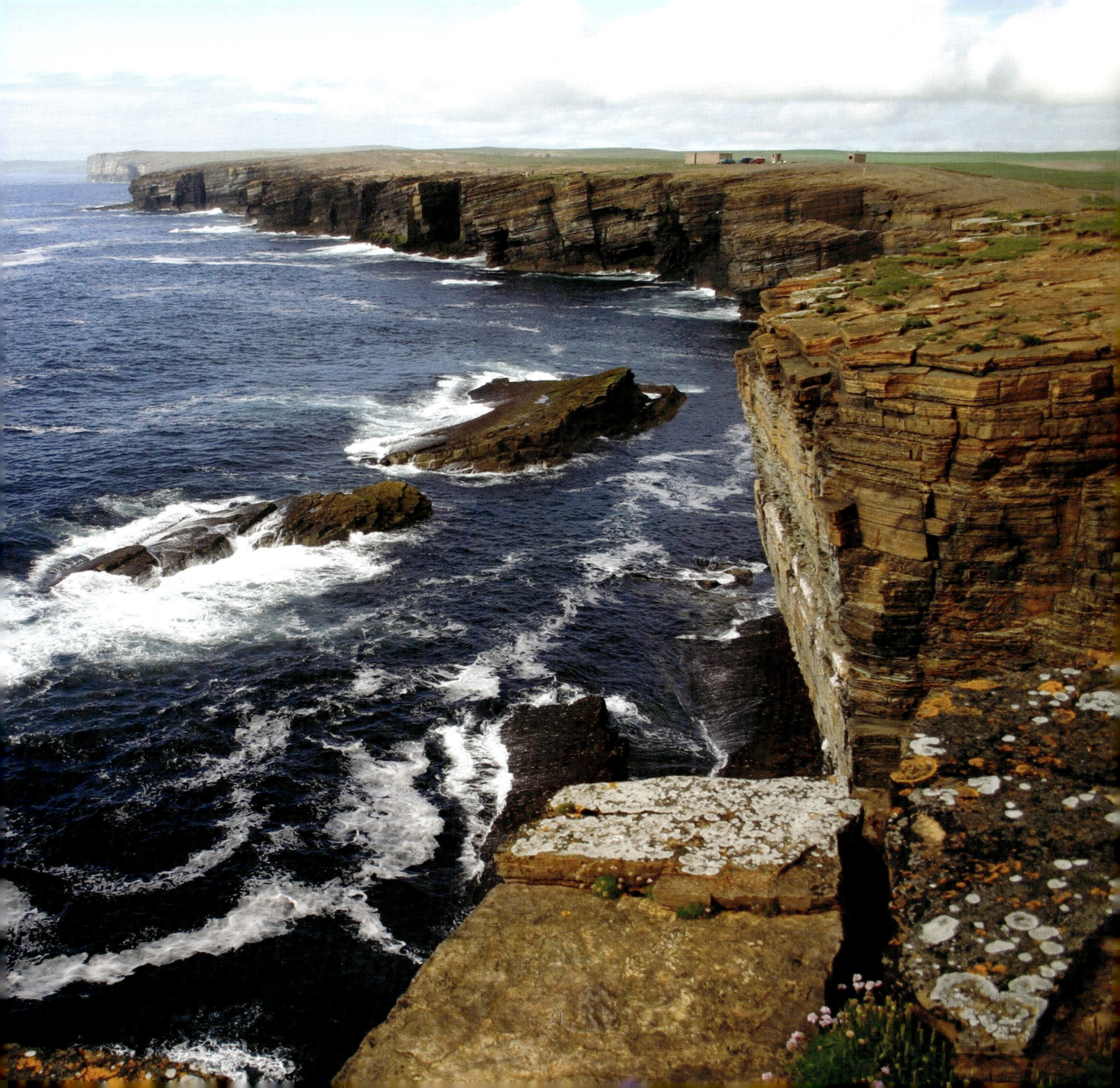

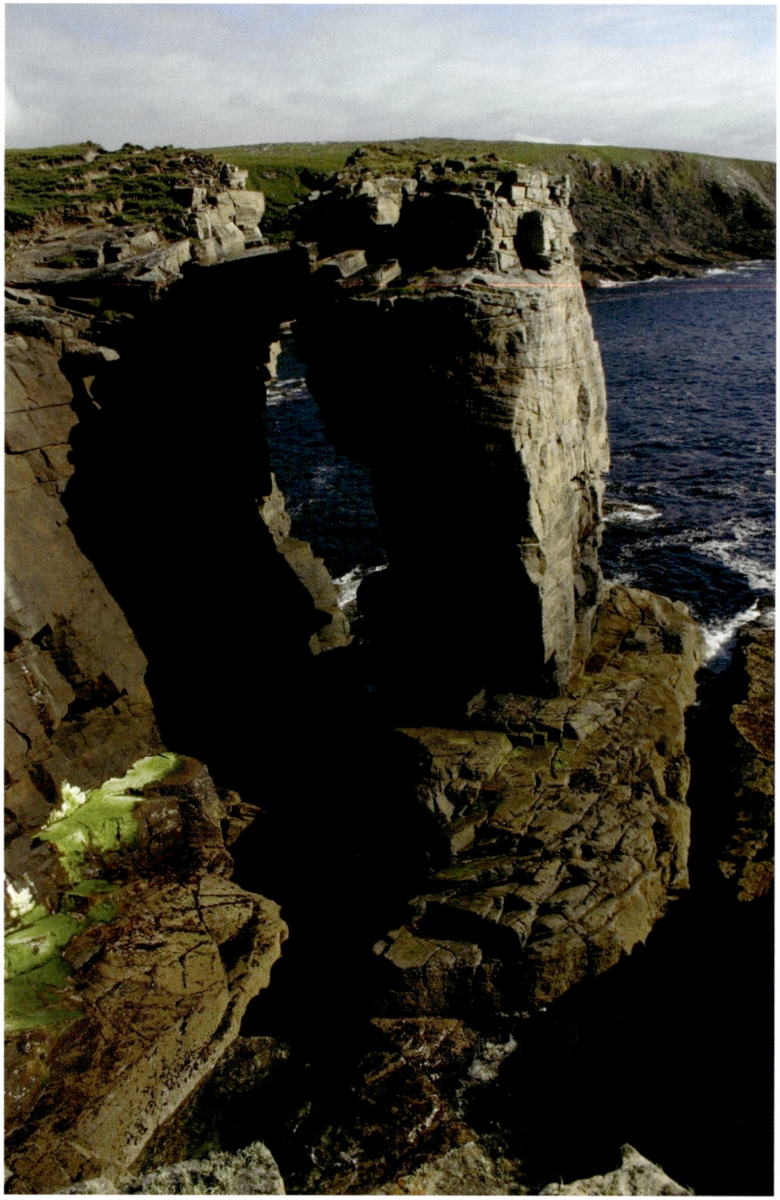

Countless sea stacks, arches, and blow-holes can be found along the cliffs at Yesnaby.

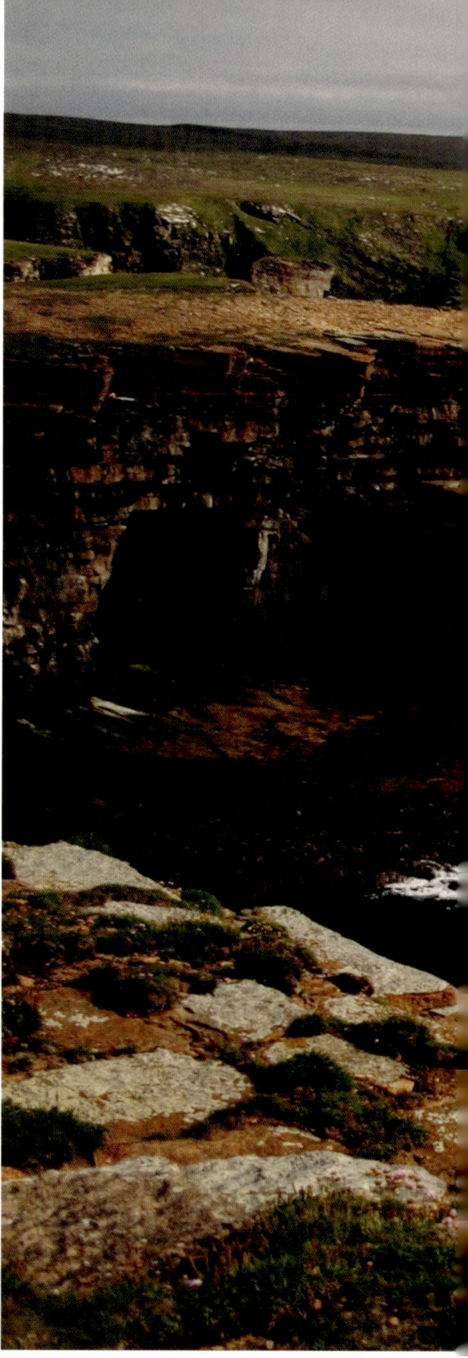

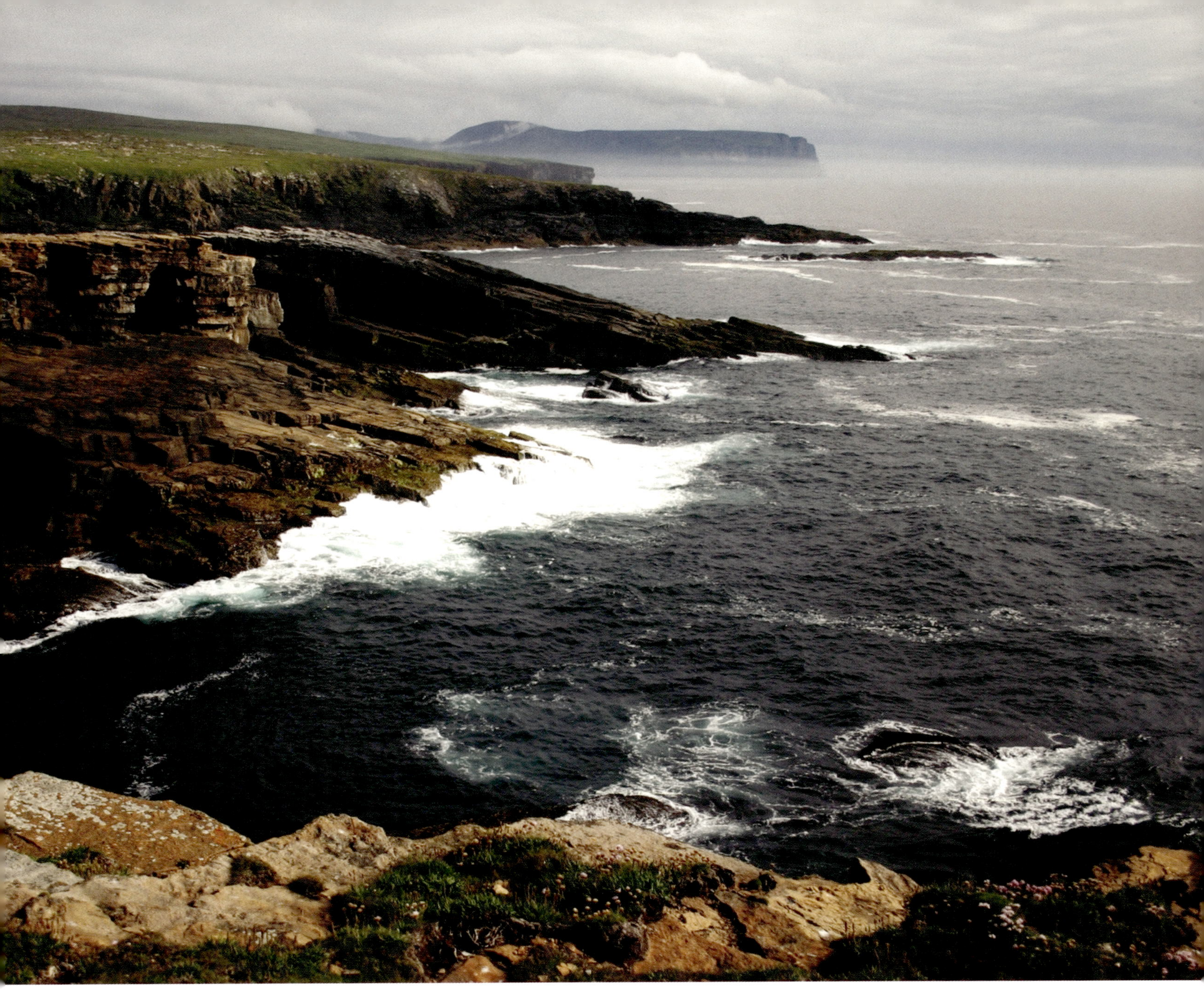

Looking south from Yesnaby towards the distant outline of the island of Hoy.

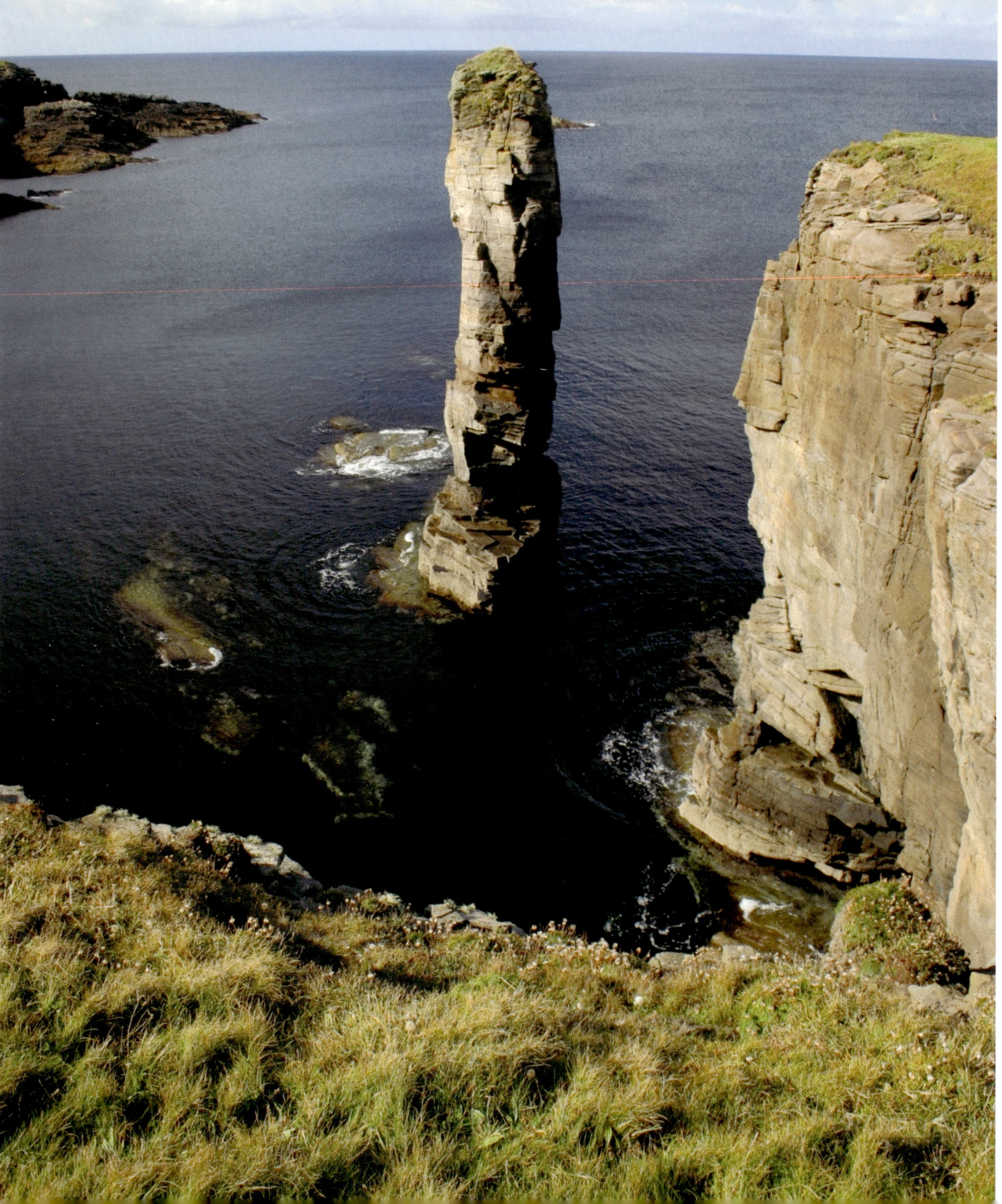

The Yesnaby Castle – not a castle at all, but a magnificent sea stack. Stacks are formed when the sea cuts an arch into a headland. Over thousands of years erosion wears down the rock, until the arch collapses, leaving these spectacular pinnacles.

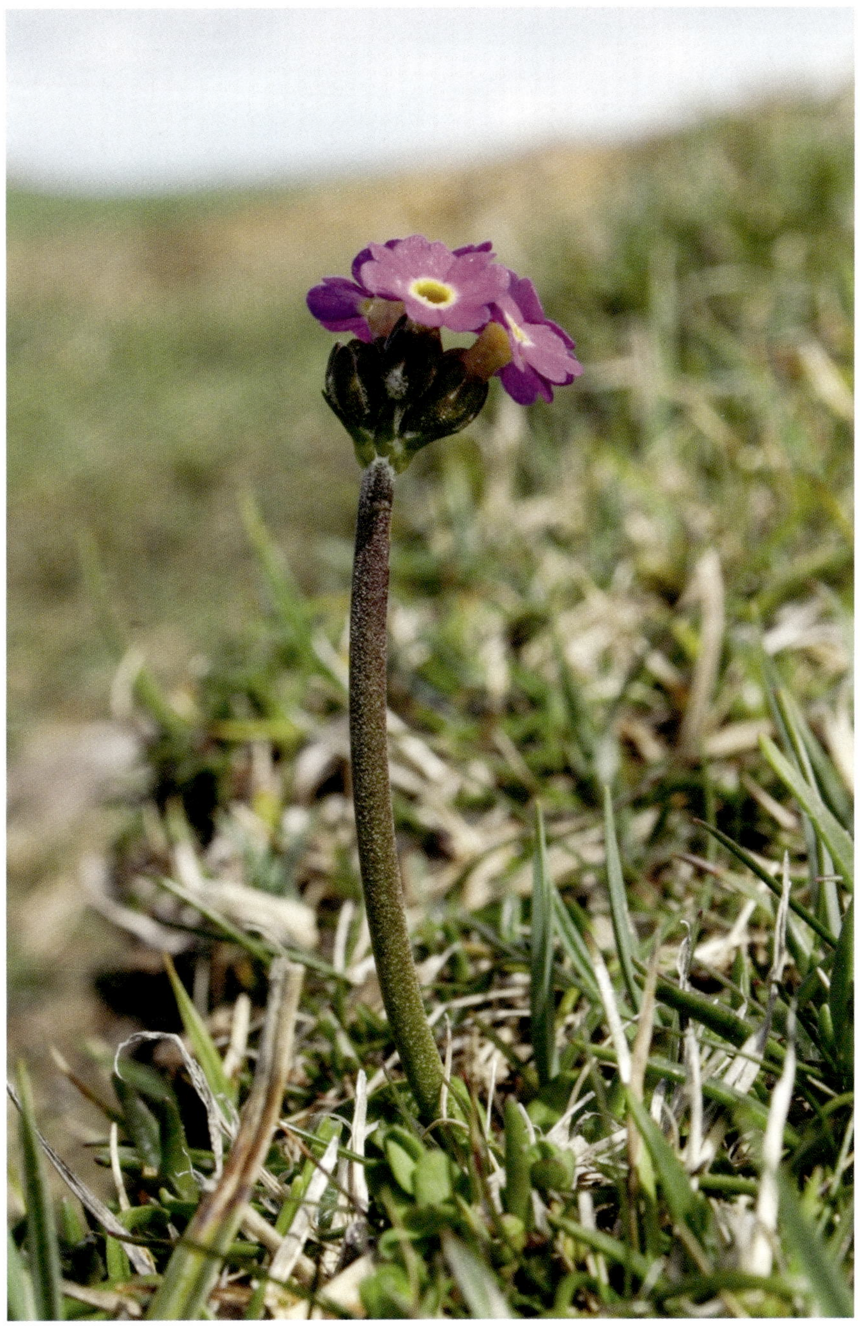

One of the rarest plants in Britain is the tiny Scottish primrose, *Primula scotica*. It grows in profusion in the close-cropped grass sward on the cliff tops at Yesnaby.

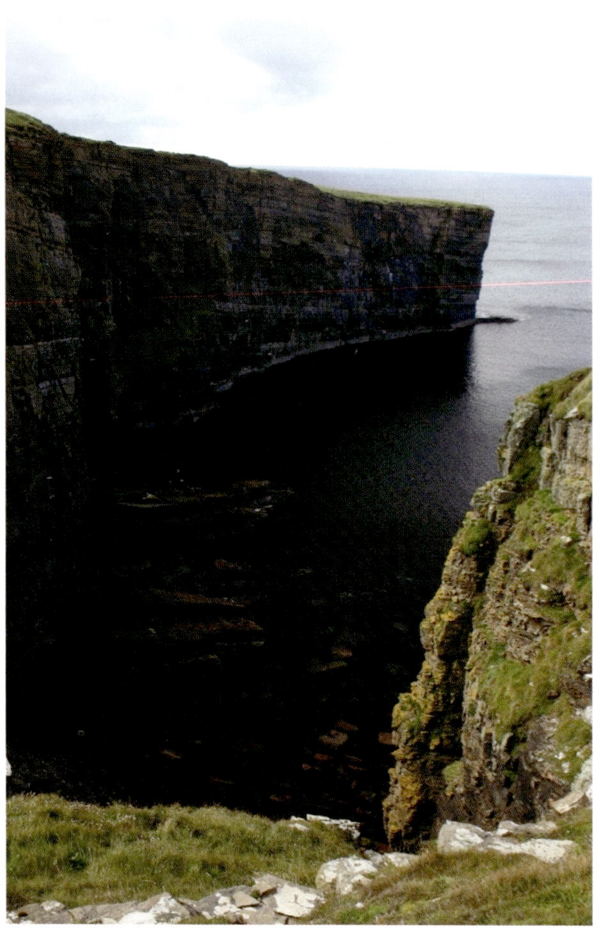

Neban Point, a magnificent headland just south of Yesnaby.

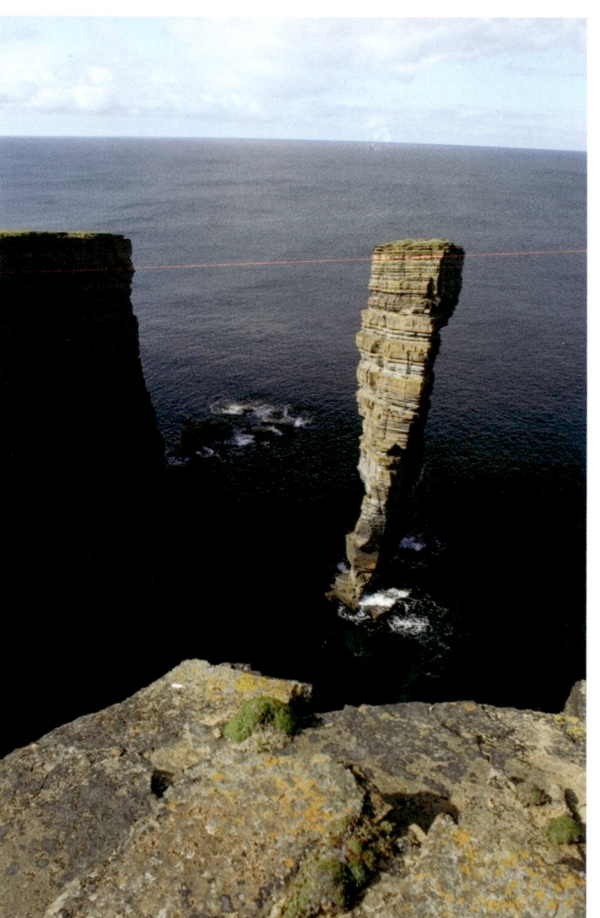

Another superb sea stack, the Neban Castle, looks as though it won't be standing for very much longer! The whole pinnacle rests on a very narrow base.

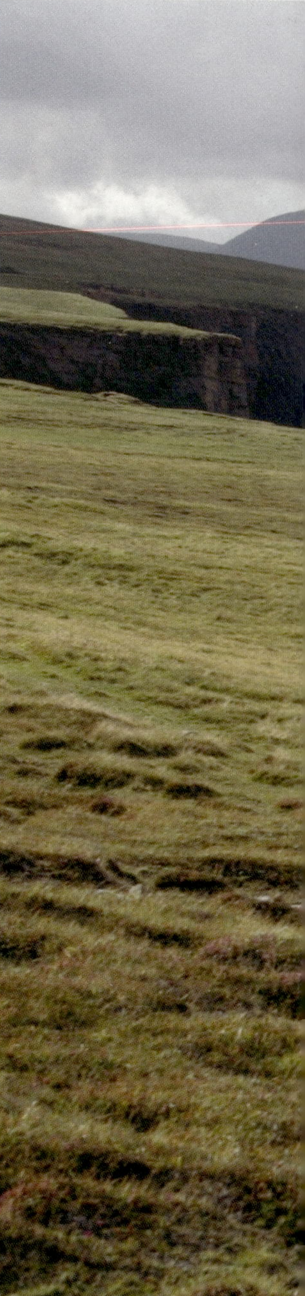

Walkers striding out southwards from Neban Point towards Black Craig. The hills of Hoy dominate the views in the distance.

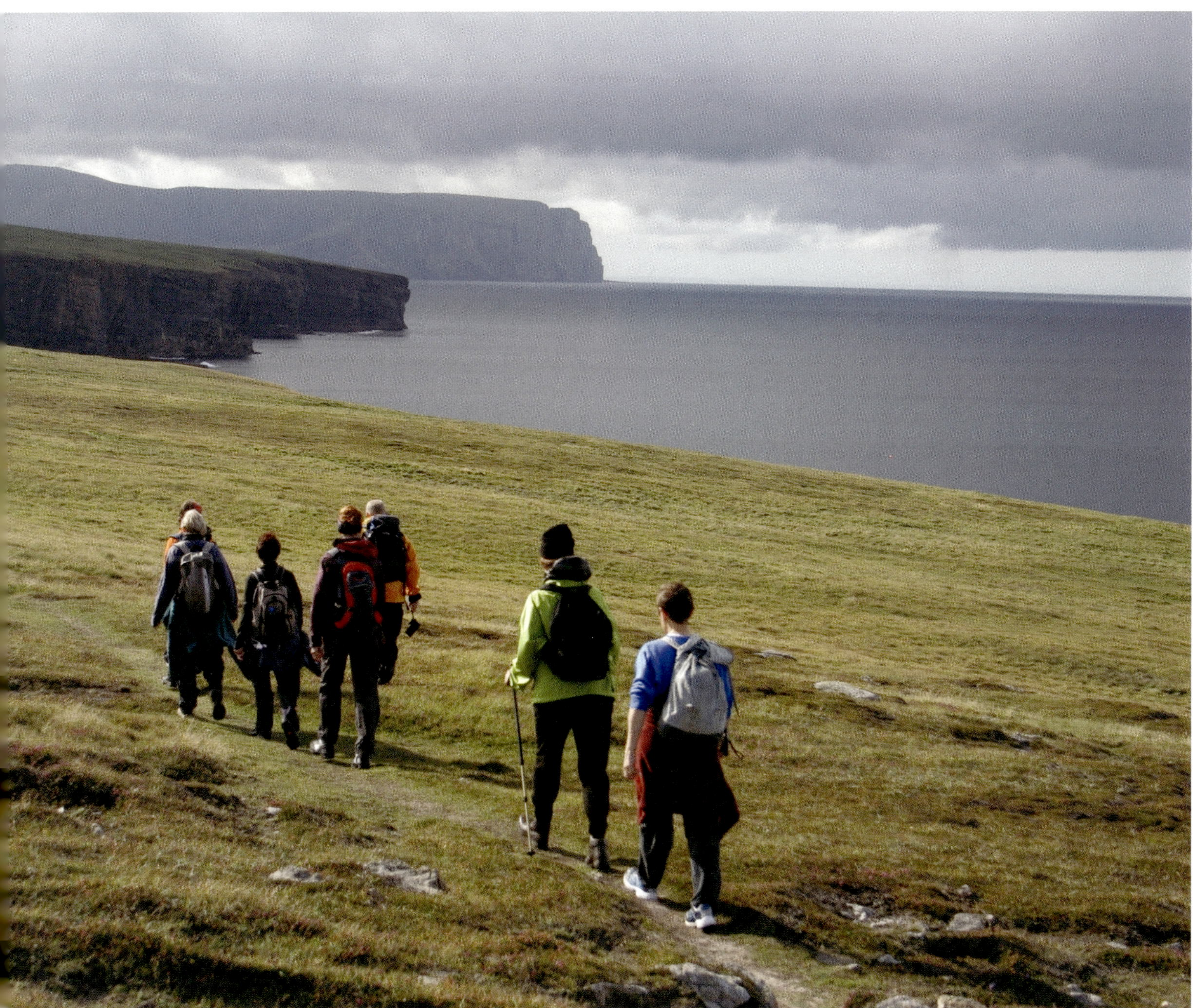

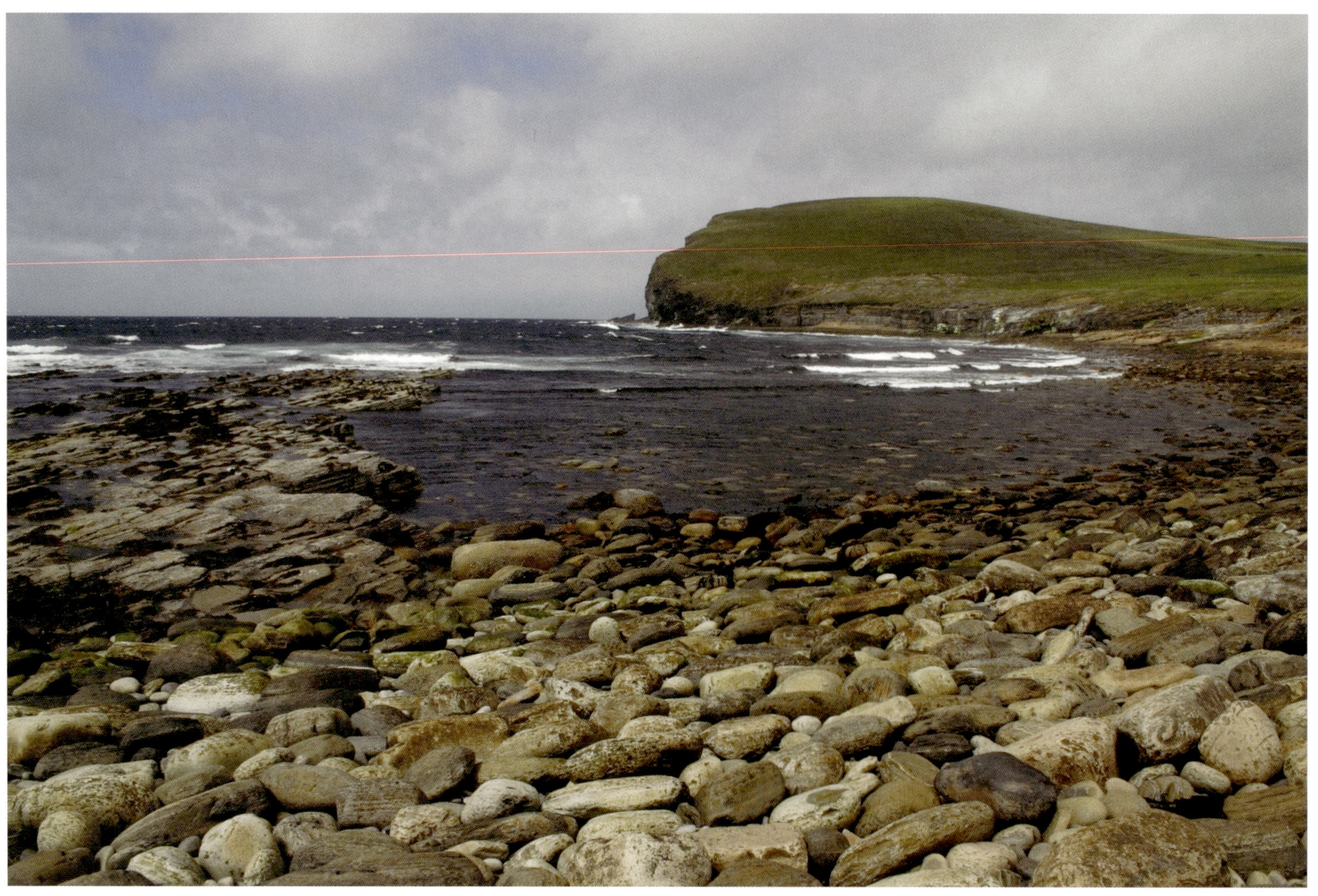

Above: The superb cover at Billia Croo and Black Craig rising beyond on West Mainland, Orkney.

Above, right: The Caithness Flags at the Sands of Warebeth. Here, sedimentary rock has been tilted by immense geological forces, then weathered over thousands of years. Pebbles now fit snugly in the gaps created in the rock.

Right: The wonderful stony beach at the Sands of Warebeth on Mainland.

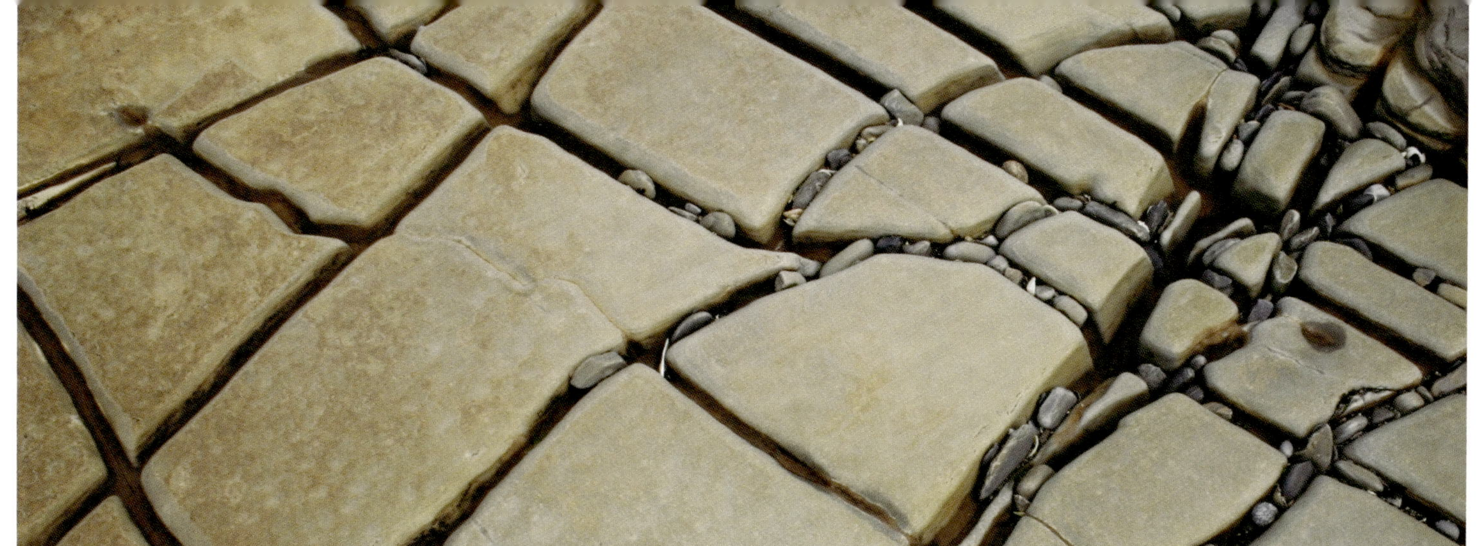

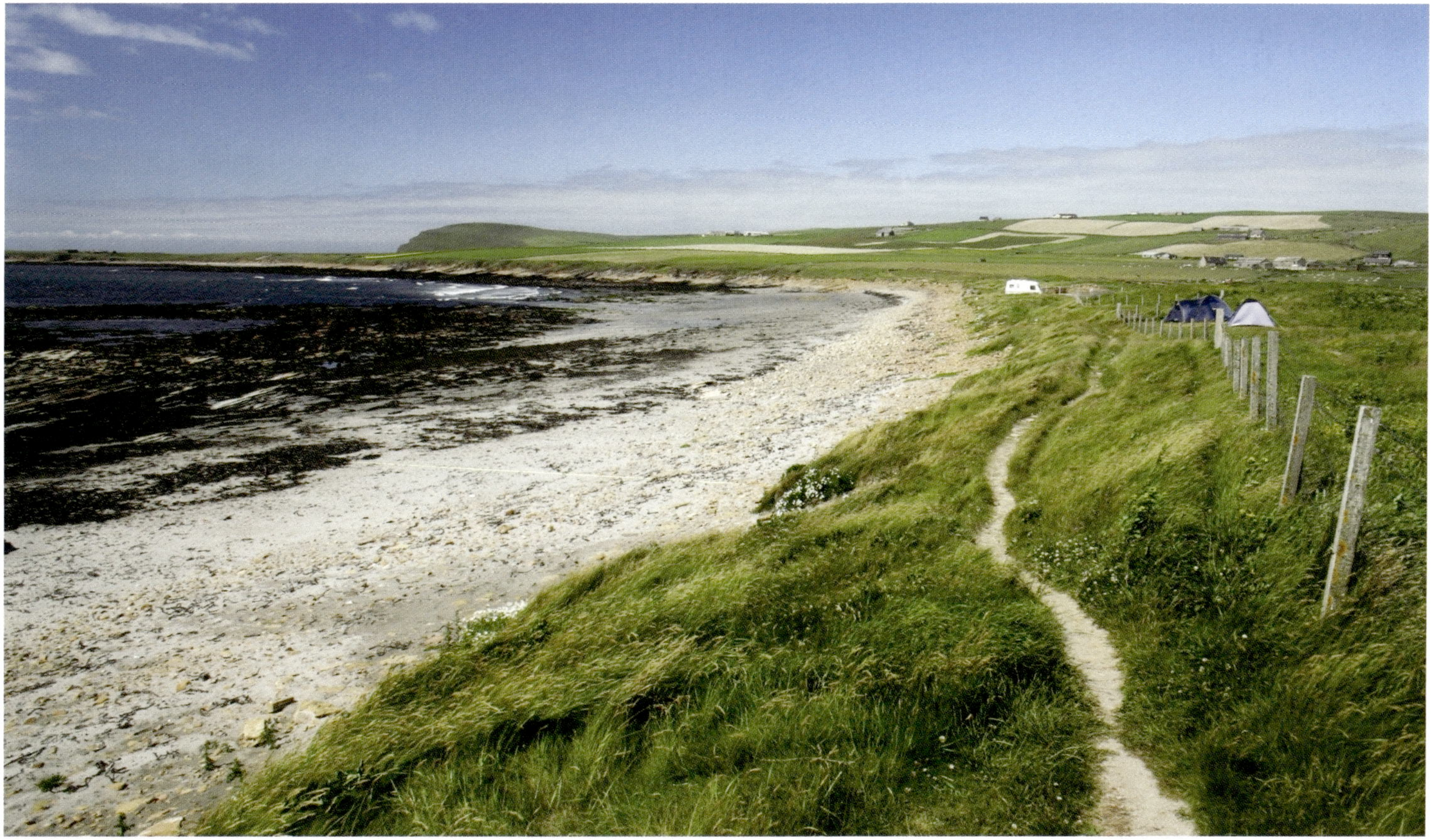

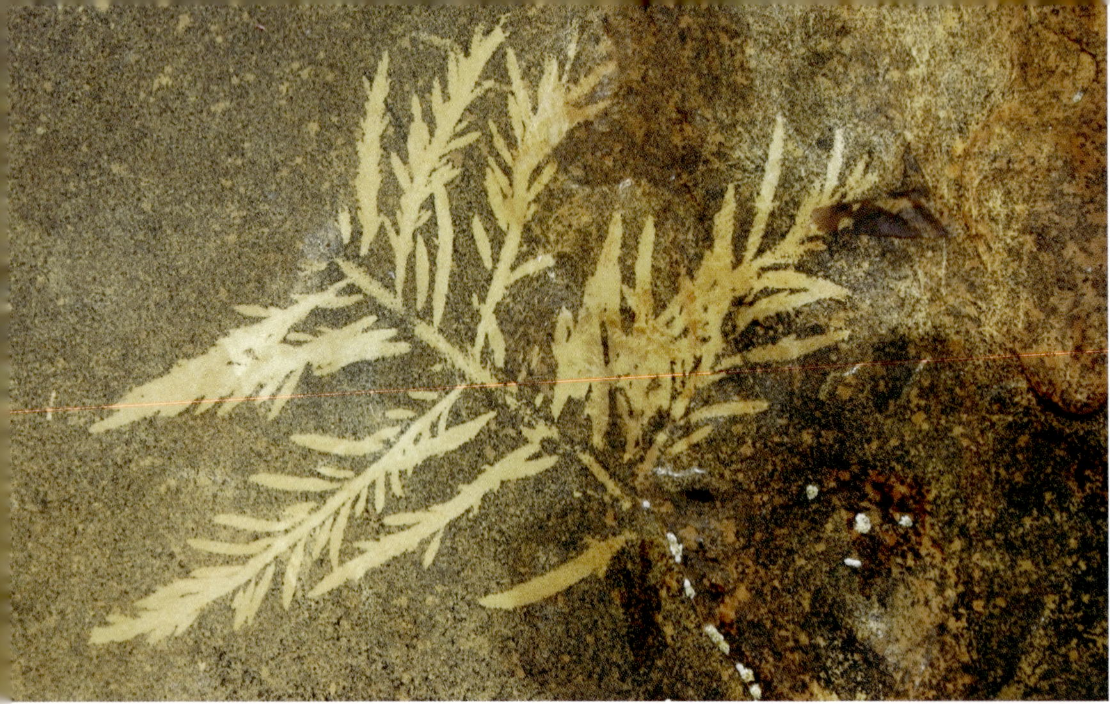

Left: On the Caithness Flags at Warebeth a frond of seaweed has stuck to the rock and remained there for a long time. When peeled off the pattern revealed was remarkable, where the rock around the weed has weathered darker than that which was covered.

Right: An interesting stone sculpture, in the form of a large cairn, perfectly formed and with a long slot running all the way through, at the Sands of Warebeth.

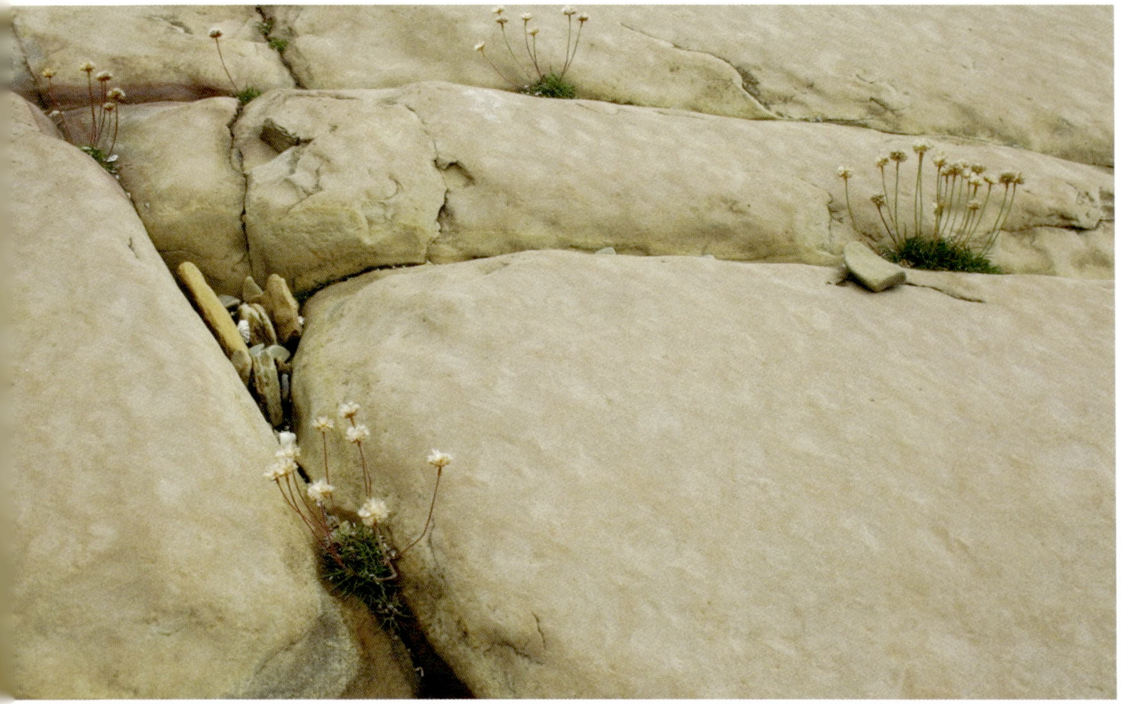

Left: Thrift clings to a harsh existence on the Caithness Flags.

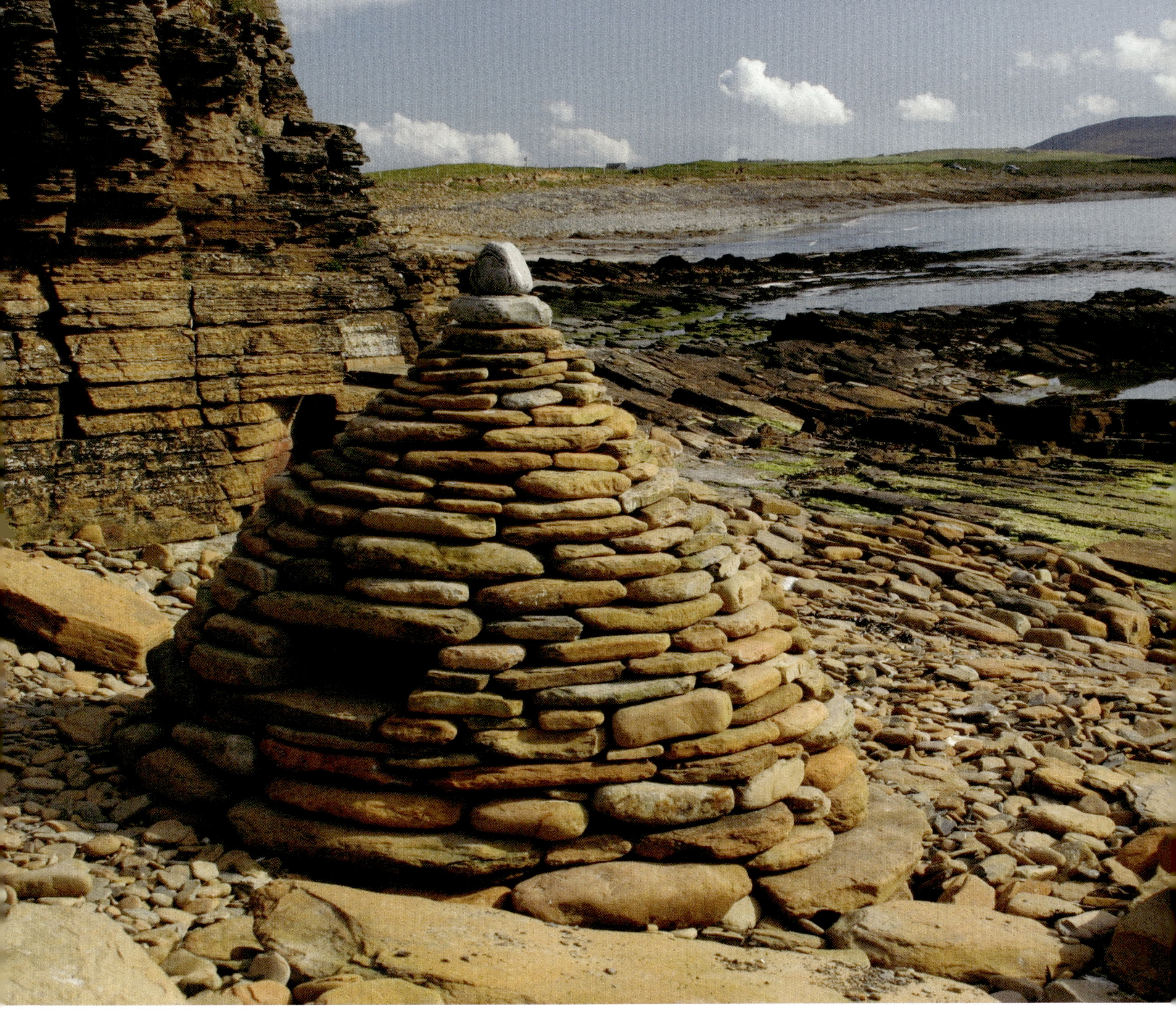

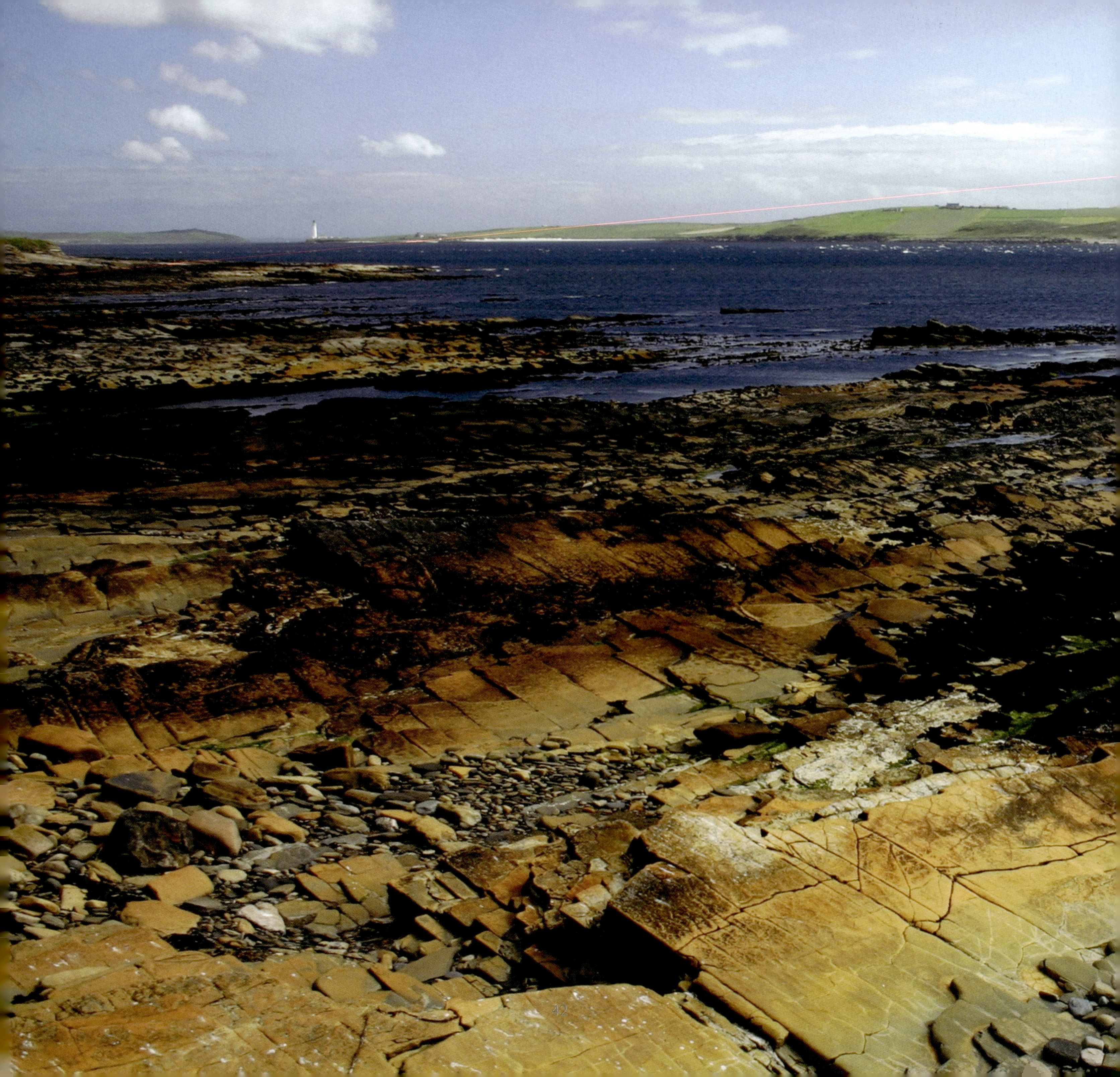

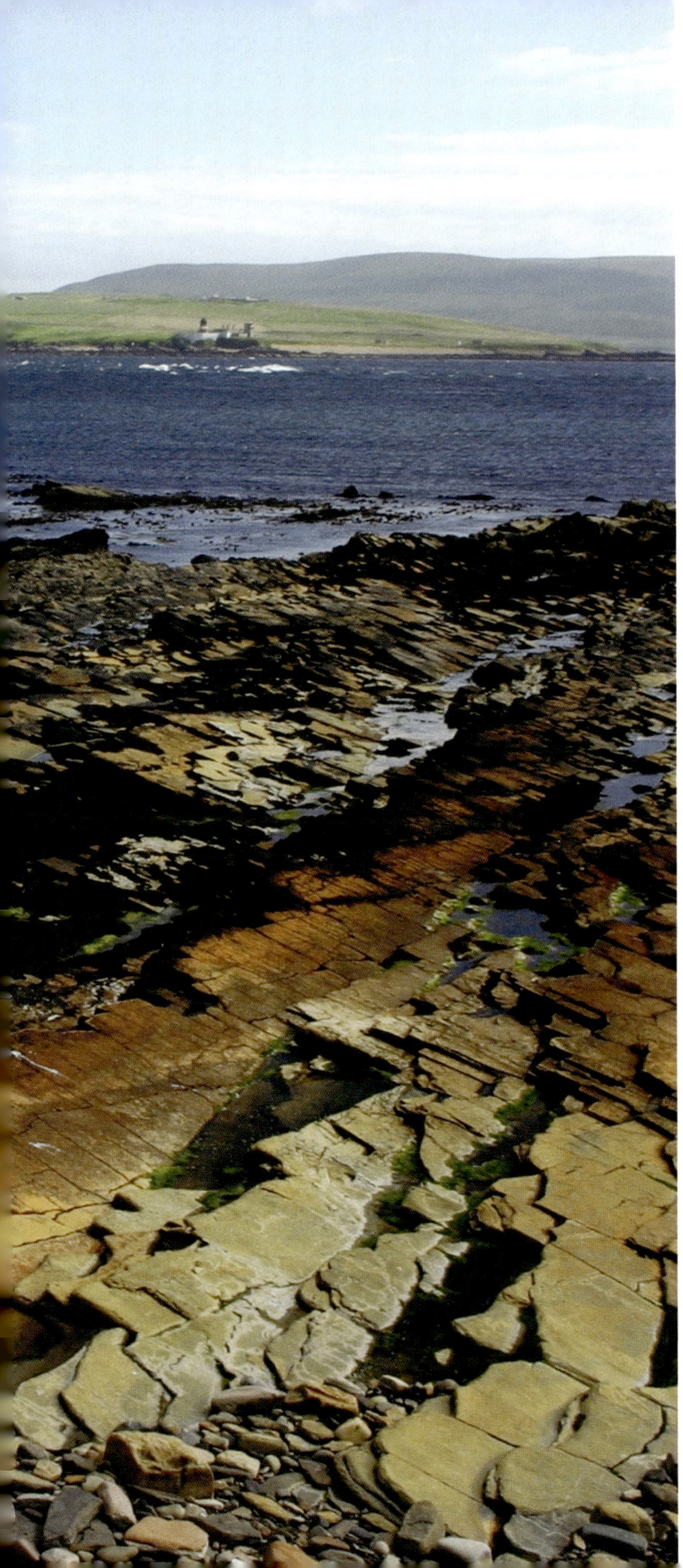

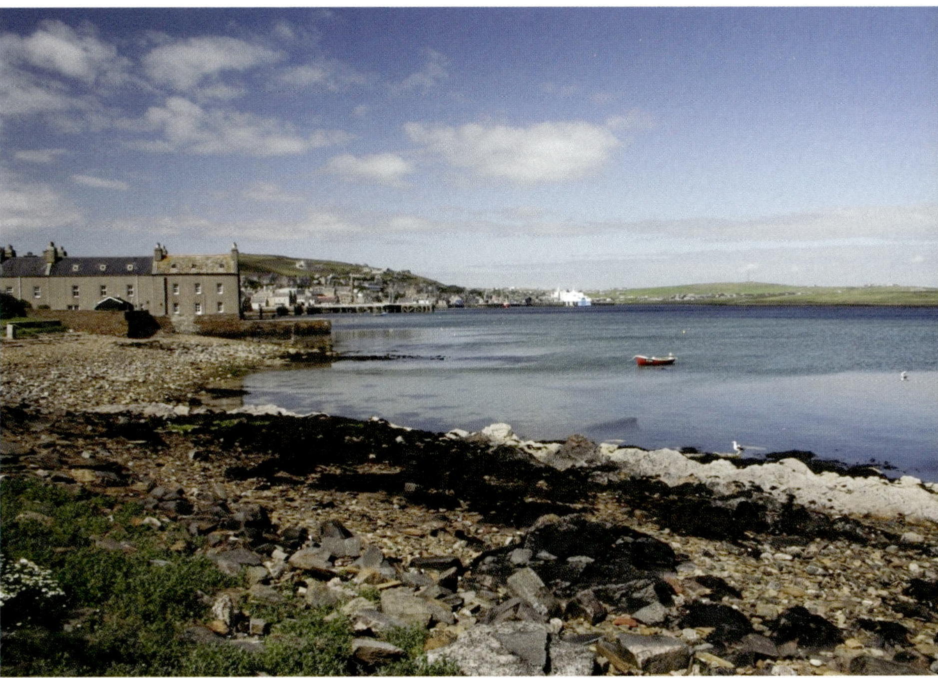

Stromness on the bay of Hamnavoe, from the Skerry of Ness.

Here you can appreciate the flat strata of sedimentary rocks, laid down over hundreds of thousands of years on the sea bed, then thrust up above the waves and tilted.

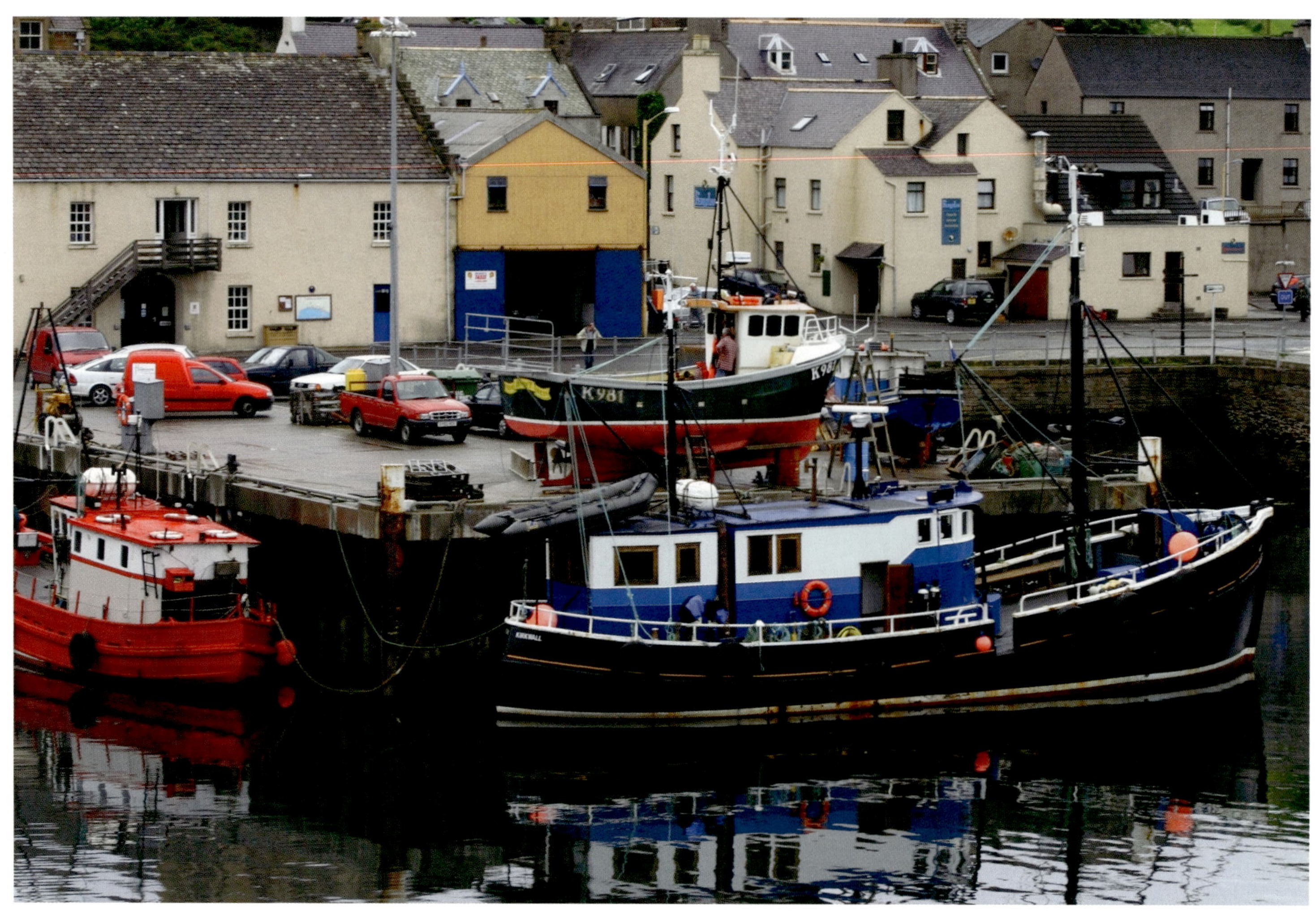


Fishing boats in Stromness. Often these boats now go out with divers into Scapa Flow, where the many wrecks make it one of the top dive sites in Europe.

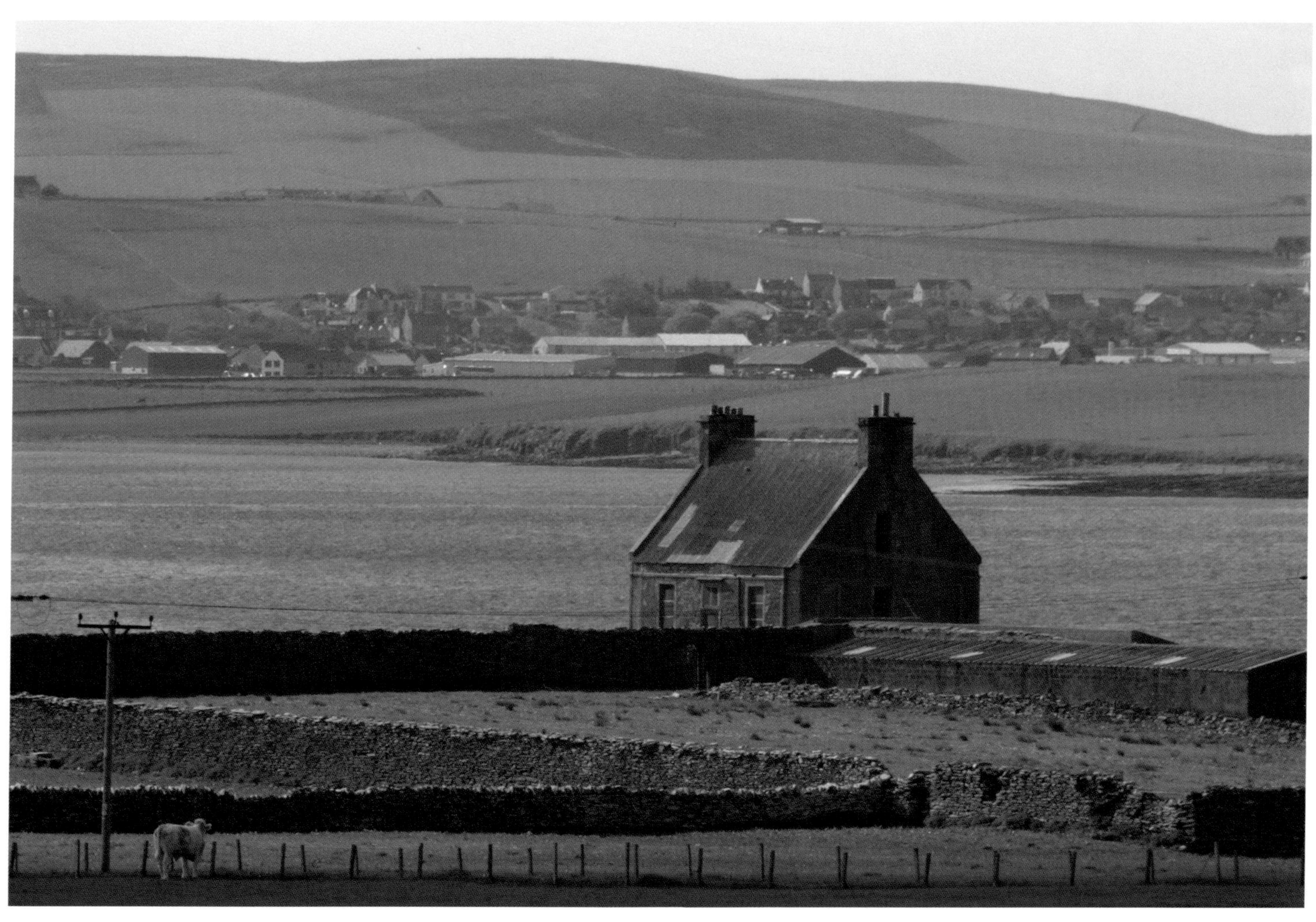

Stromness across the Bay of Ireland.

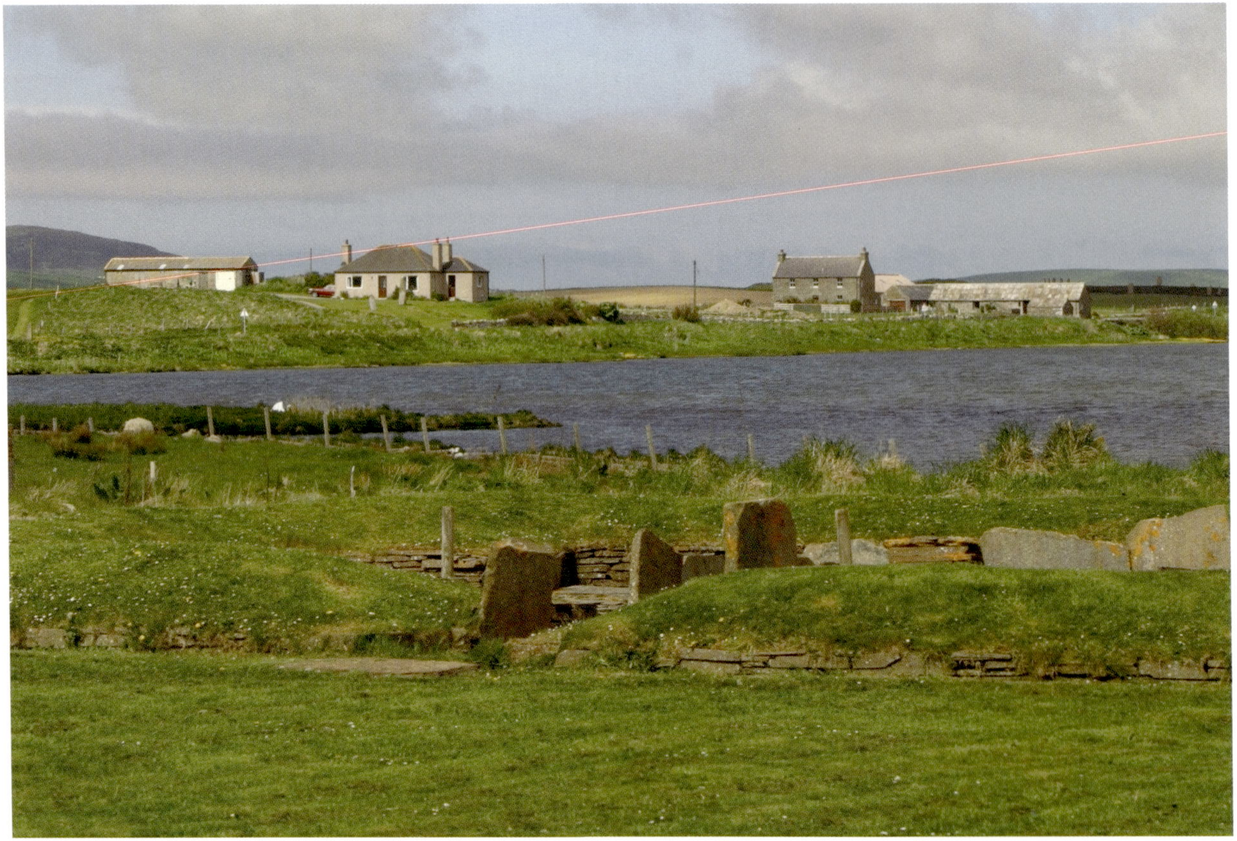

Overlooking the Loch of Harray at Stenness there is a Neolithic village settlement known simply as the Barnhouse. Today all you see is a reconstruction, but it is well worth a visit if you're in the area.

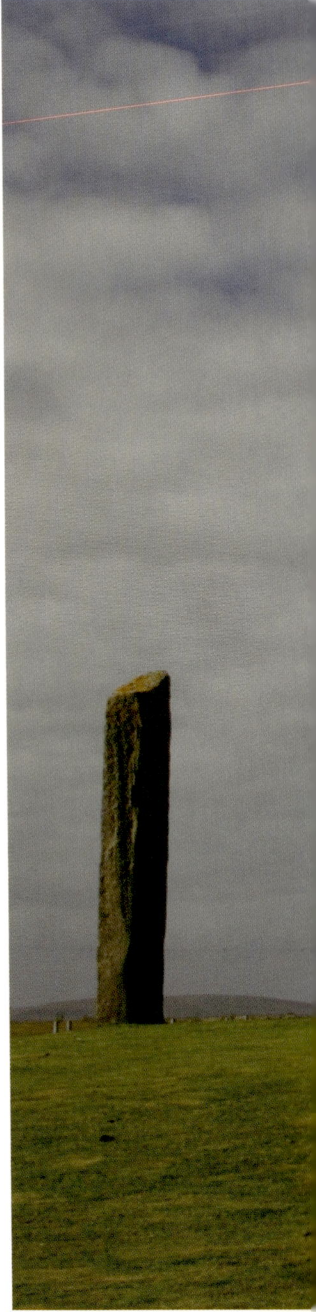

The amazing Stones of Stenness, situated near the narrow spit of land that lies between the brackish Loch of Stenness, and the freshwater Loch of Harray. This impressive Neolithic site is just one of the magnificent ancient monuments around these lochs, with the Ring of Brodgar, the Barnhouse village, Maes Howe, and the Knowe of Onston all close by. Clearly this was a very important place in Stone Age times.

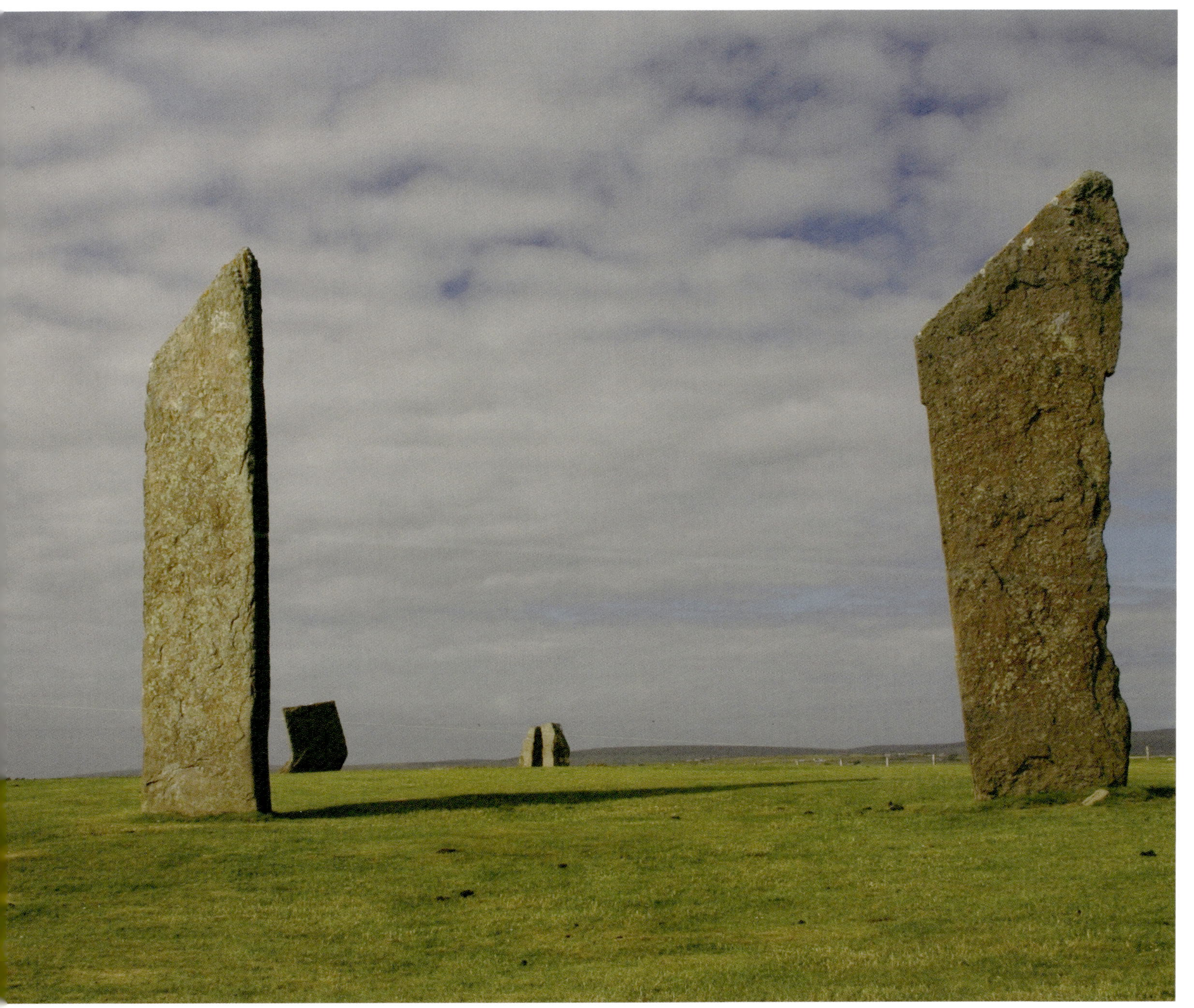

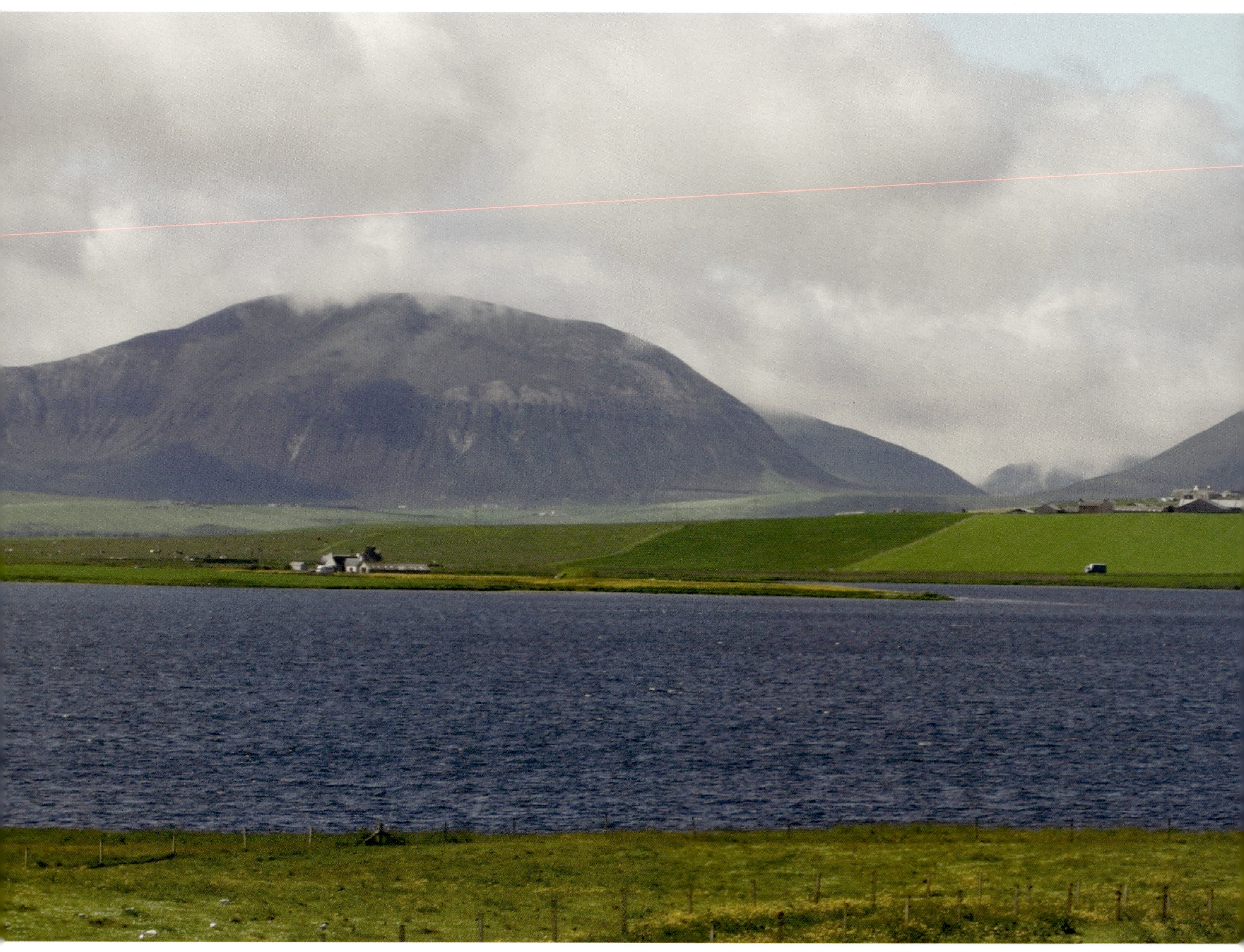

The view across the Loch of Stenness to the hills of Hoy, from the Stones of Stenness.

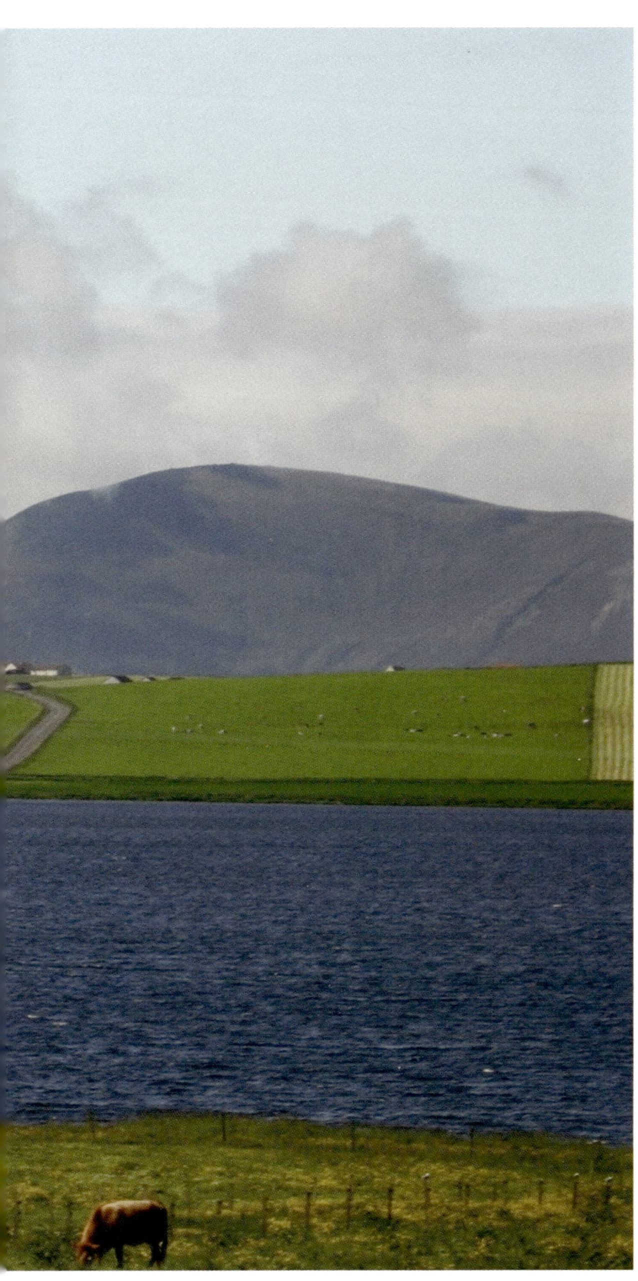

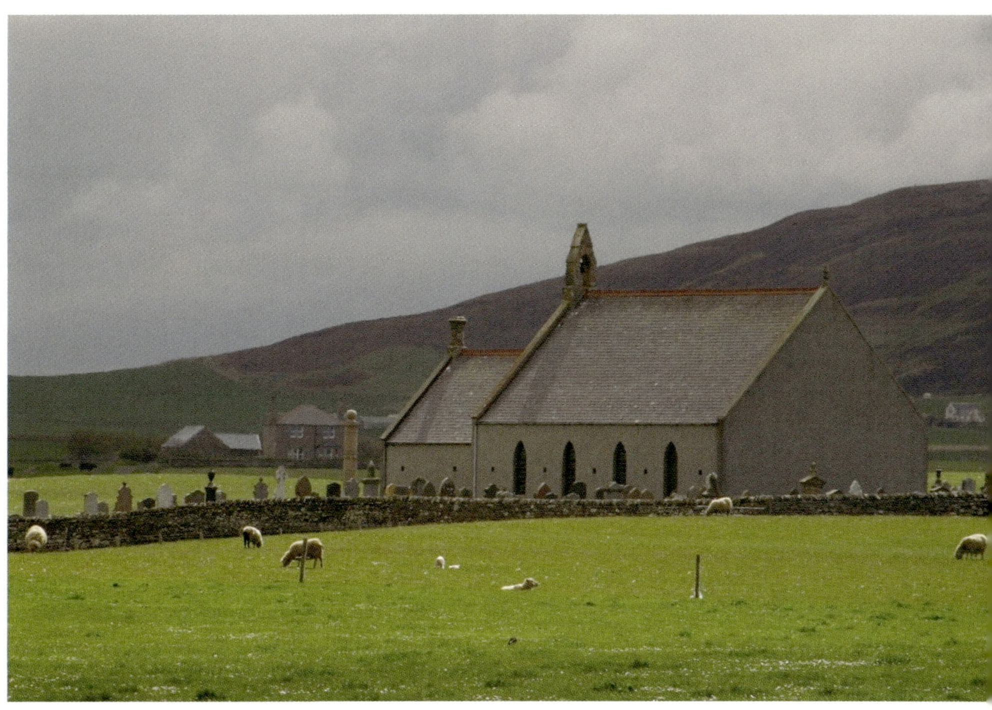

The chapel at Stenness, with Ward Hill behind.

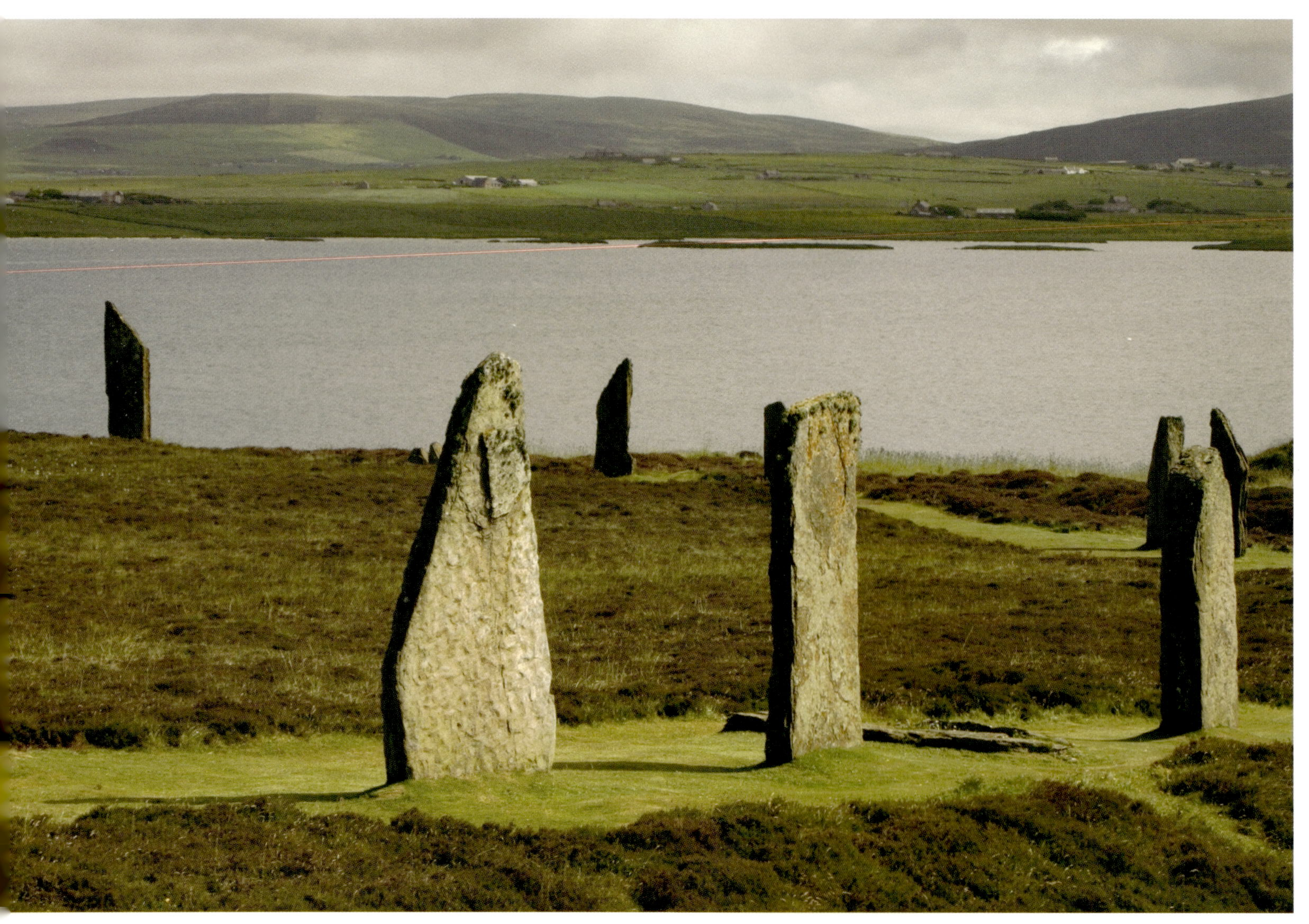

The Ring of Brodgar overlooking the Loch of Harray.

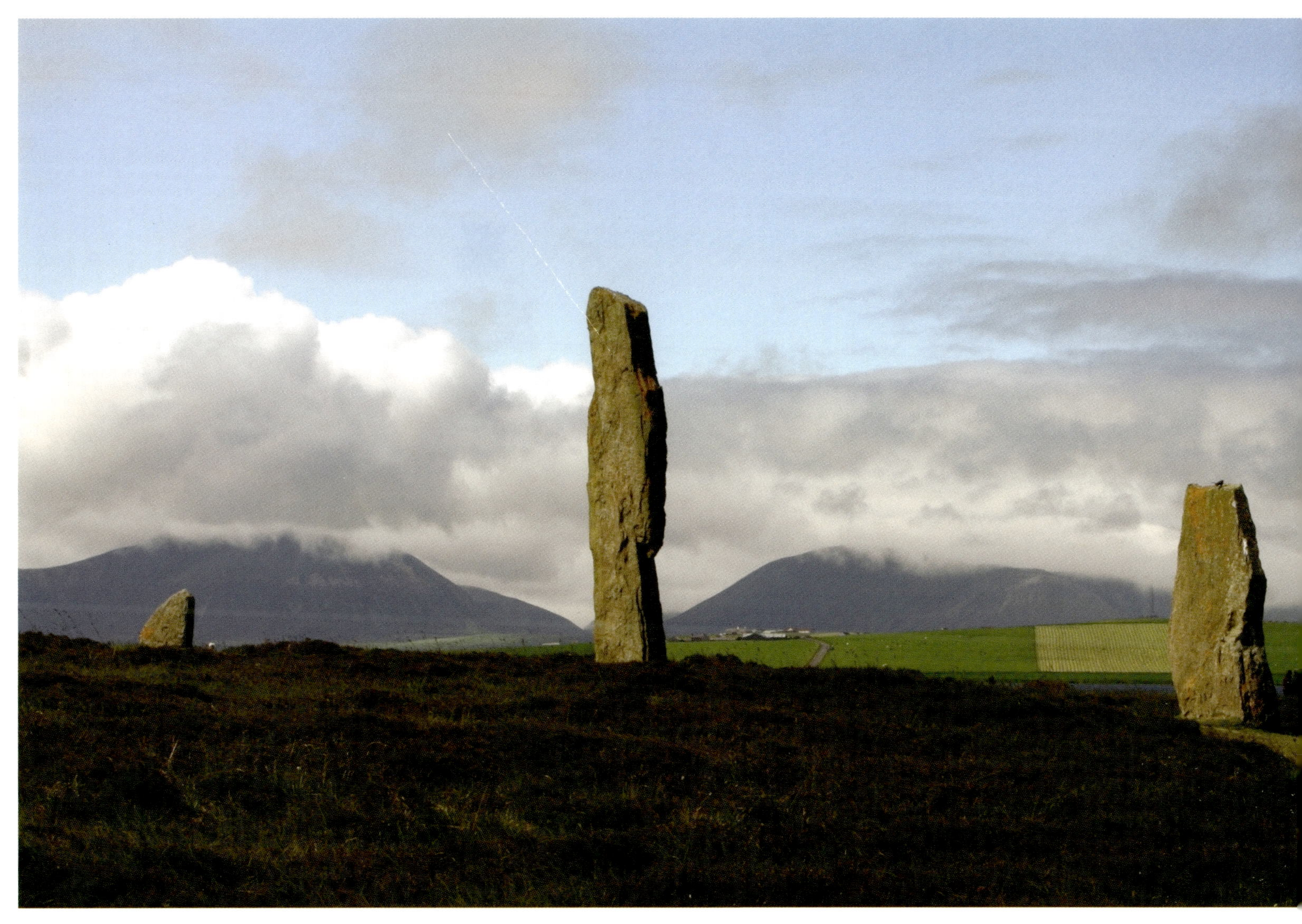

The Ring of Brodgar framing the hills of Hoy, with Ward Hill, the highest in the Northern Isles at 481 metres, to the left, and Cuilags to the right.

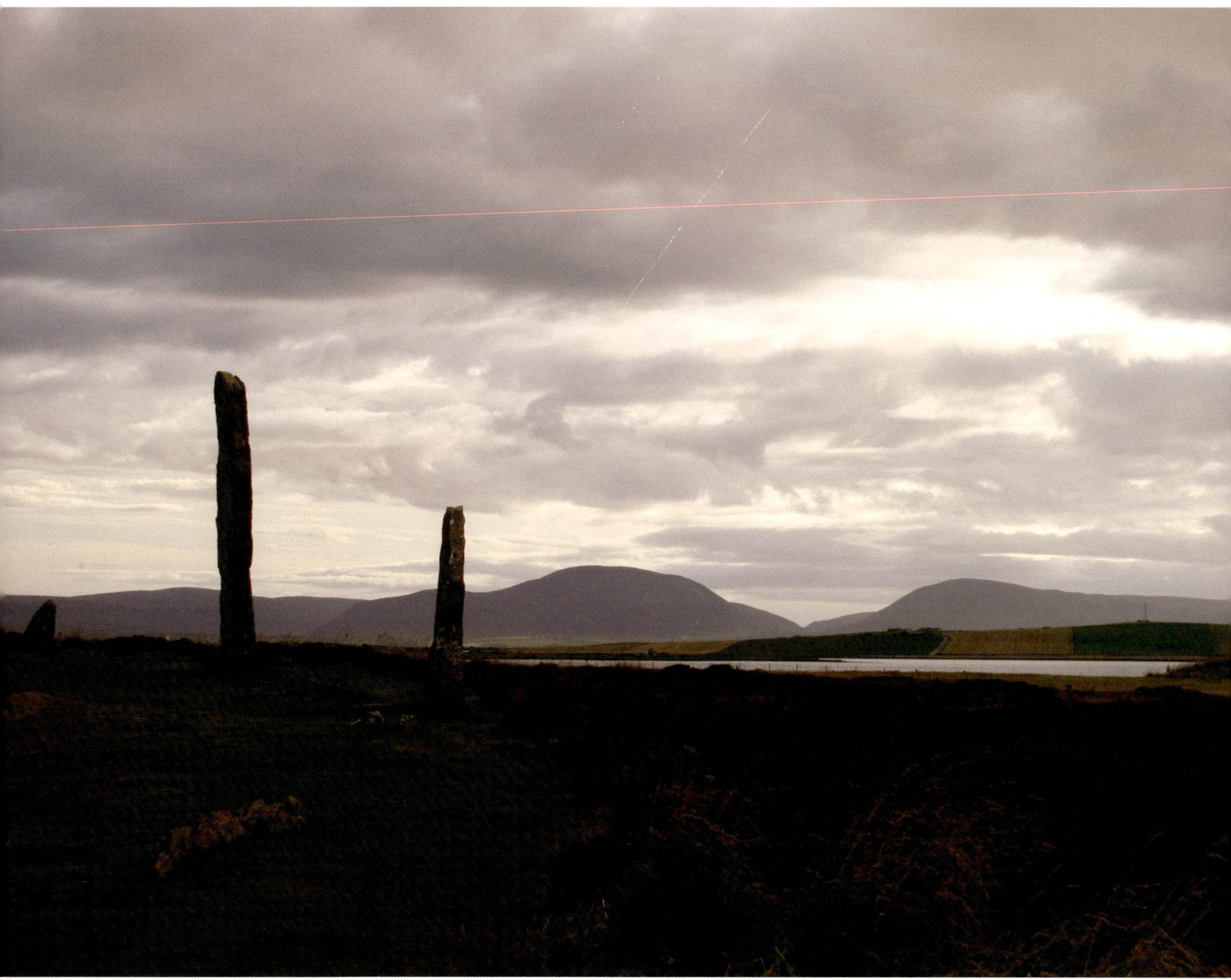

Left: Given the importance of the Ring of Brodgar, it is no surprise that UNESCO described the henge as being at the heart of the Neolithic Orkney World Heritage Site.

Right: On the narrow isthmus between the Loch of Stenness and the Loch of Harray stands the important henge known as the Ring of Brodgar. Its exact age is not known, although many archaeologists believe it to have been built around 2500BC. It is the third largest henge in Britain, and originally had 60 standing stones around its circumference. Today however, only 27 remain.

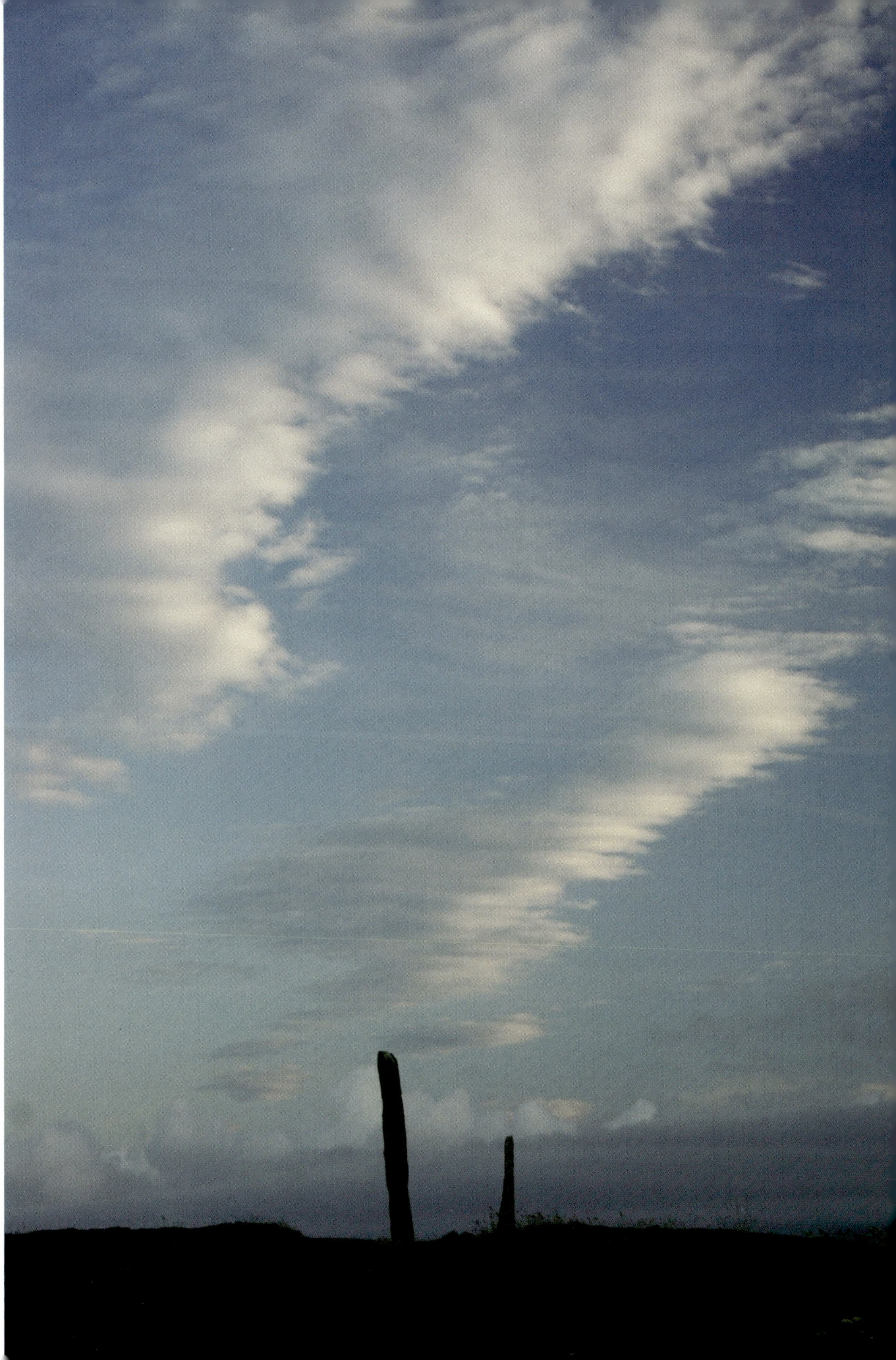

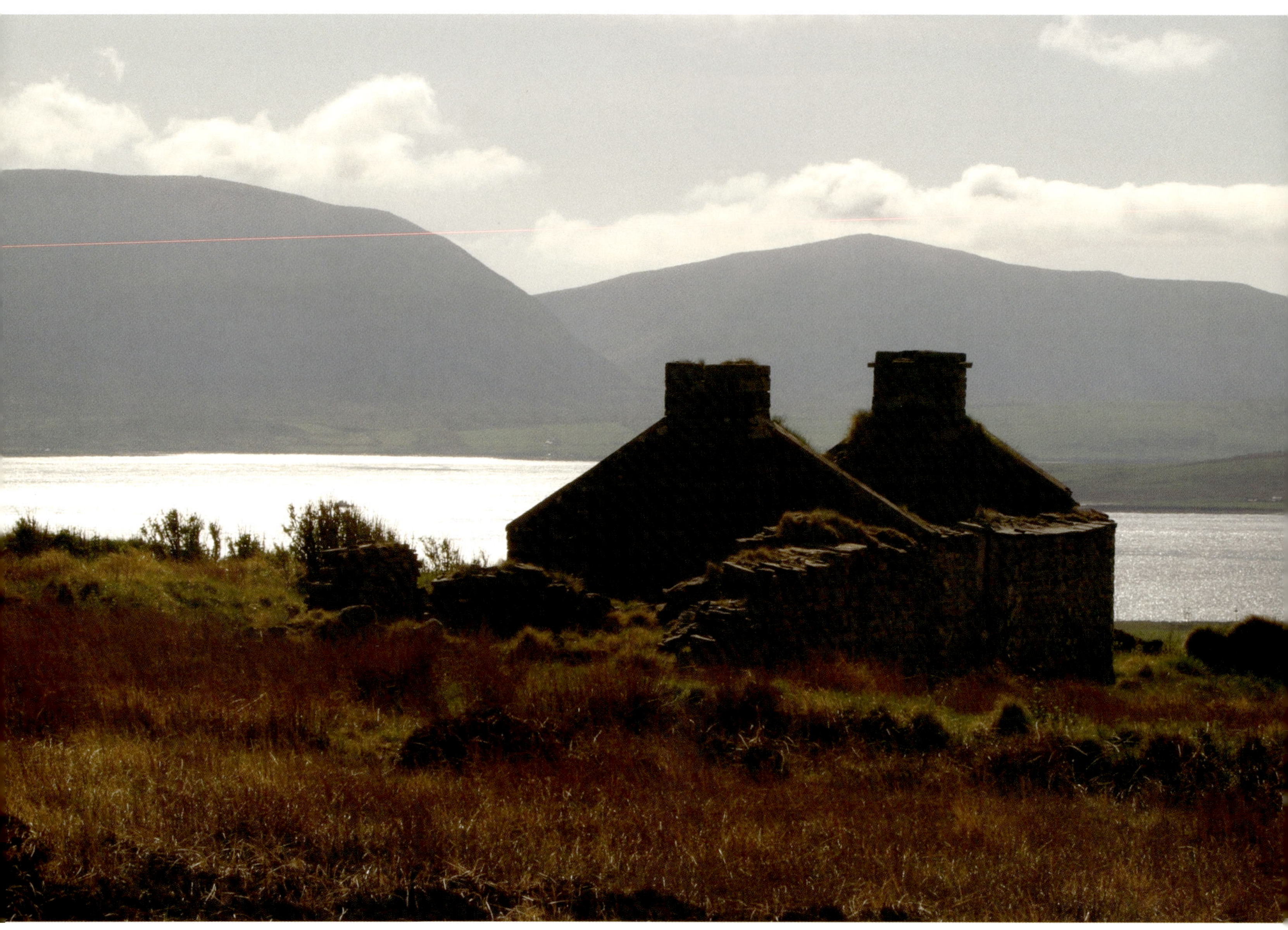

An old cottage at Langwell beneath Gruf Hill. Across the Clestrain Sound the hills of Hoy dominate the view.

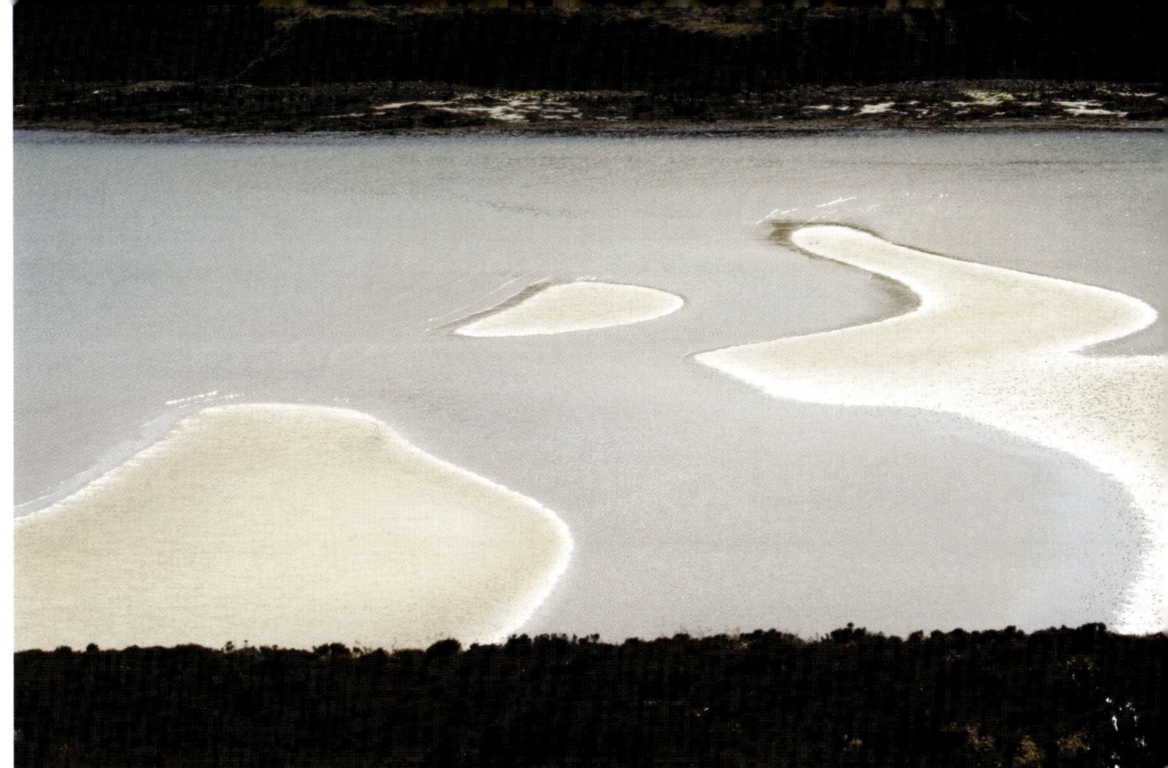

Sand patterns at the delightful Waulkmill Bay.

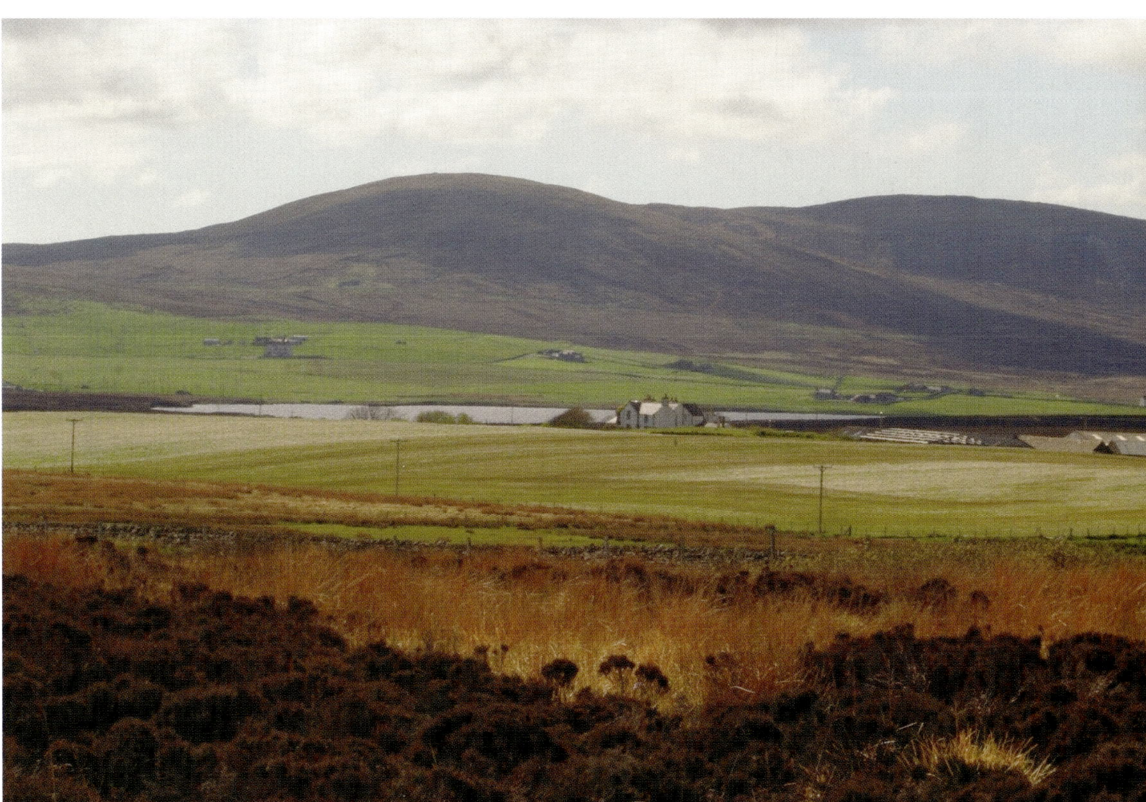

Ward Hill on Mainland Orkney from Hobbister.

The Italian Chapel on the tiny island of Lamb Holm.

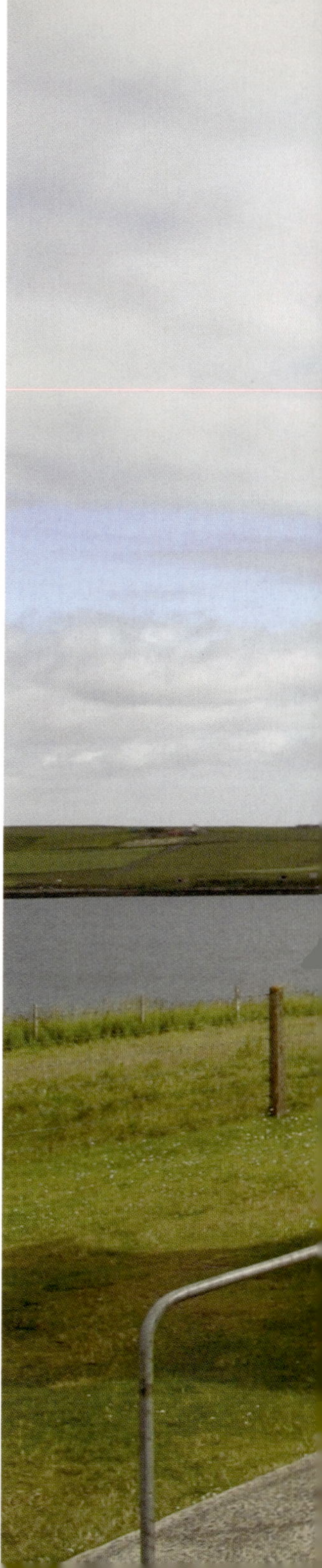

Inside the Italian Chapel. The island of Lamb Holm is where Italian Prisoners of War were kept during World War Two while they were working on the Churchill Barriers. On the island, they built this remarkable chapel, using two Nissen huts and any bits of scrap that they could find or scrounge.

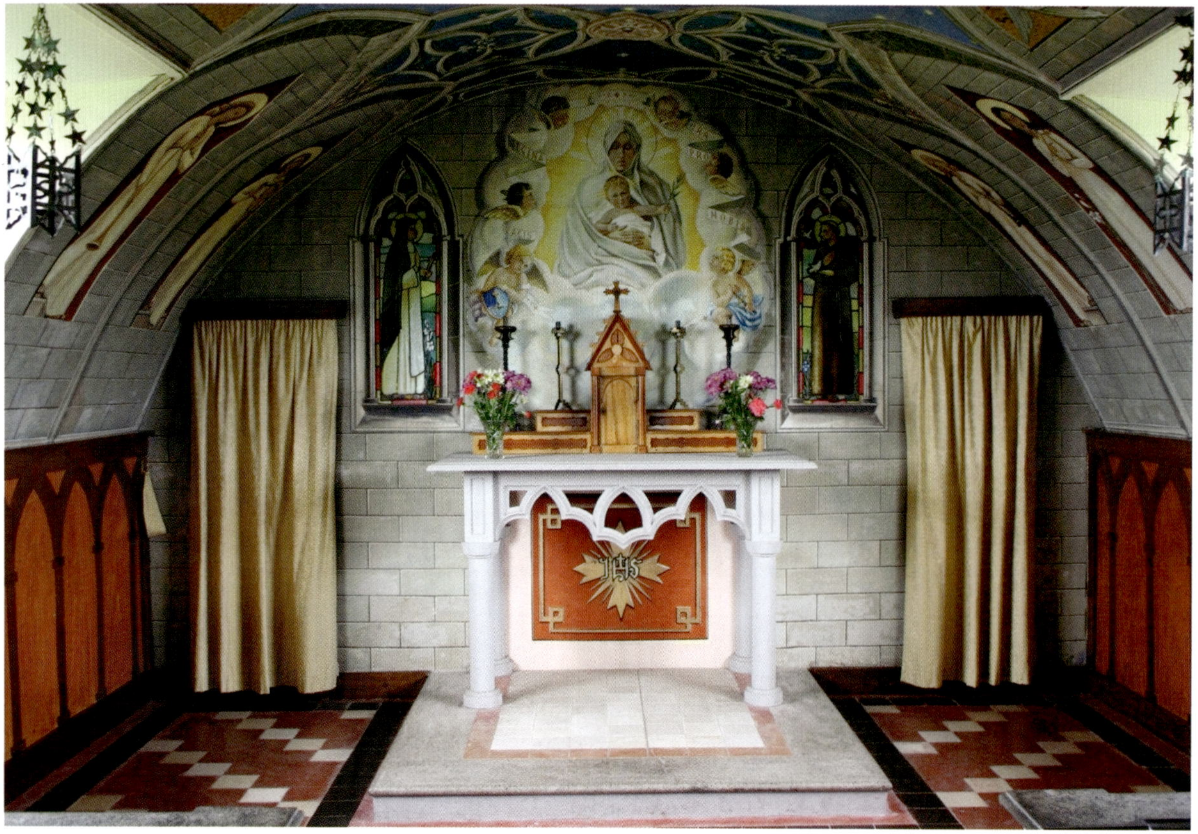

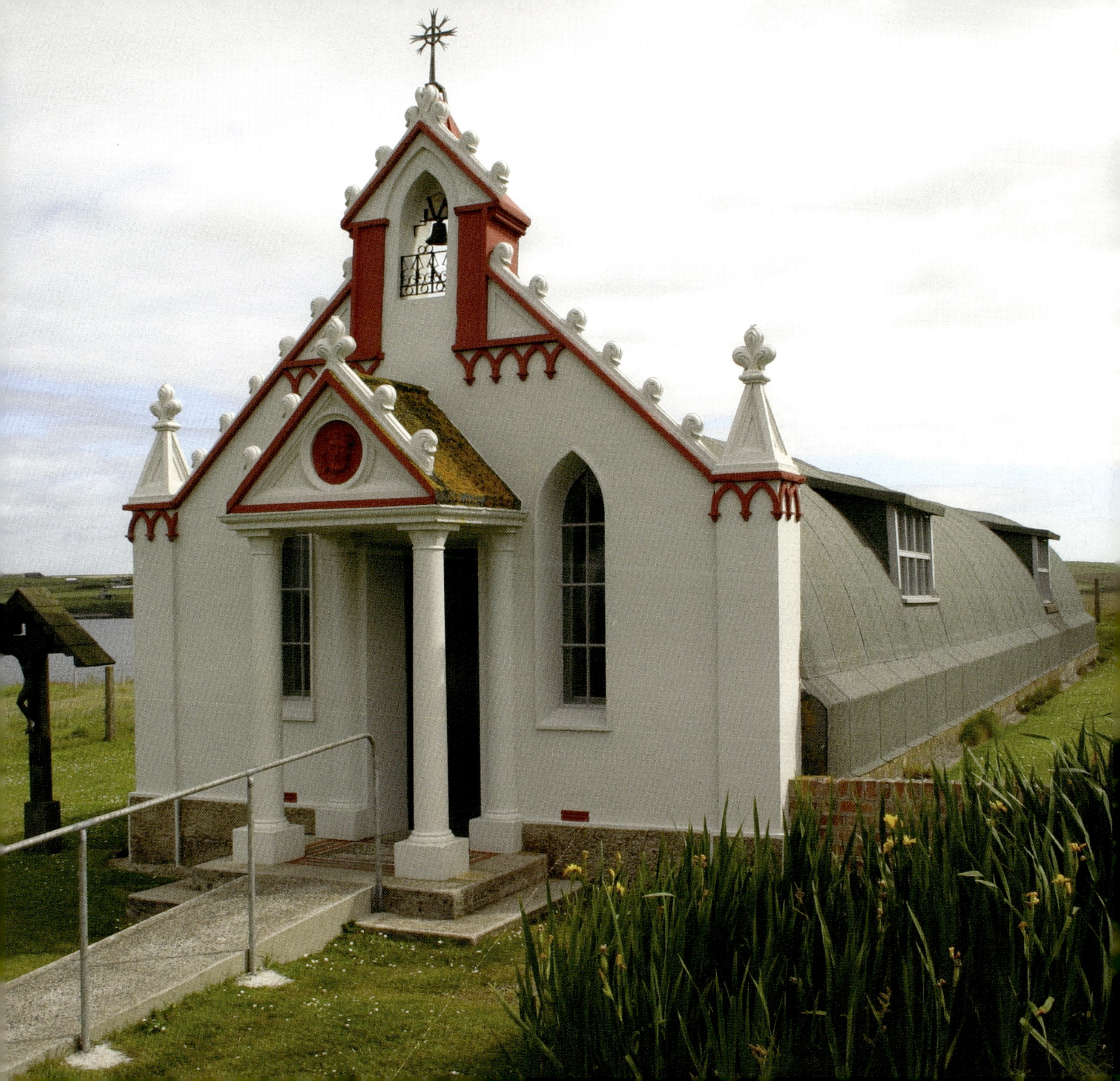

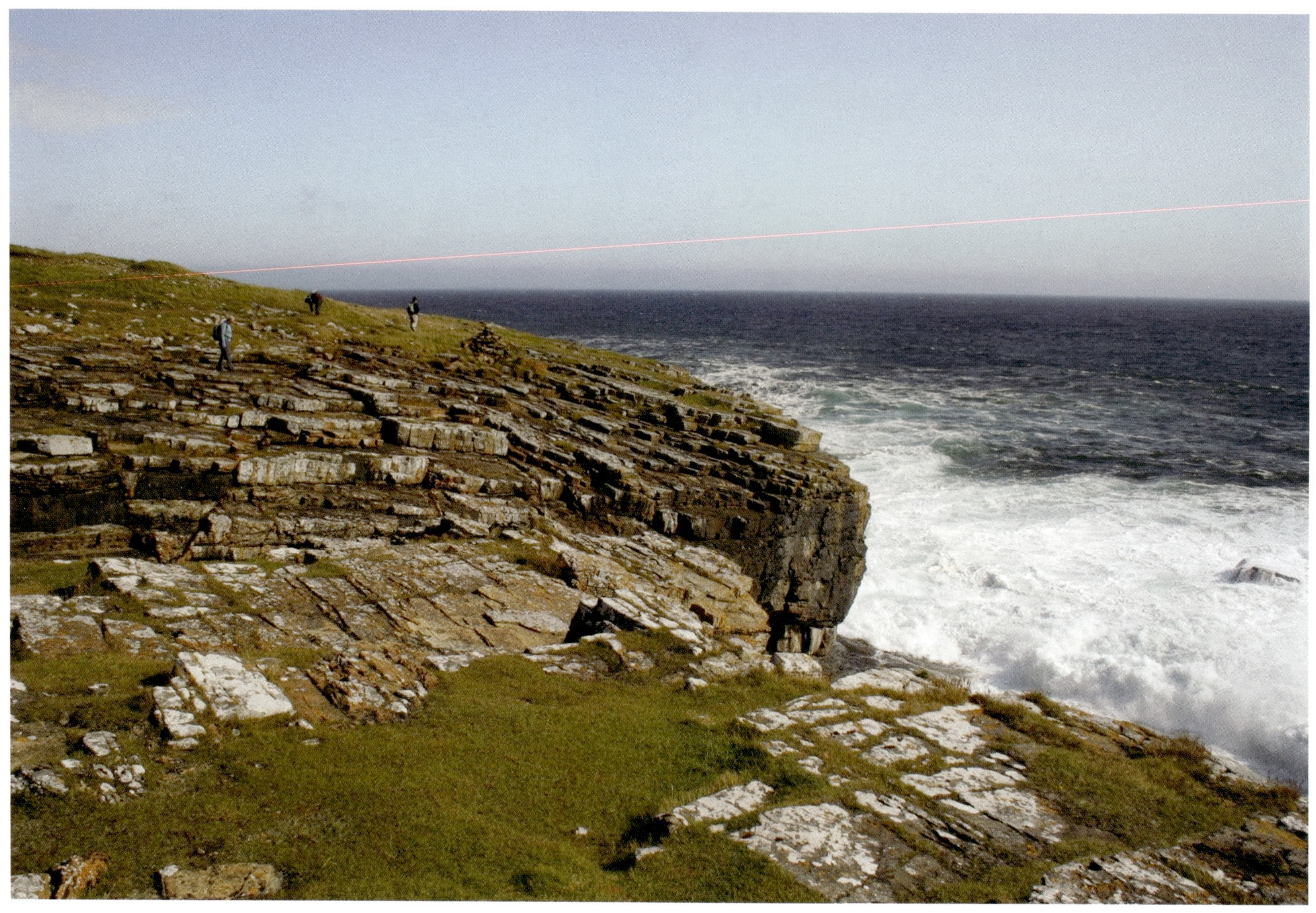

Above: On the east side of Mainland at Deerness. The seas pile in to the shore near The Gloup.

Above right: A stone cairn on the flat cliff tops at Deerness.

Right: A girl explores the coast at Deerness, stopping to look for seals on a tiny skerry.

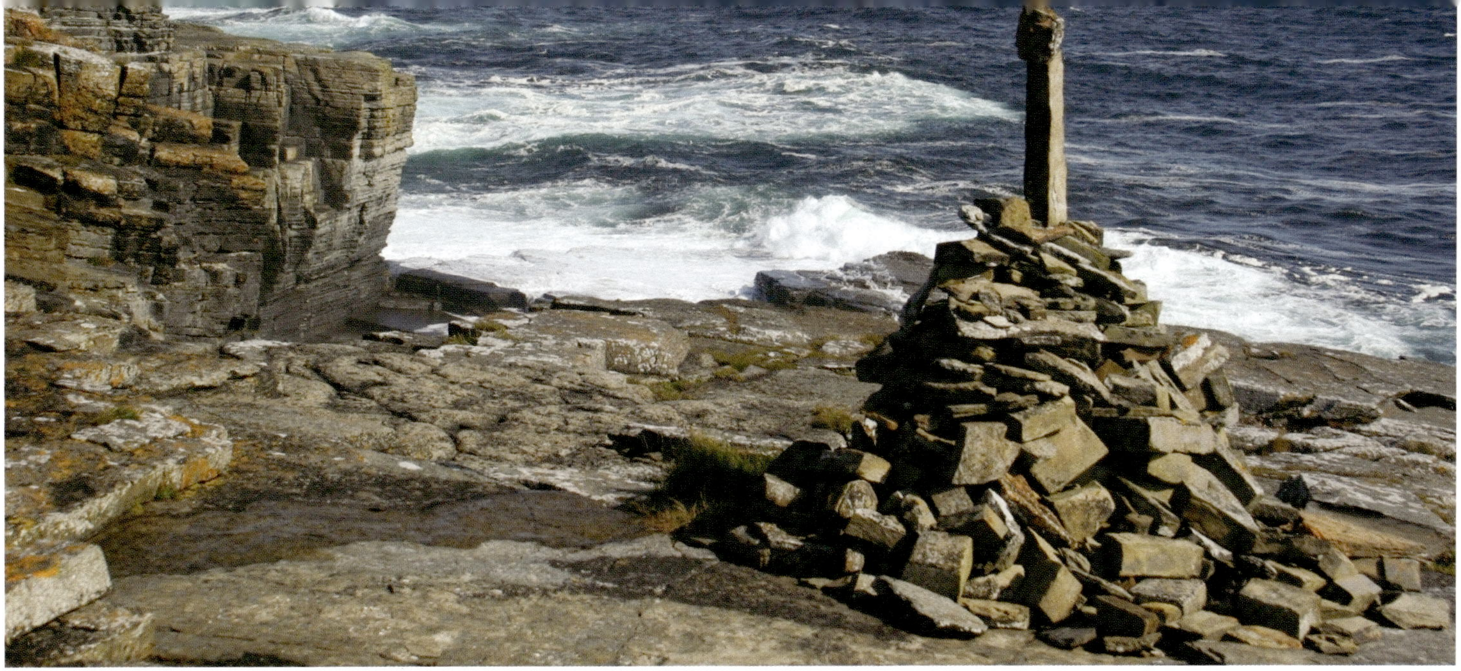

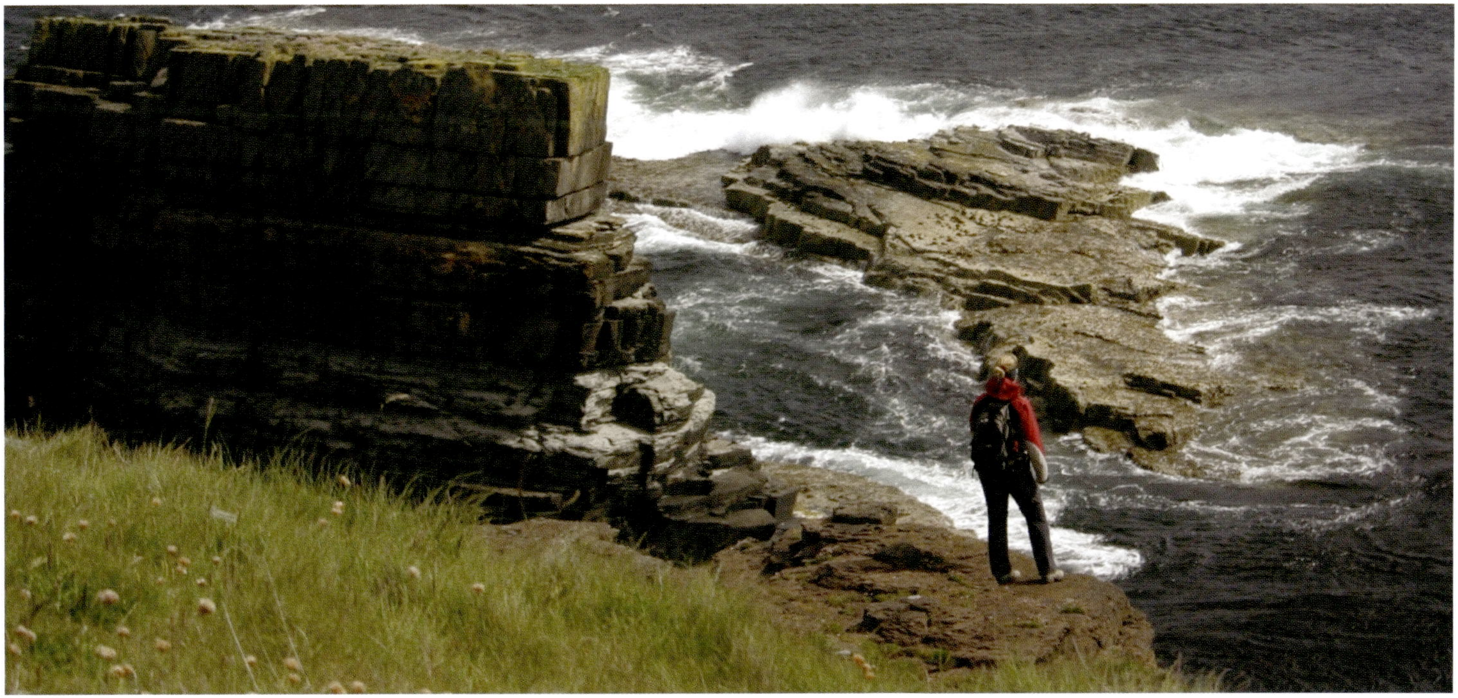

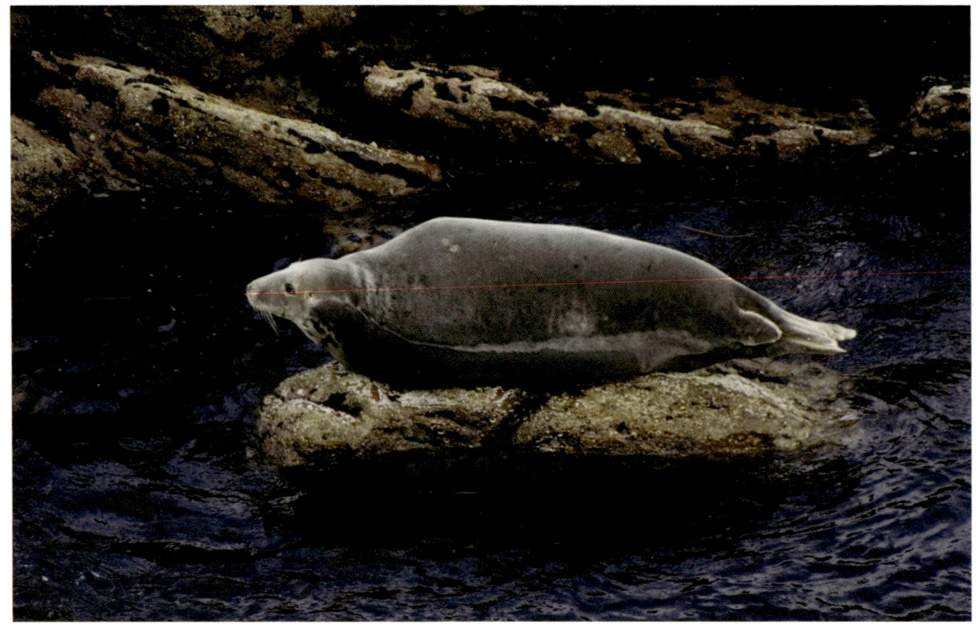

Grey seals are very common in the Northern Isles. You can often see them hauled out on rocks and skerries.

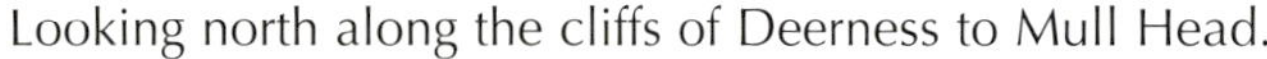

Looking north along the cliffs of Deerness to Mull Head.

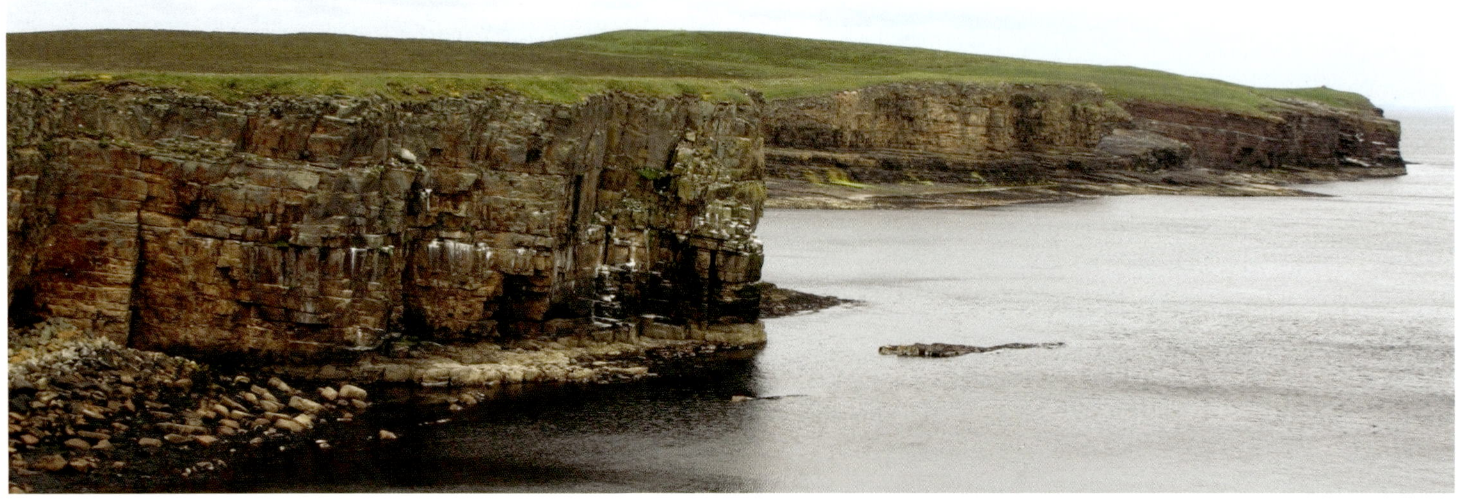

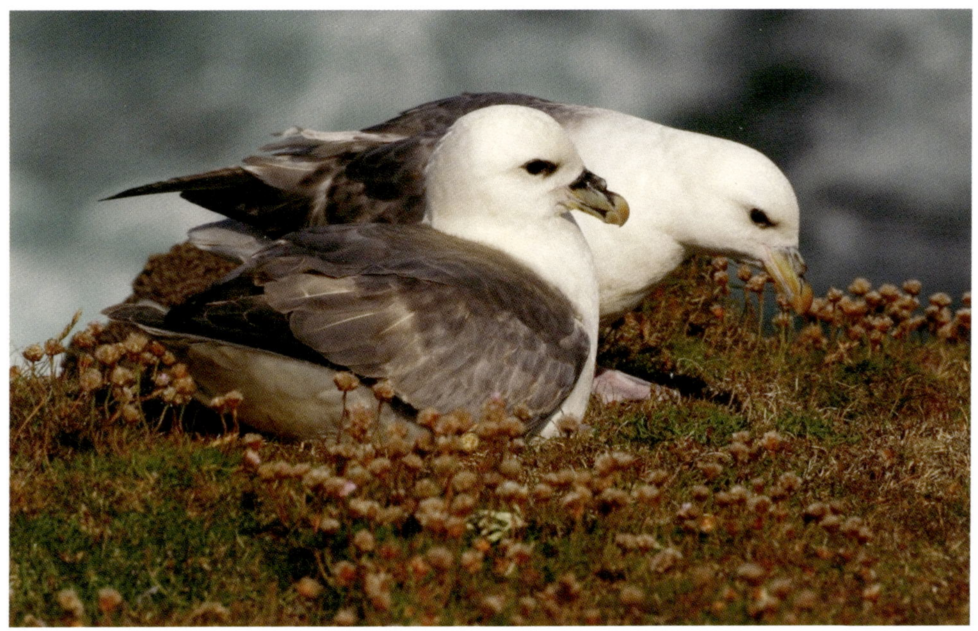

Fulmar petrels nest on practically every sea cliff in the Northern Isles. Here they are at Mull Head.

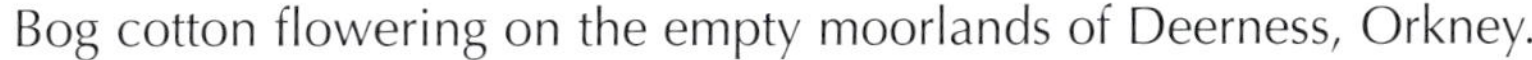

Bog cotton flowering on the empty moorlands of Deerness, Orkney.

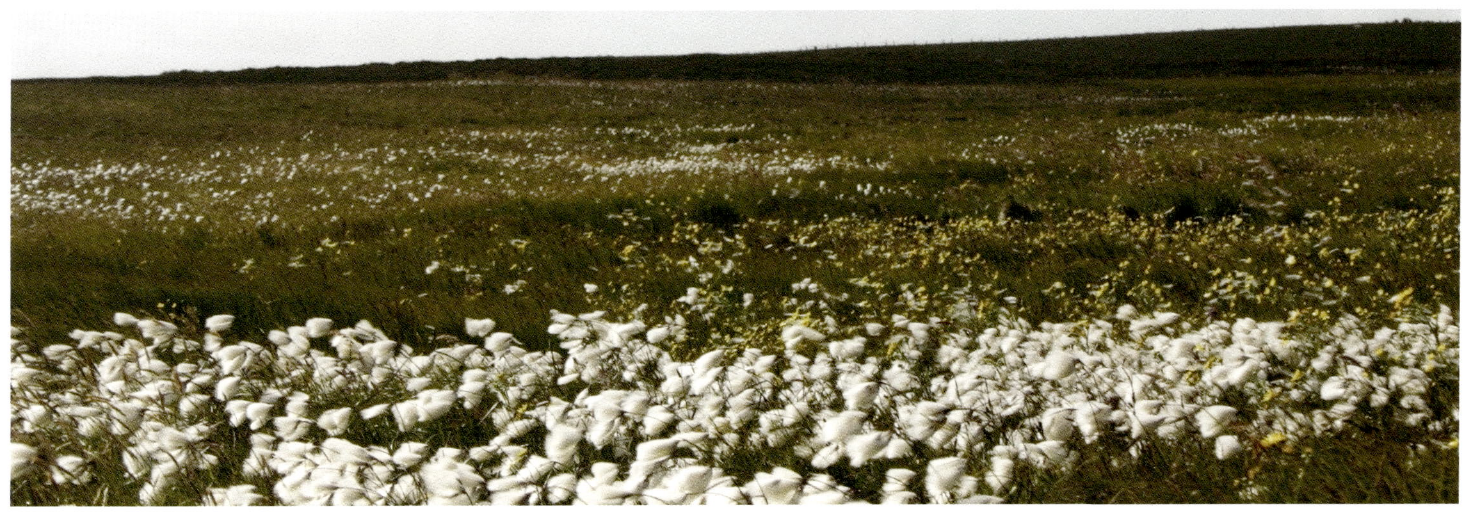

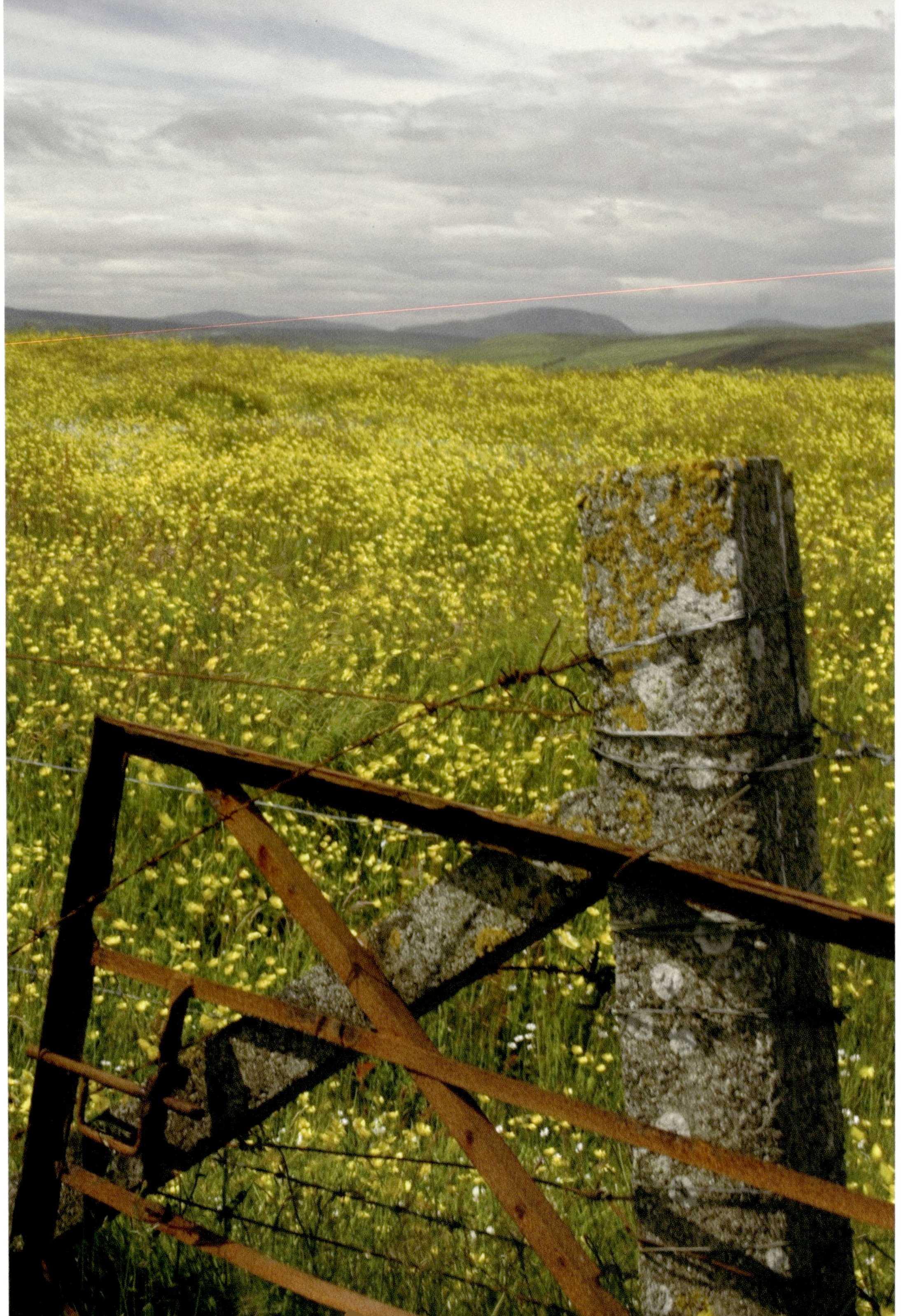

Left: Wildflower meadows
on Enyas Hill.

Right: An old stone wall
leads the eye off Enyas Hill
towards the island of Gairsay,
out in Gairsay Sound.

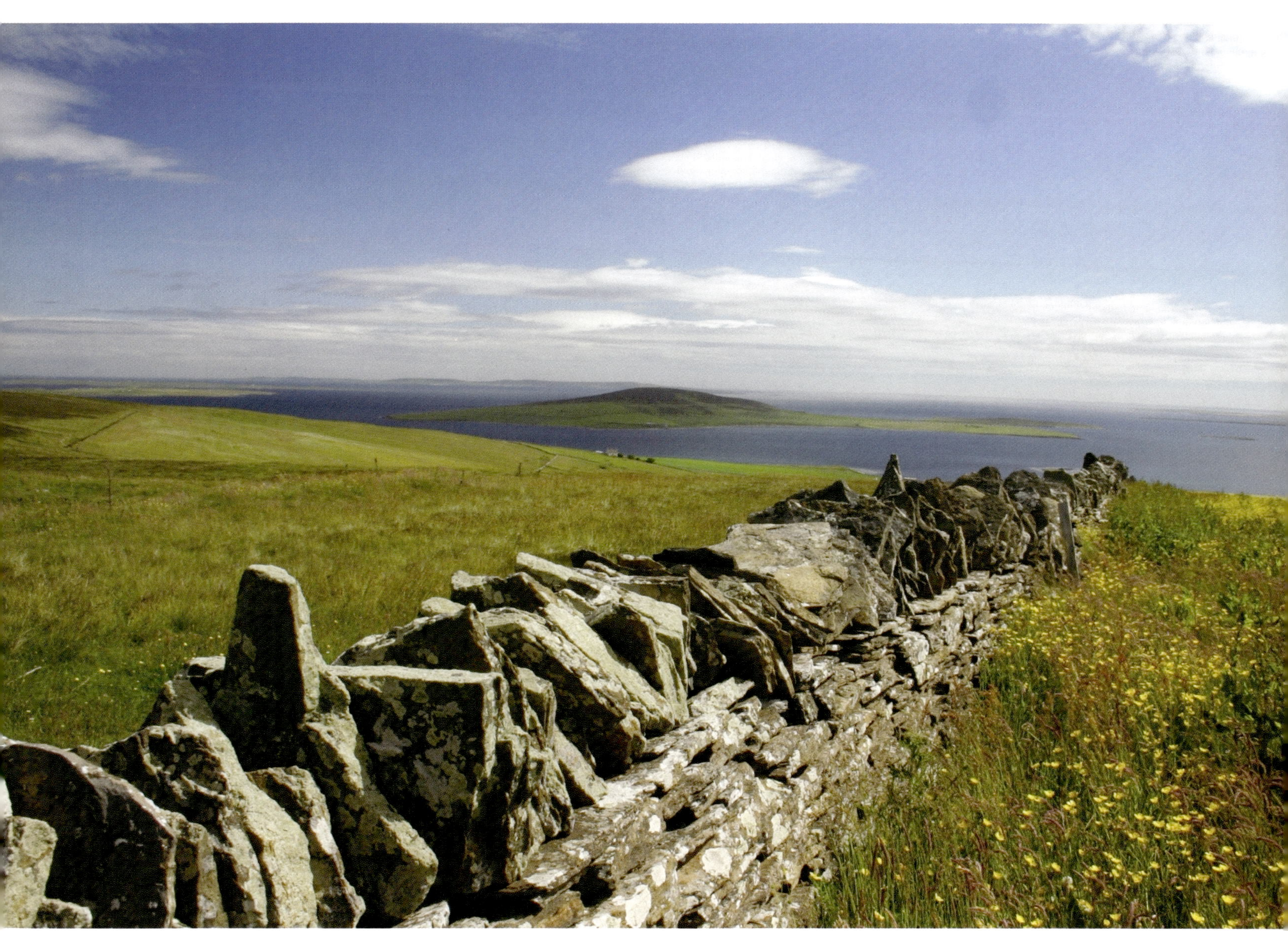

Gairsay is a wonderful, little visited island just off the north side of Mainland Orkney.

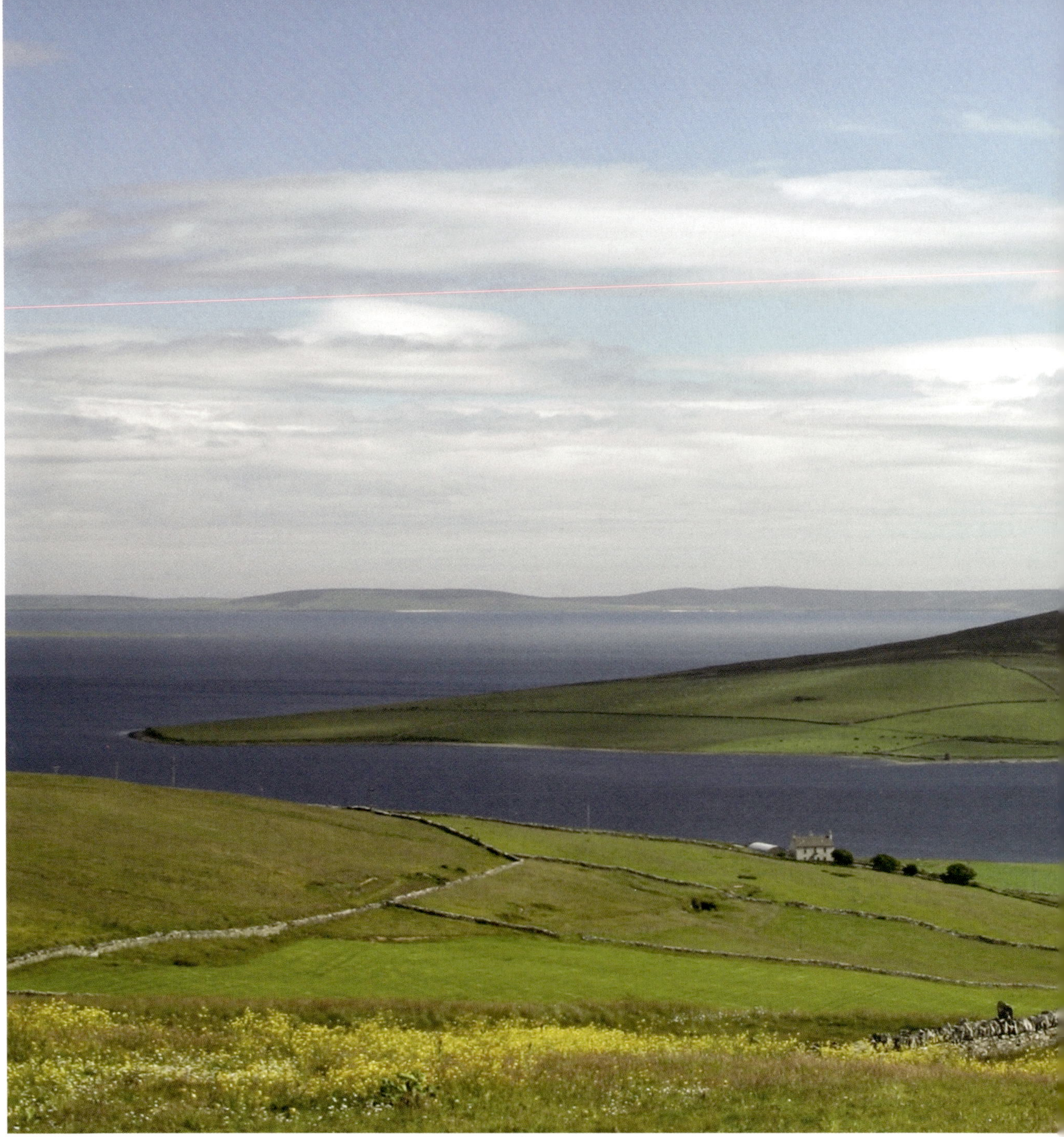

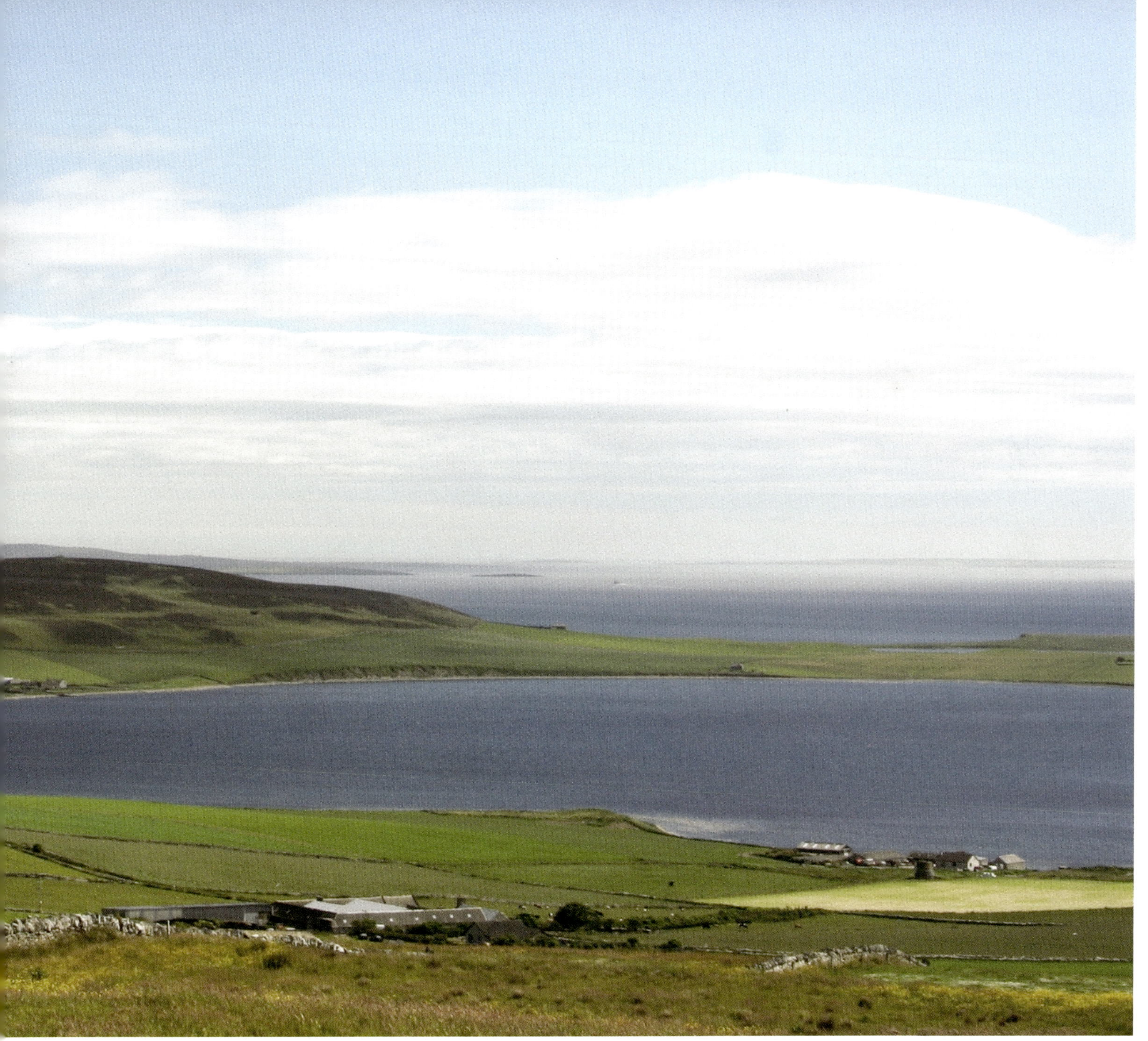

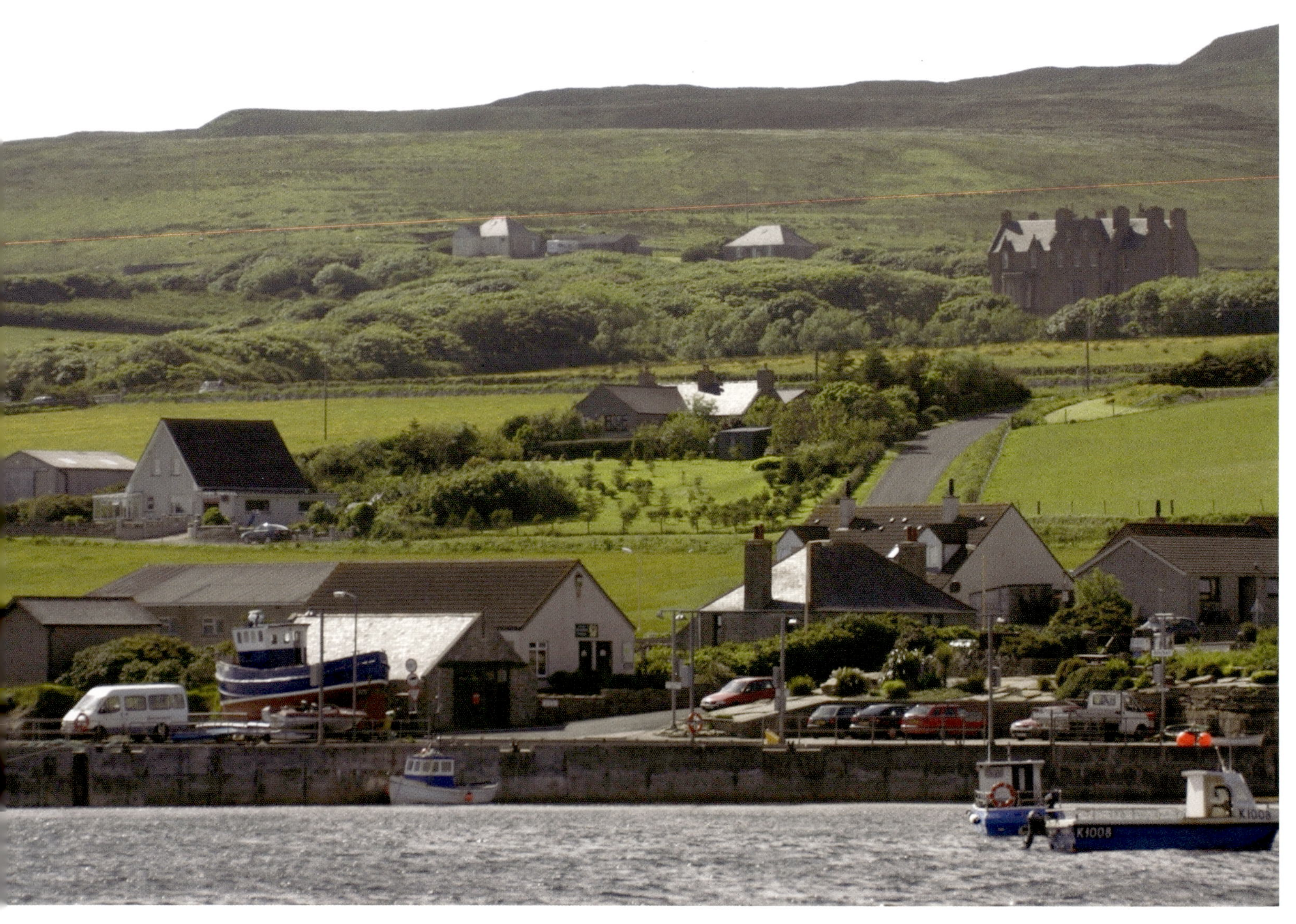


Just north of Mainland Orkney the island of Rousay is one of the few in this group that can truly be described as 'hilly'. This is Trumland, which is where the ferry comes in from Mainland.

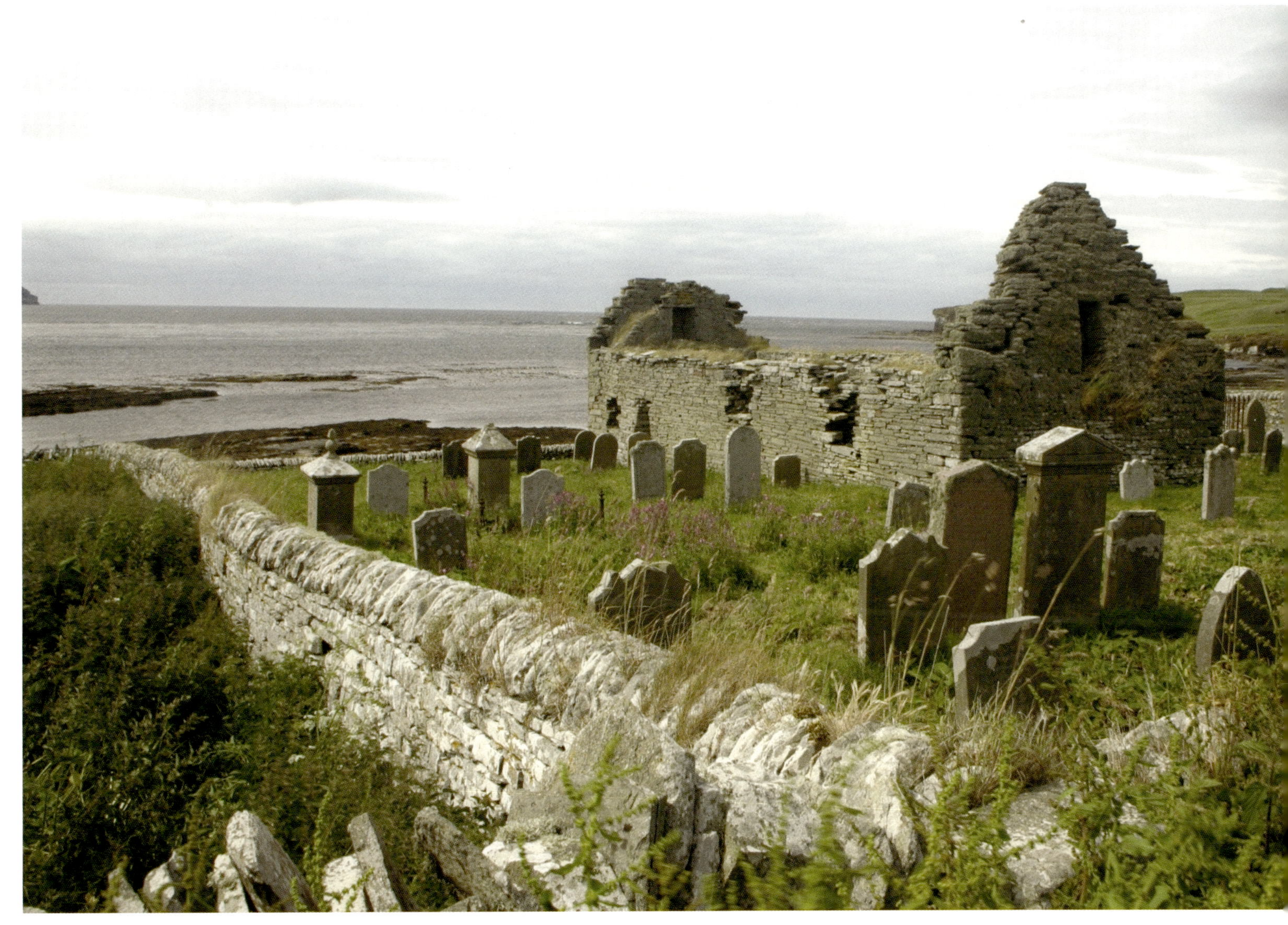

Along the south-west coast of Rousay there are countless old village sites. This one at Westness dates back to Viking times.

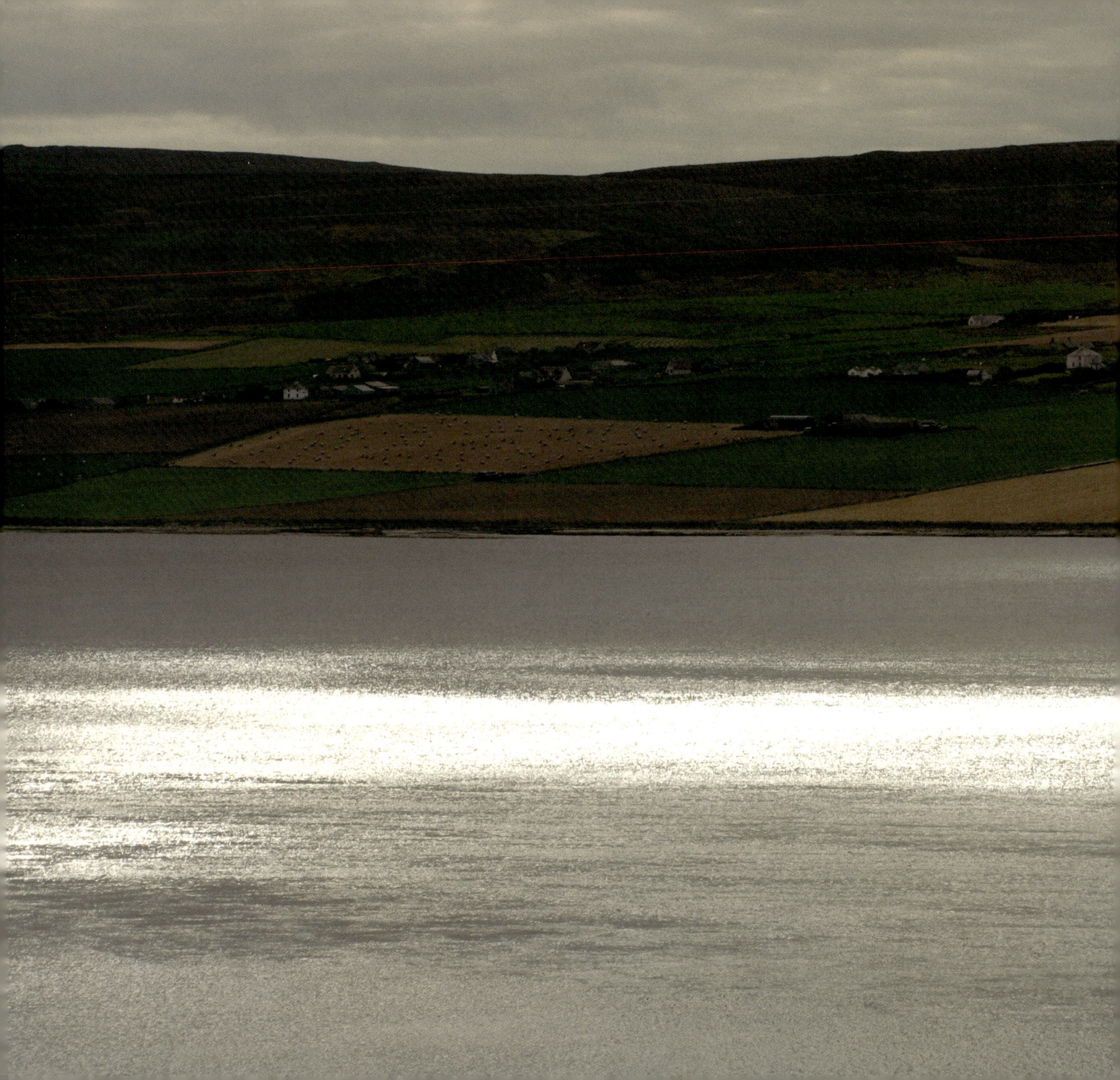

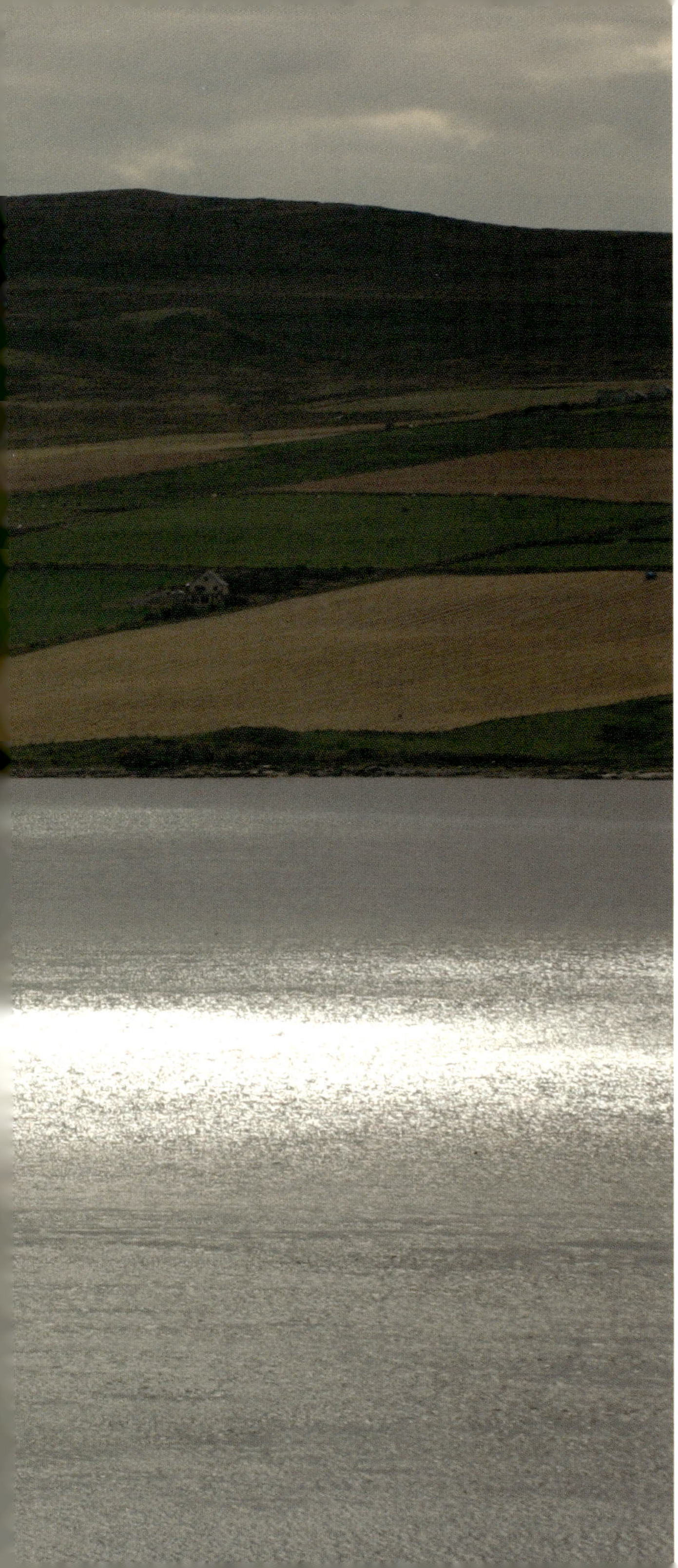

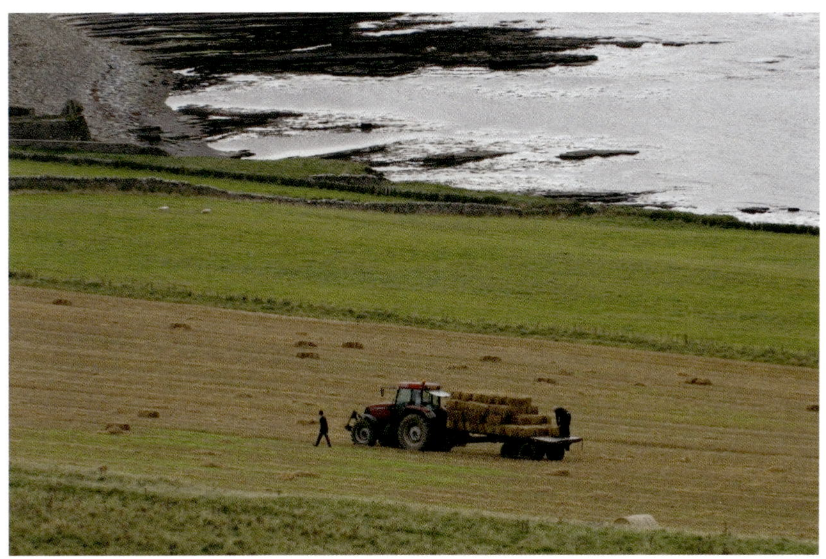

Bringing in the sheaves at Westness, Rousay.

Waters sparkling on the Eynhallow Sound, between Rousay and Mainland.

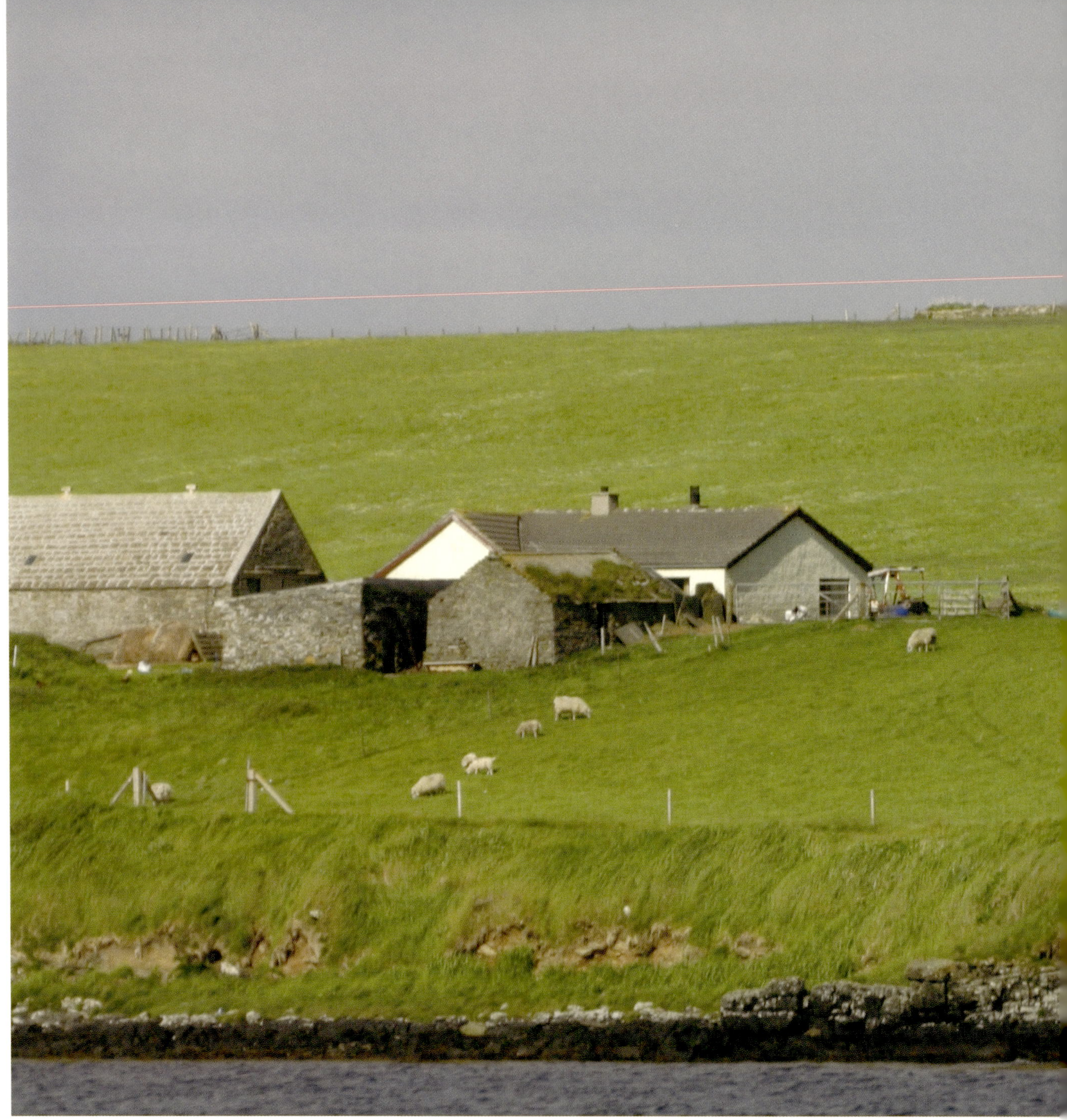

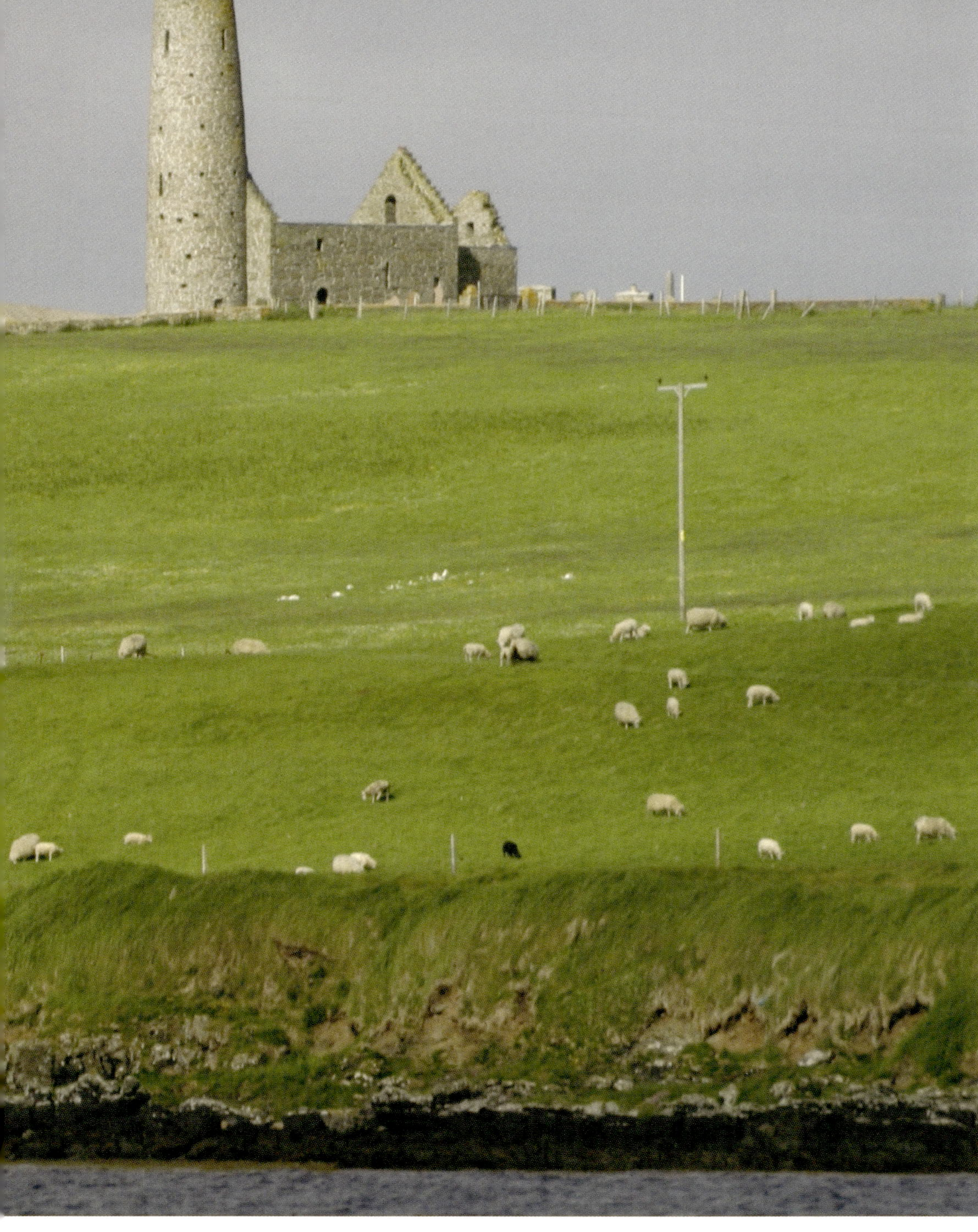

The island of Egilsay is dominated by the tower of St Magnus's Church. Some believe that this church may be the root of the name of the island, as 'eaglais' is Gaelic for church. However, if it were Norse, which seems more likely, it would simply translate as 'Egil's island' – Egil being a common Norse first name. St Magnus was killed on Egilsay in 1117, although the church's foundation is much older.

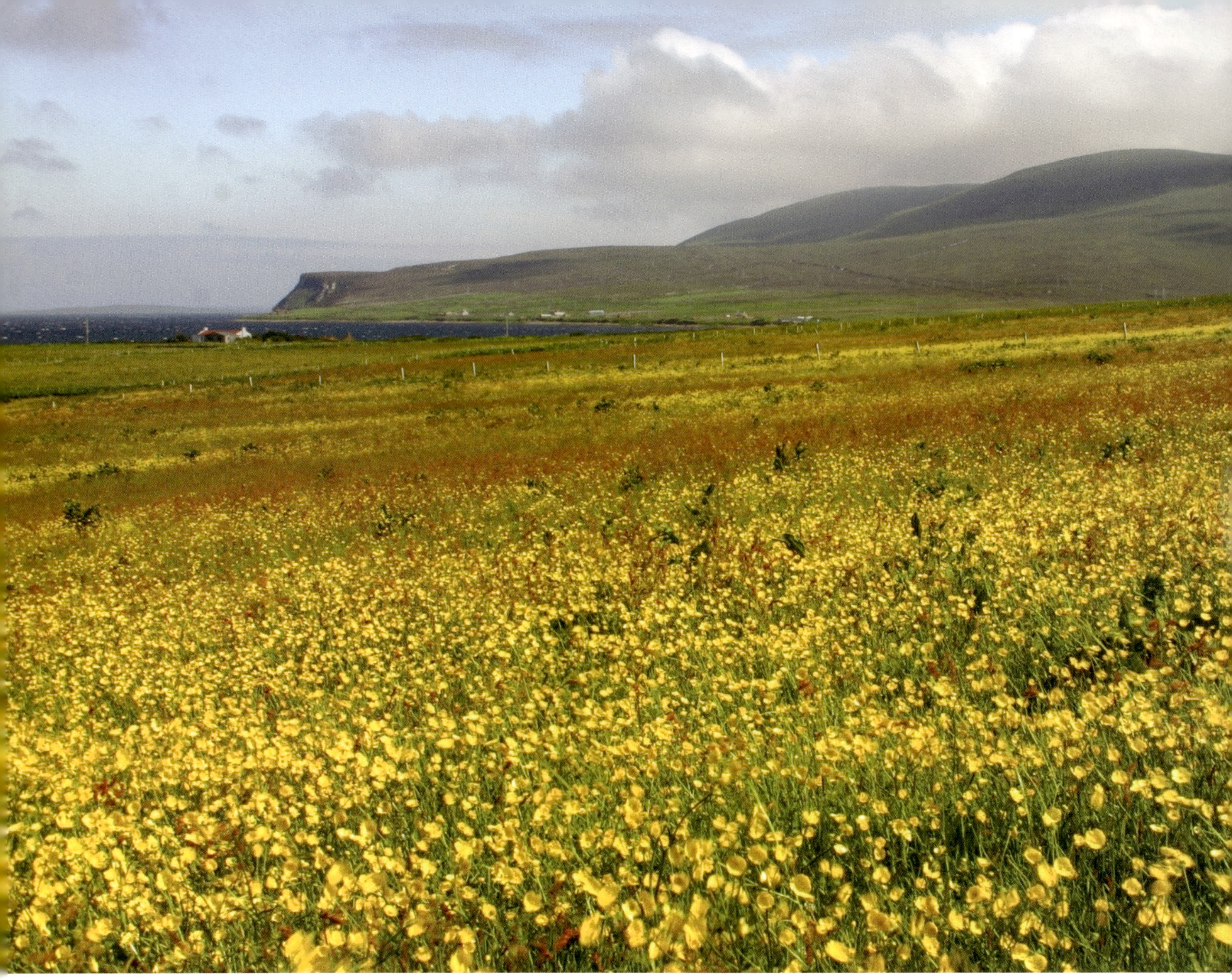

On Hoy buttercup meadows stretch along the shore-side at Moaness.

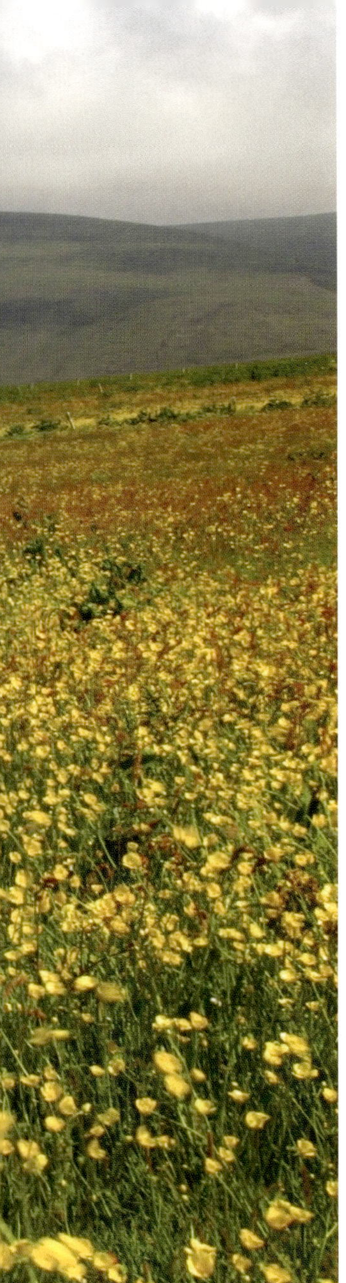

Rackwick means 'Rock Bay' in Old Norse, and has the same root as Reykjavík. There, the similarity between the two places stops! Rackwick on Hoy is a small village facing out into the brunt of the Atlantic storms.

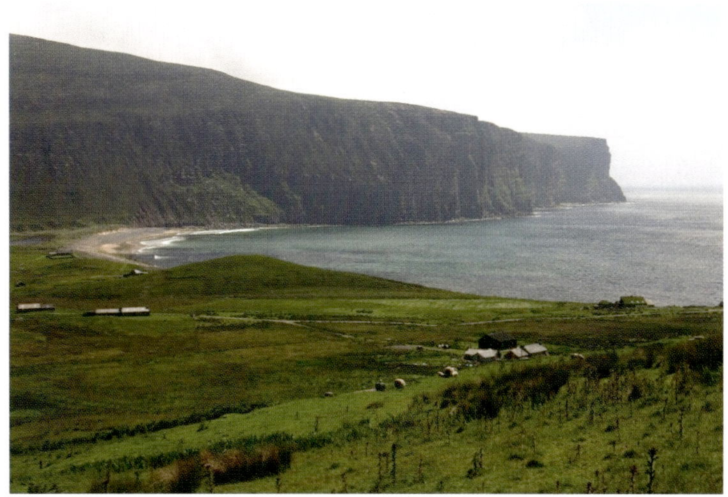

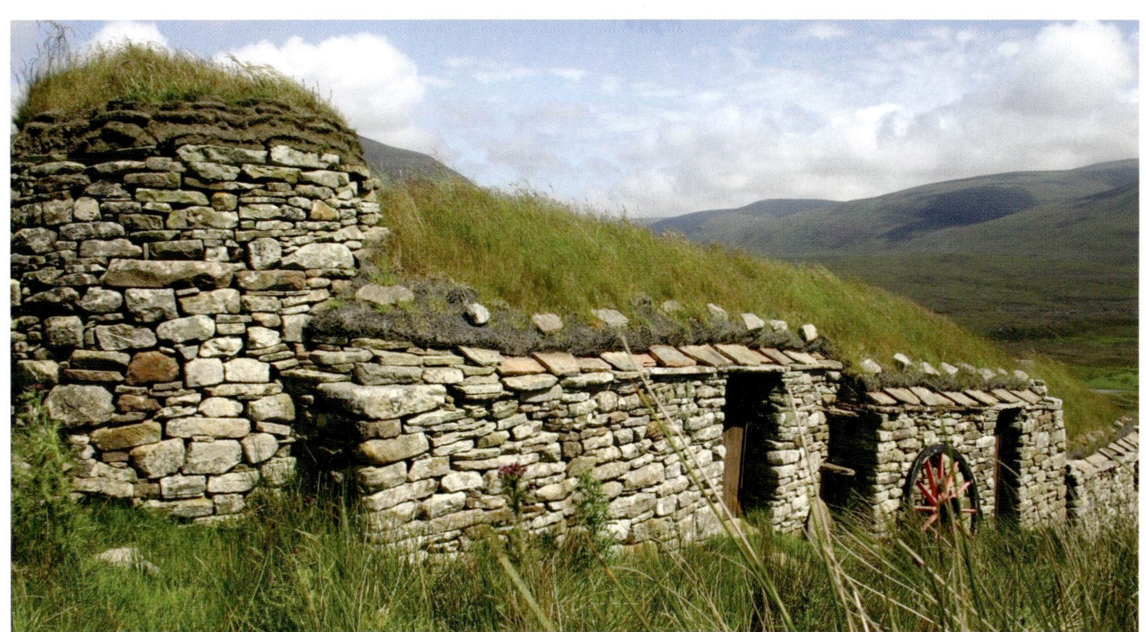

There's a fascinating croft museum at Rackwick, and it was here, believe it or not, that the lady's suspender belt was invented!

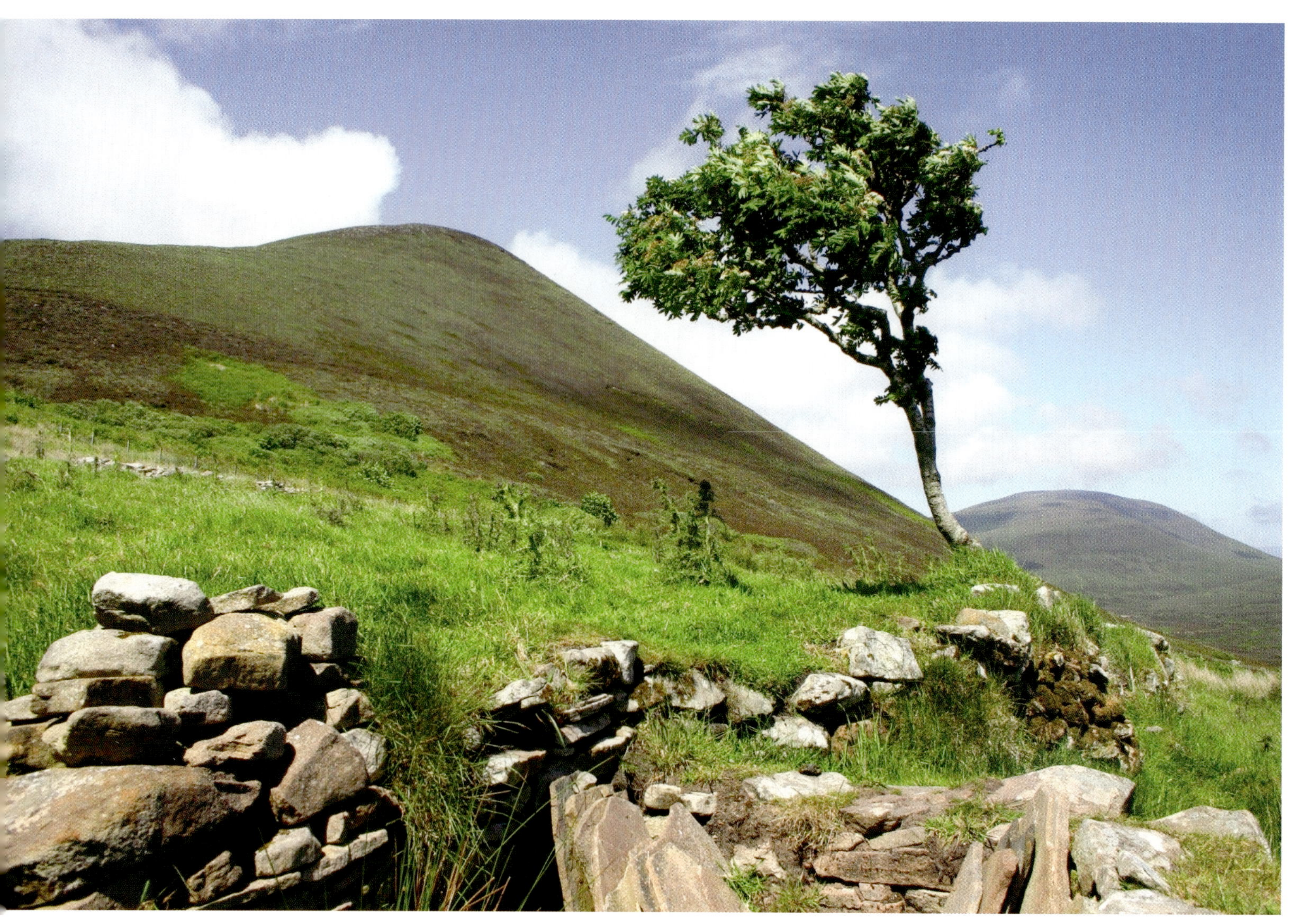

A fine old rowan tree grows on the slopes of Cuilags on Hoy.

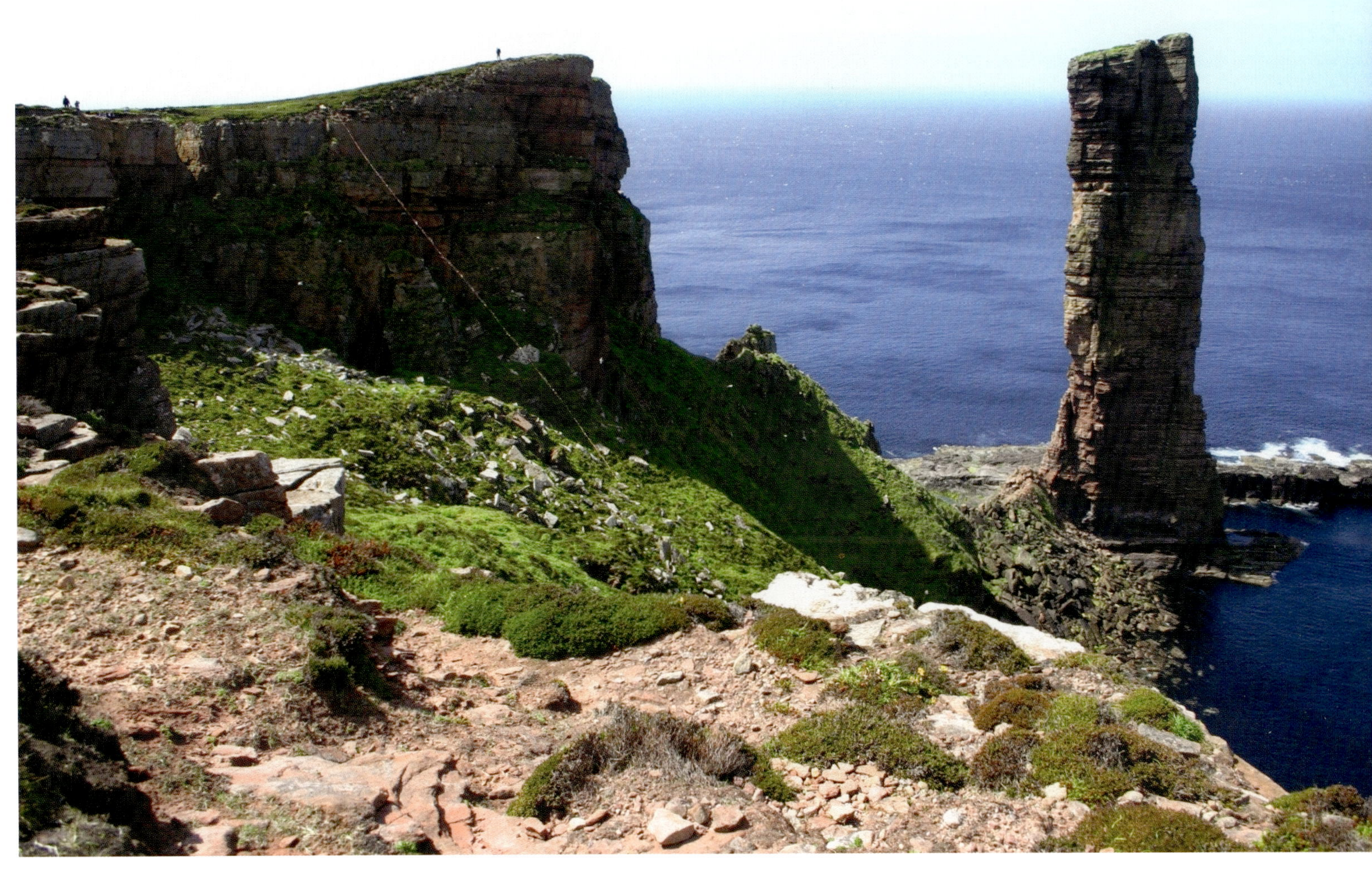

The Old Man of Hoy is one of the most recognisable natural features in the whole of the Northern Isles. It rises 450 feet above the sea, and is fairly popular with climbers. Geologists tell us that the stack is slowly falling over! The stack was first climbed in 1966 by Tom Patey, Rusty Baillie and Chris Bonington over a period of three days. The following year it featured in the first live BBC outside broadcast, when it was climbed again, this time by Bonington and Patey repeating their original route, while two new routes were put up on the same day by the teams of Pete Crew and Dougal Haston, and Ian McNaught-Davis and Joe Brown. On 16 May 2008 the first person to base jump off the stack was announced by BBC Radio Orkney.

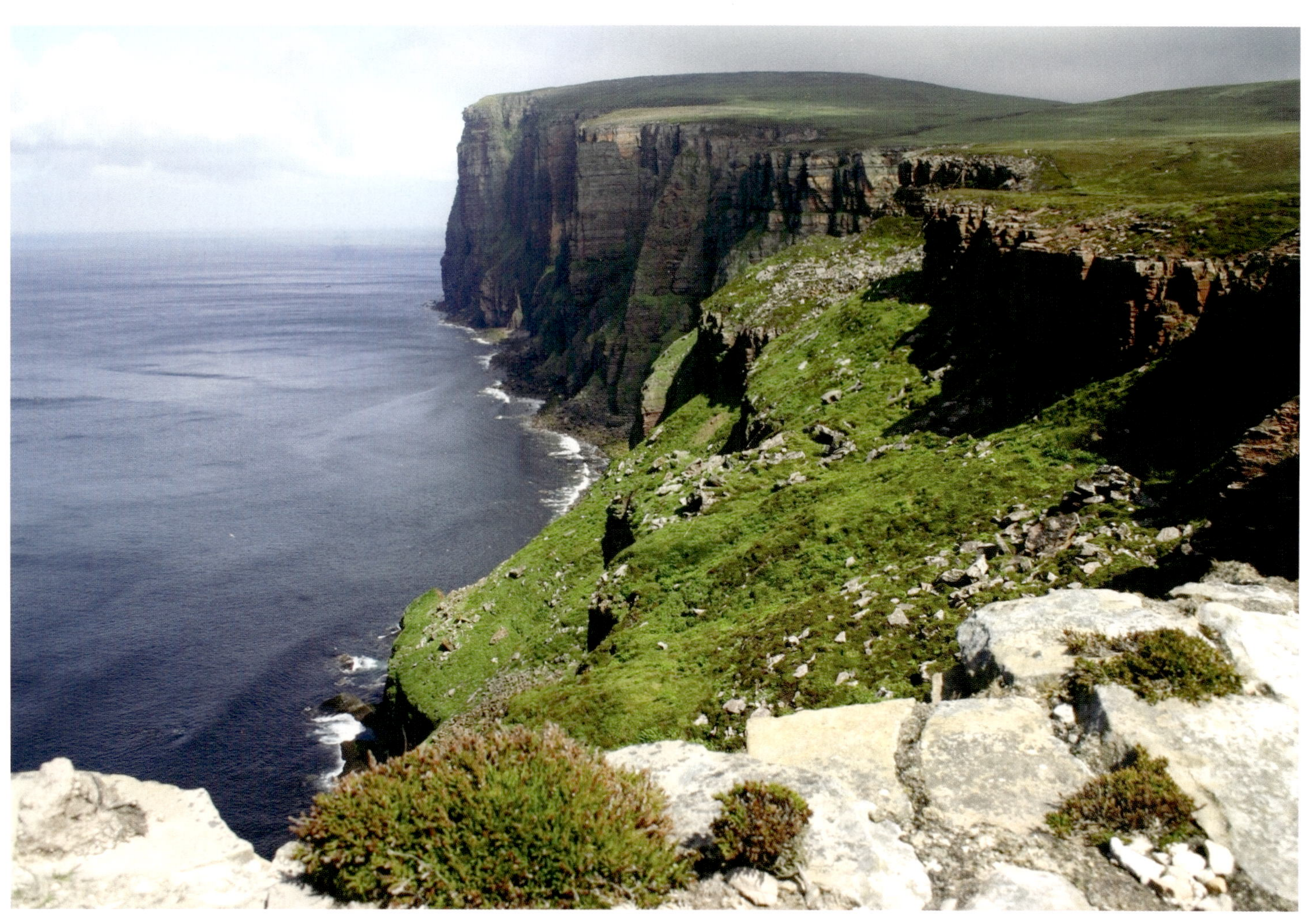

The massive sea cliffs at St John's Head, Hoy. These are pretty much the highest vertical sea cliffs in Britain. It is no surprise, given the hilly nature of Hoy, that the island's name derives from the Old Norse meaning 'high island'!

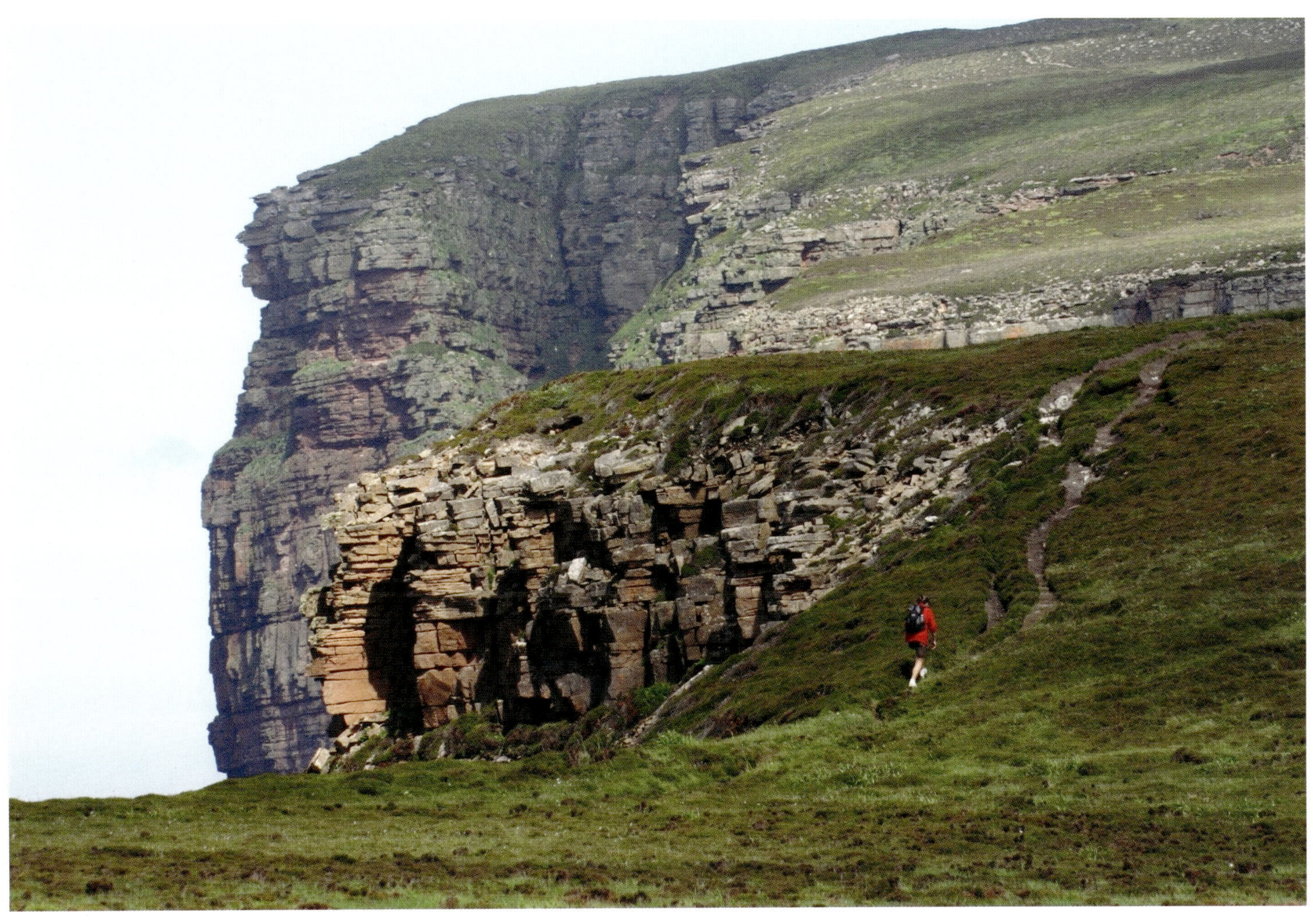

A walker heads off around the coast from the Old Man of Hoy, her sights set firmly on St John's Head and Cuilags.

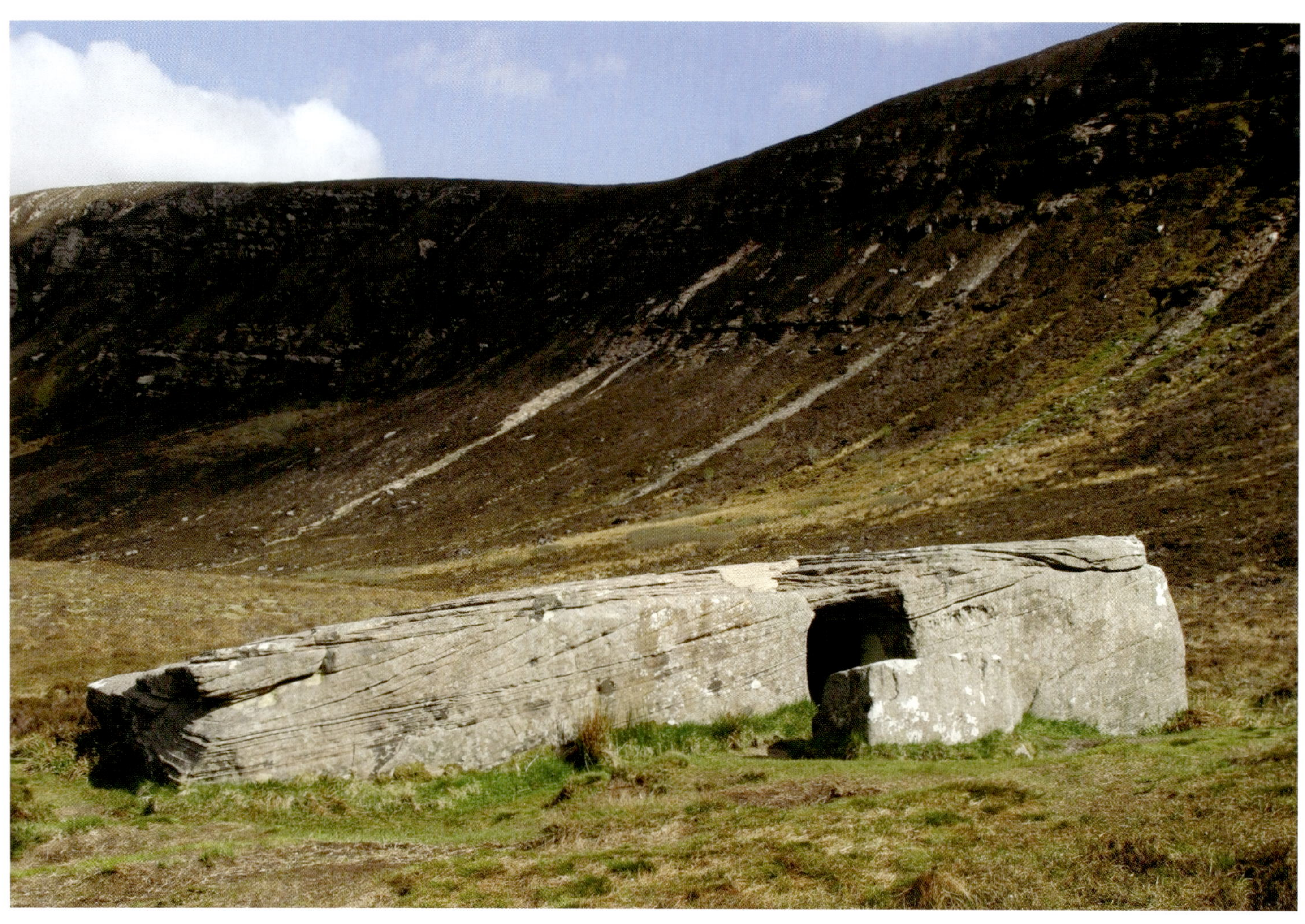

In the Trowie Glen (Troll Glen) you'll find the 5000 year old tomb that is the Dwarfie Stane.

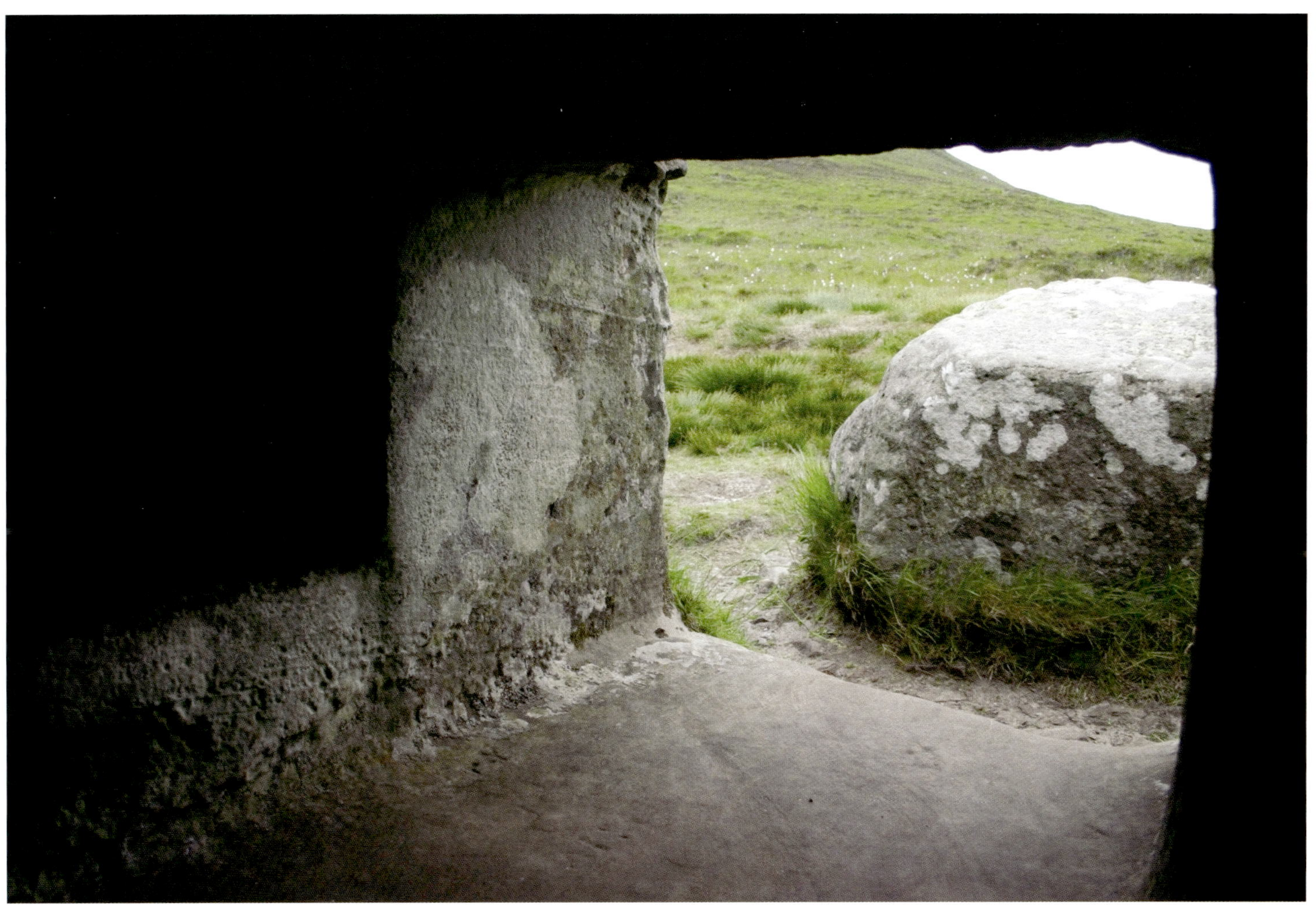

The Dwarfie Stane was hollowed out of a huge block of red sandstone, although no-one knows why. It has two side compartments, and a large blocking stone at the entrance. In 'The Pirate', Sir Walter Scott wrote about the rock that, 'this extraordinary dwelling which Trolld, a dwarf famous in the Northern sagas, is said to have framed for his favourite residence'. Rather him than me!

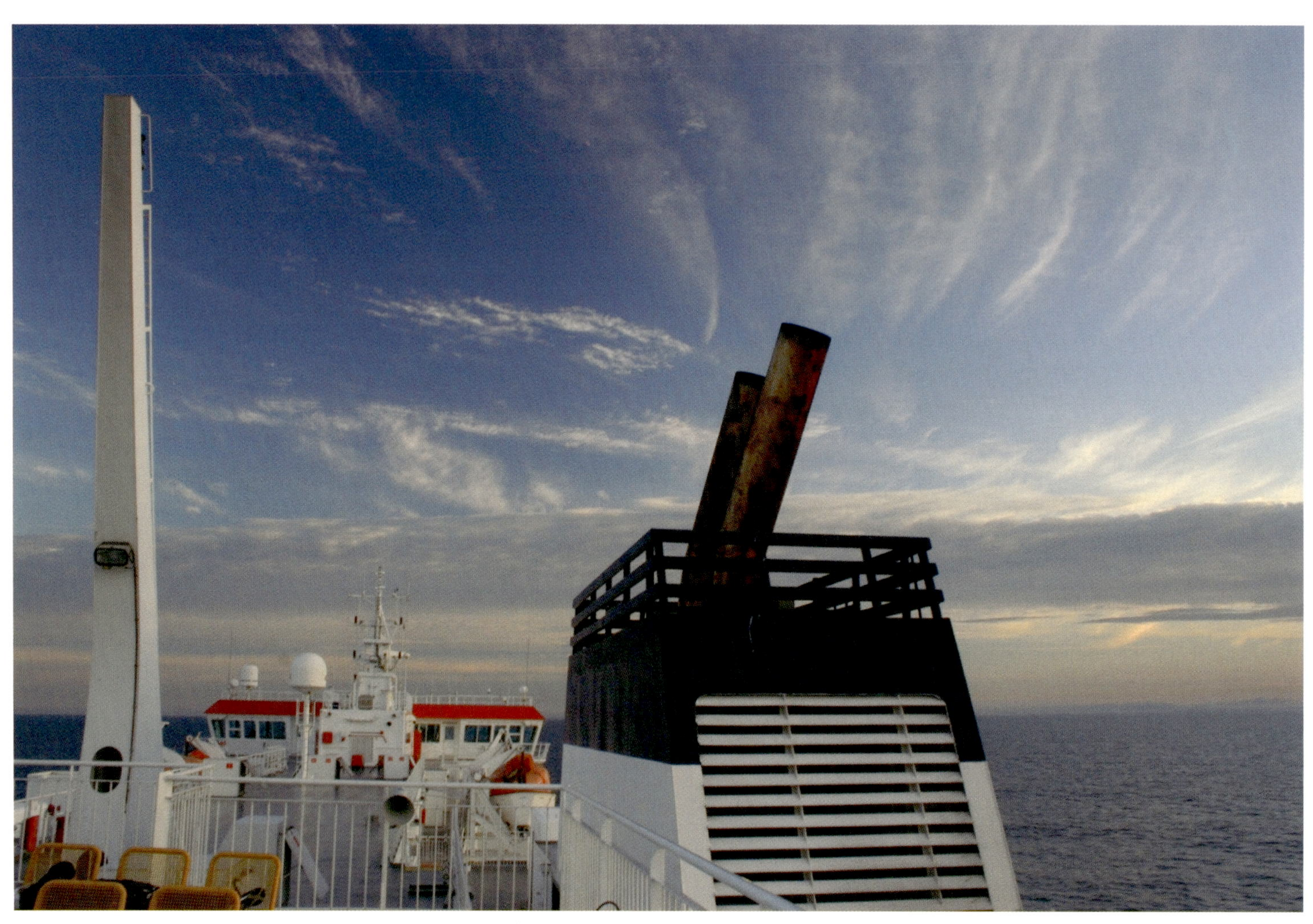

A summer sky from the Northlink ferry between Orkney and Shetland.

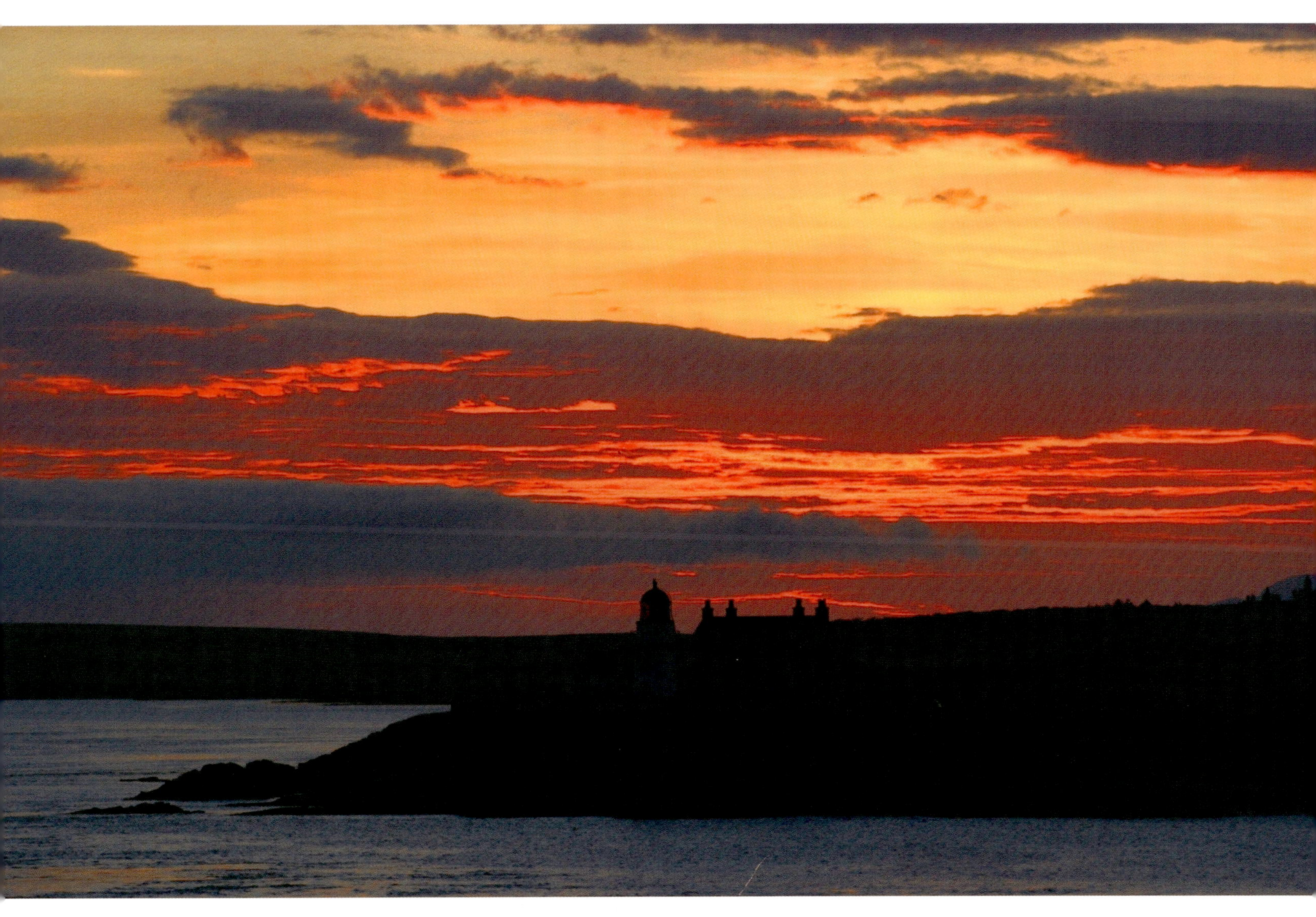

Saeva Ness lighthouse on the little island of Helliar Holm, south of Shapinsay, looks out across the channel The String to the Head of Work on Mainland, Orkney, while a vivid summer sun sets behind. The lighthouse was built in 1893, and was automated in 1967.

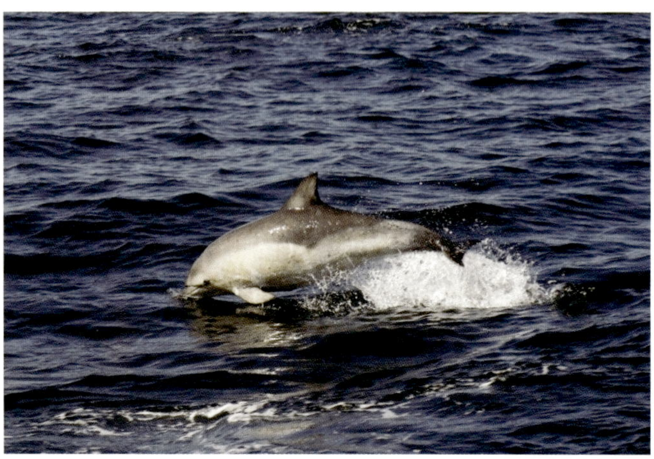

On ferry crossings you just never know what you might see, especially if the sea is calm. Here a common dolphin follows the Northlink ferry *Hamnavoe*.

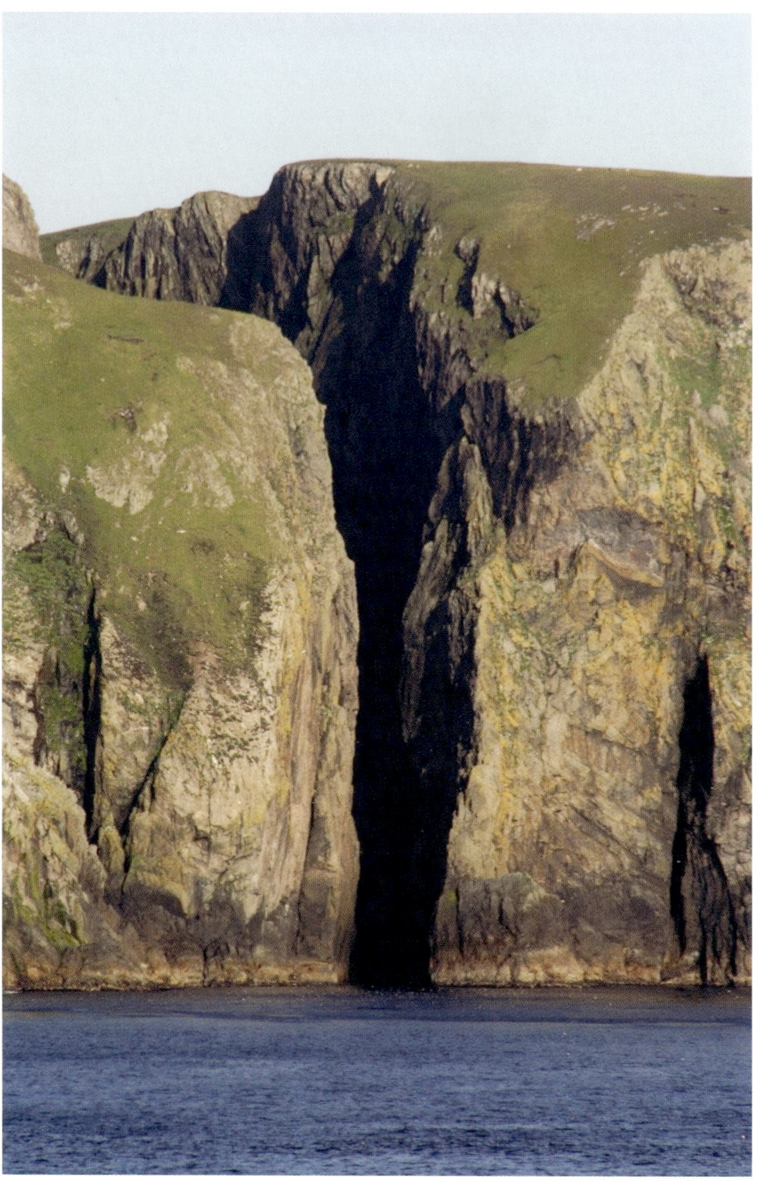

The Fair Isle cliffs hold impressive numbers of nesting seabirds, and some exciting migrant birds turn up here from time to time too. There is a bird observatory on the island which is popular with serious birdwatchers.

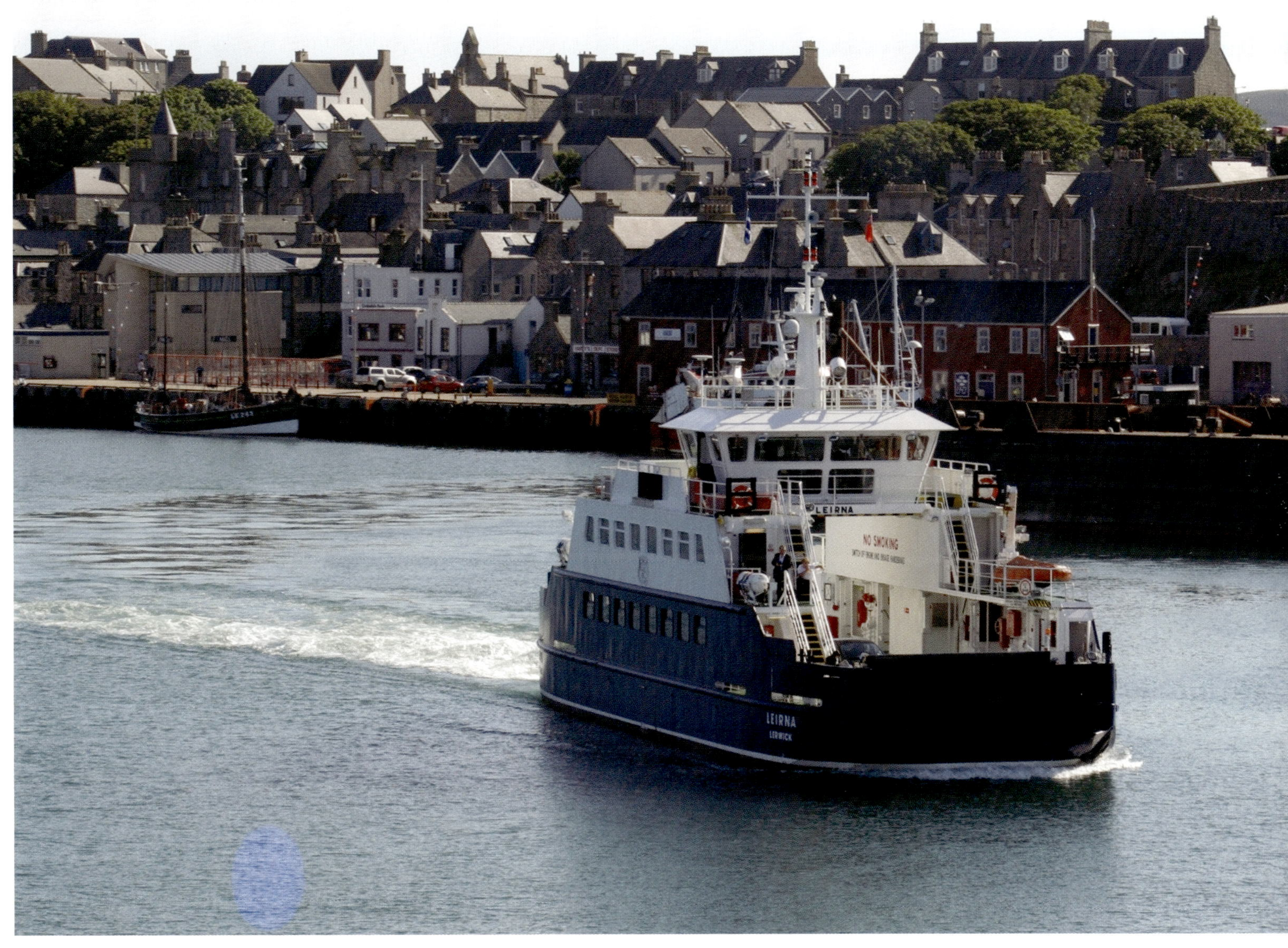


The *Lierna* plies her trade between Lerwick and the island of Bressay, which lies just across the Bressay Sound from the capital of Shetland.

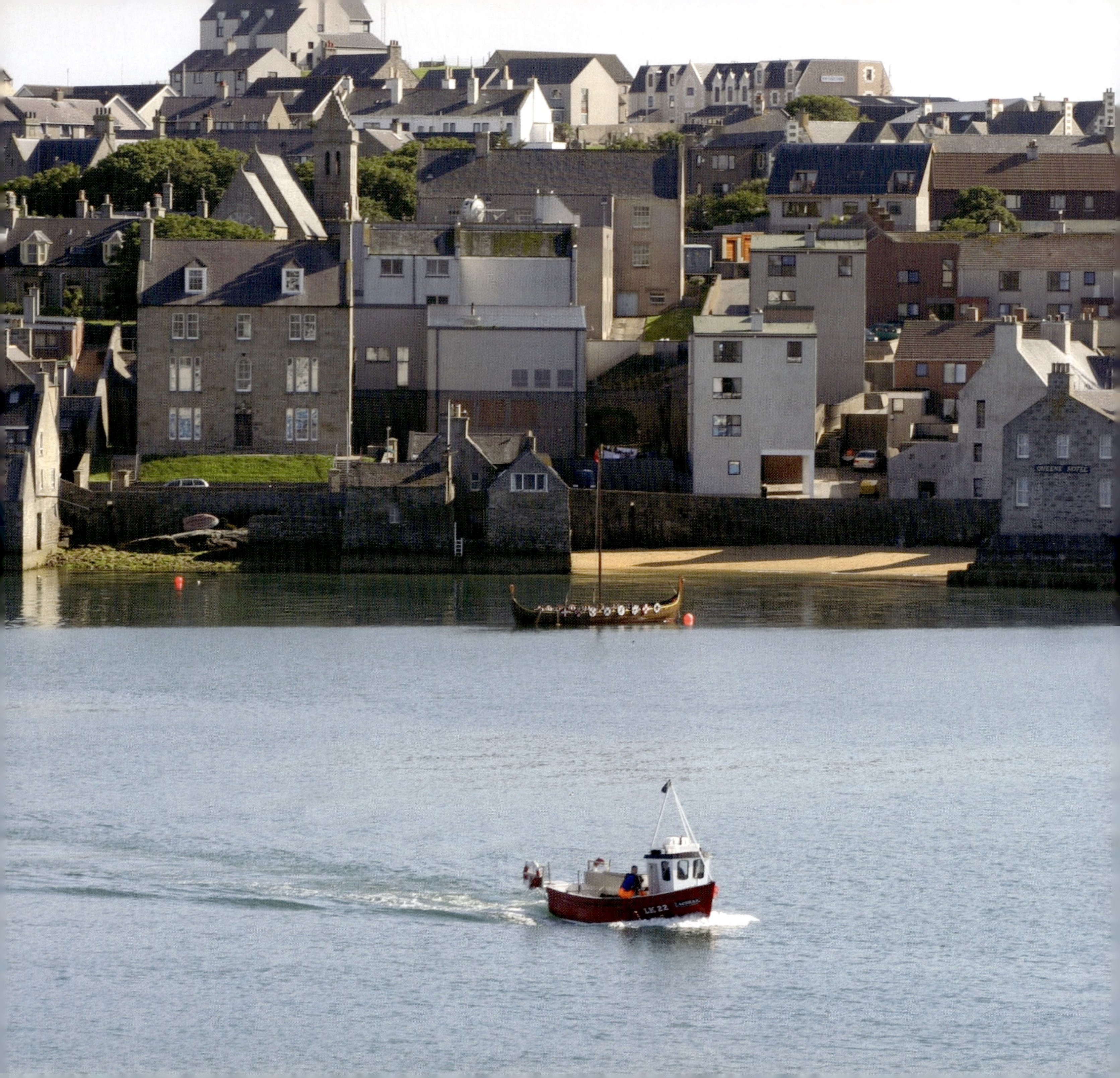
LK 22

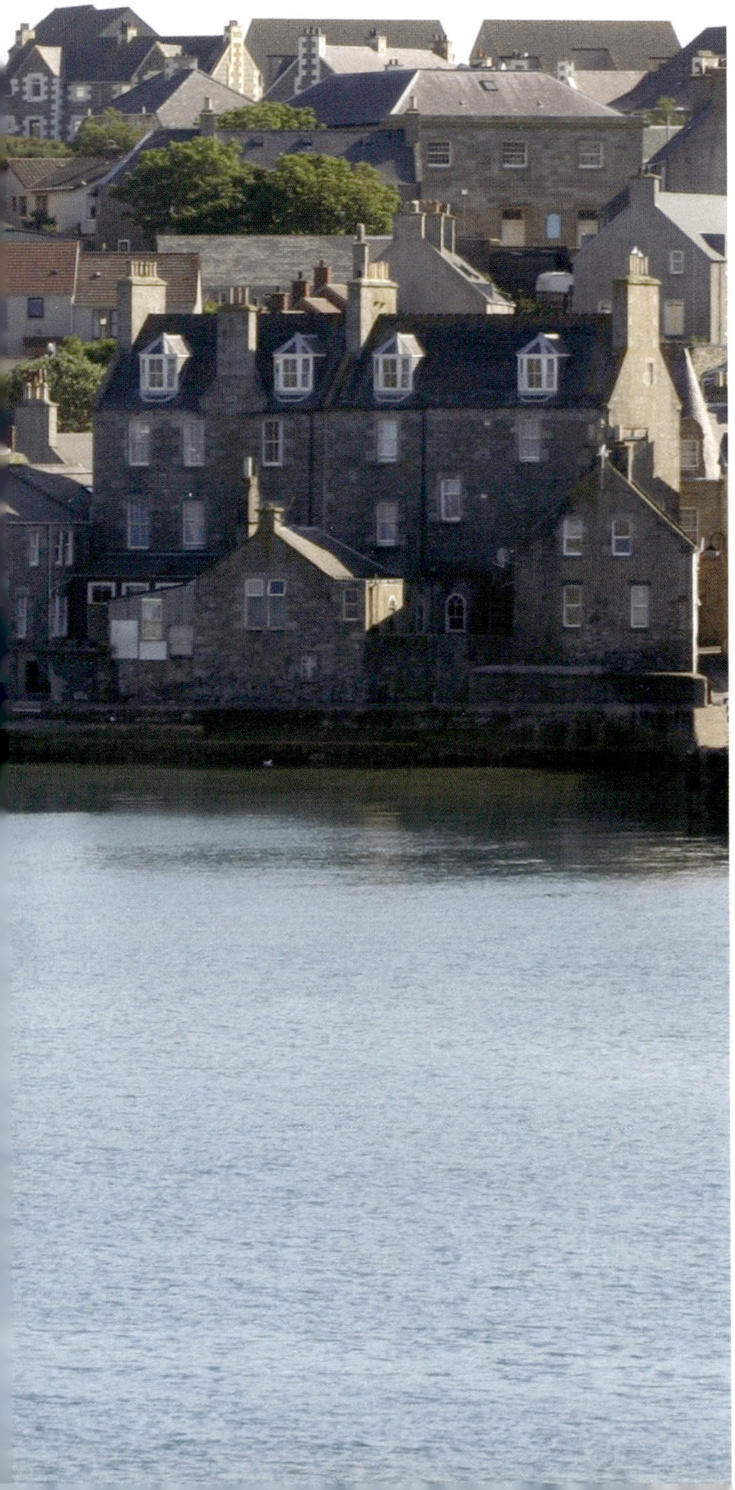

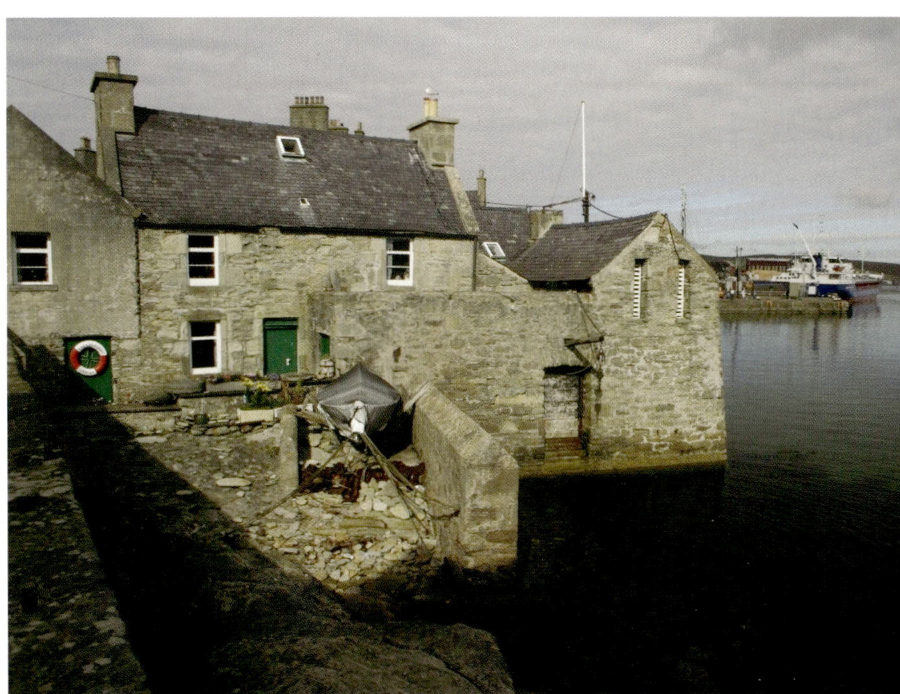

Above: The Lodberrie in Lerwick is just one of many wonderful old fishermen's cottages. They sit right down on the waterside overlooking the Bressay Sound.

Left: Lerwick in the summer.

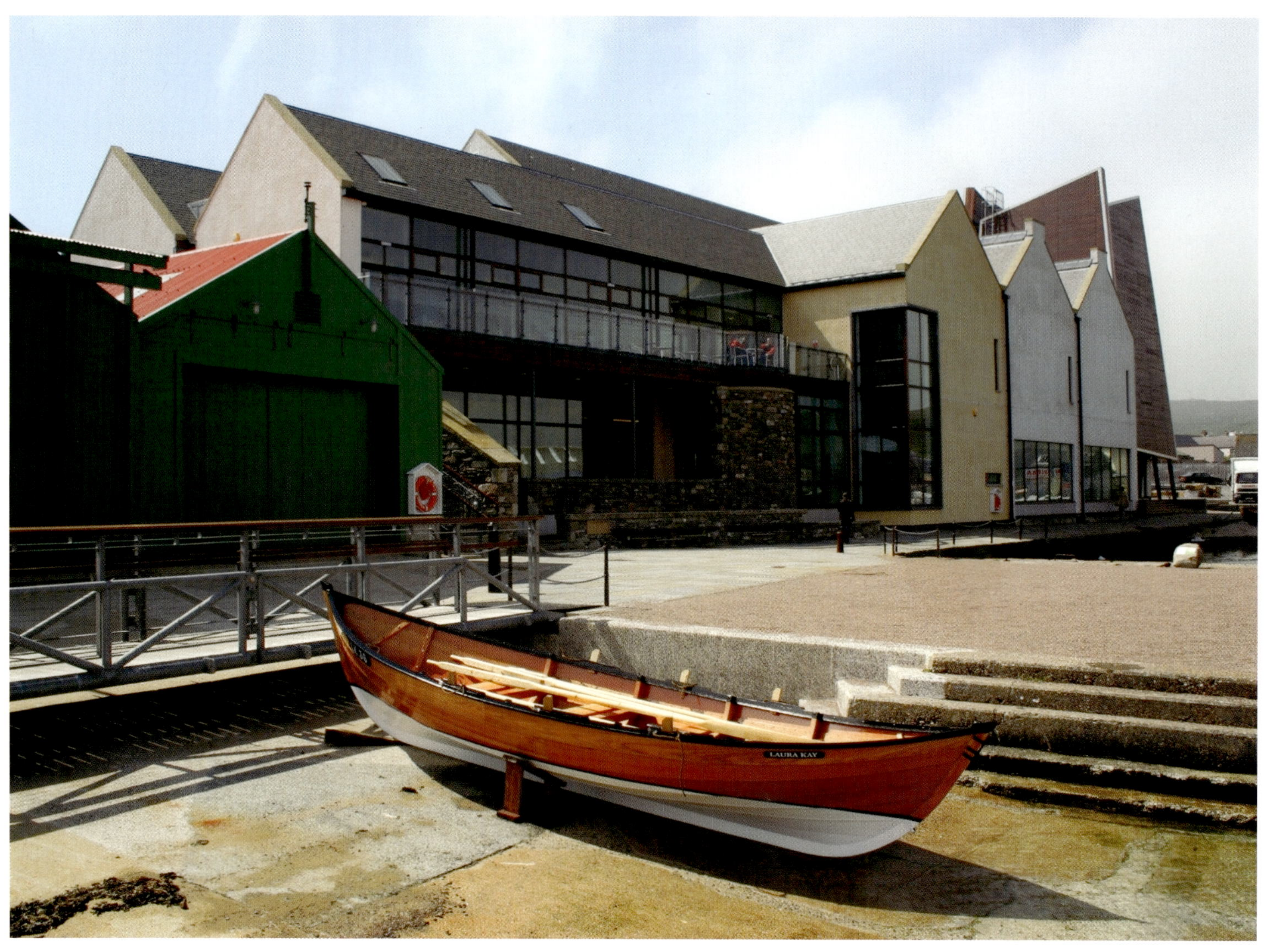


The wonderful new Shetland Museum and Archives at Hay's Dock. It houses over 3000 artefacts, and has a wealth of archival material, as well as public art displays, an auditorium, shop, café, and of course, the famous Boat Hall and Sheds.

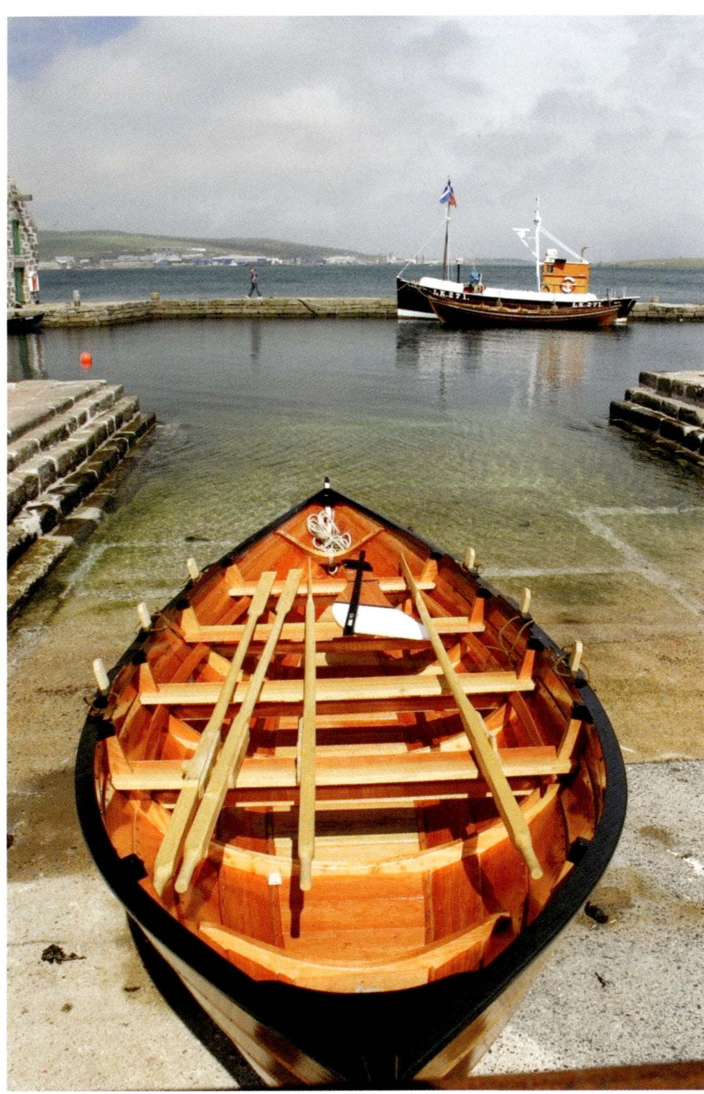

A superb new sixareen outside the Shetland Museum and Archives at Hay's Dock. The sixareen is thought of as being the ultimate development of the traditional Shetland boat. In these 30 foot open boats, the men rowed or sailed up to 40 miles from land to fish.

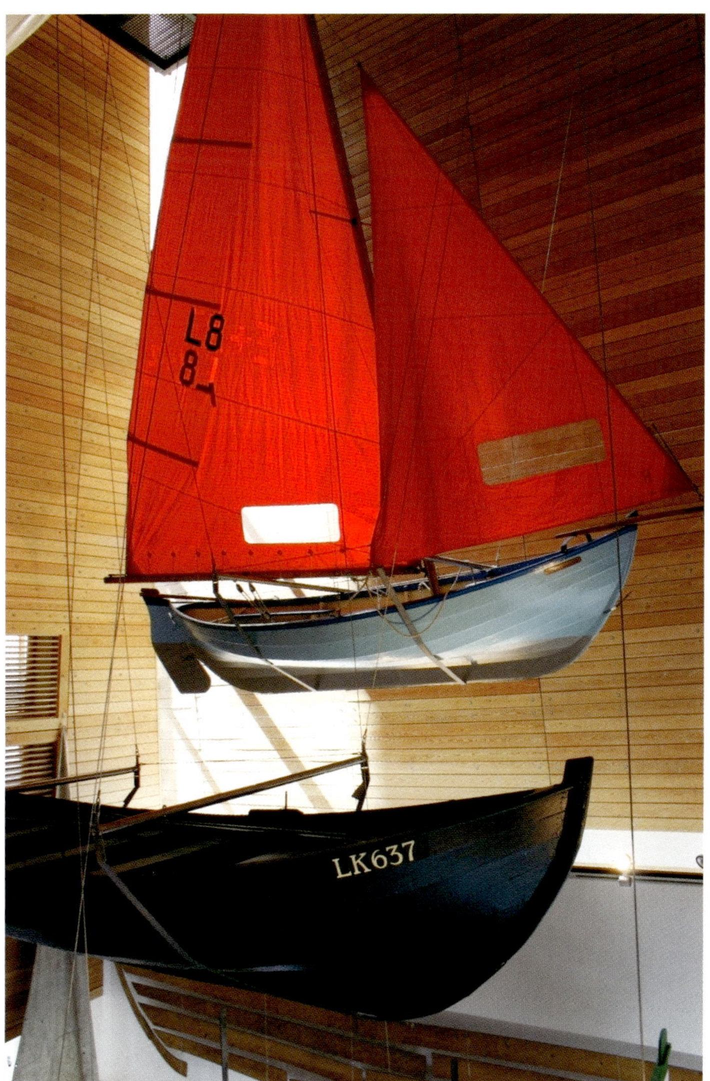


Inside the Shetland Museum and Archives.

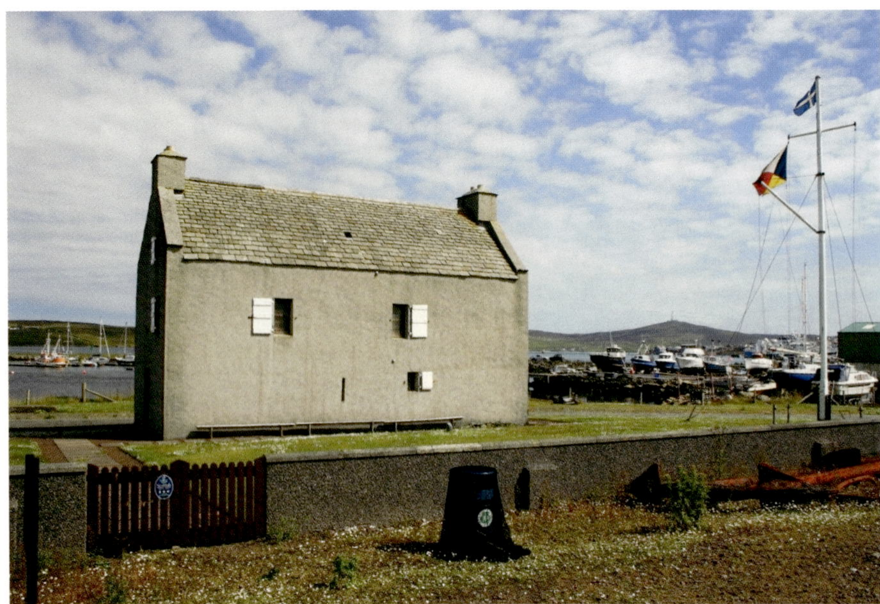

The Bod of Grimista in Lerwick is the birthplace of Arthur Anderson. He worked in fish processing as a boy, and then in 1808 he joined the Royal Navy. After various merchant shipping enterprises he launched a steamship service in 1837 between Britain and the Iberian Peninsula. He called his company the Peninsula Steam Navigation Company, which soon became known as P&O.

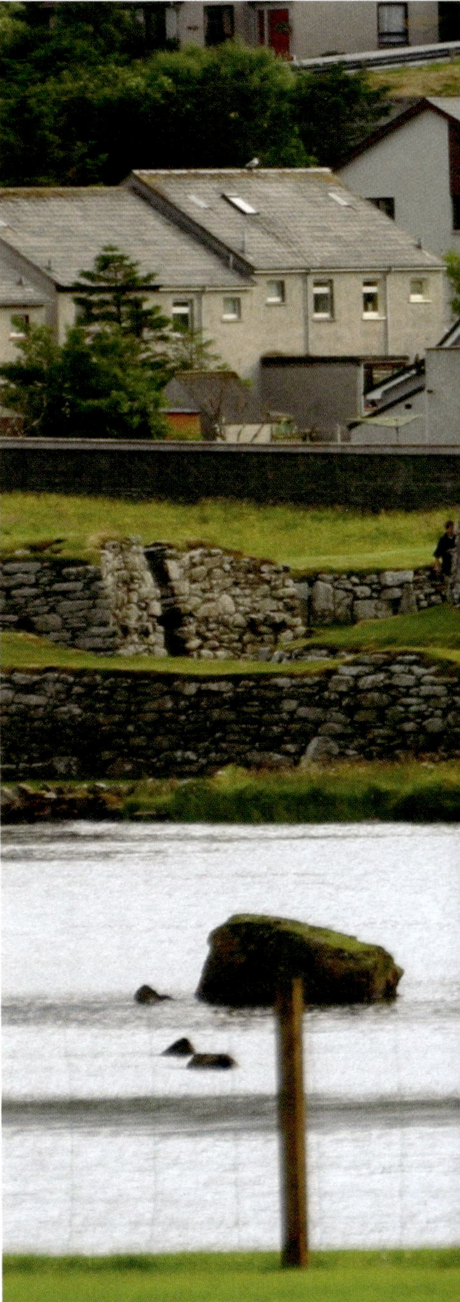

In the centre of a housing area in Lerwick stands one of the oldest houses in Britain, the Clickimin Broch. It dates back 3000 years to the Bronze Age.

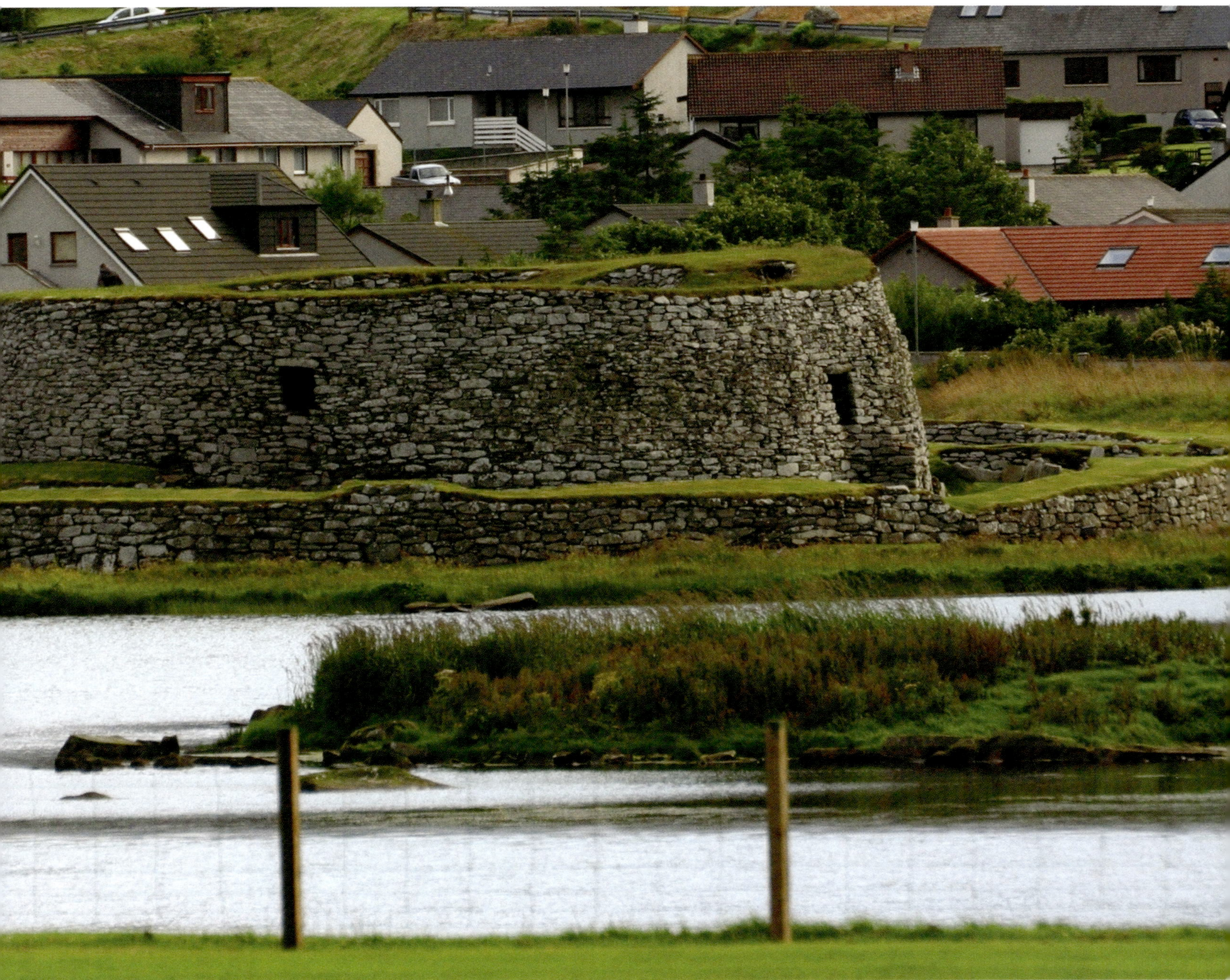

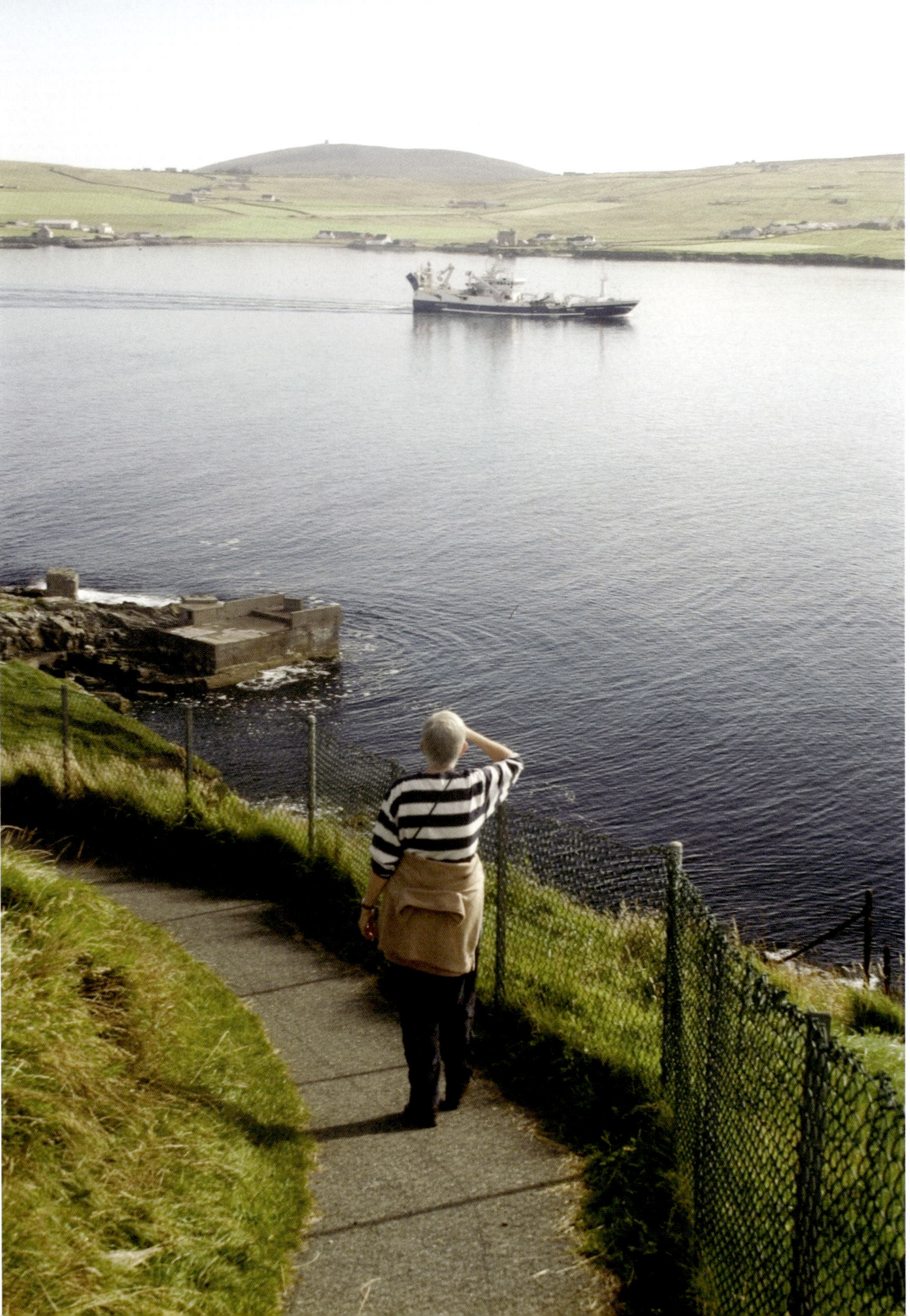

Ships come and go through the Bressay Sound while a woman enjoys a sunny stroll around The Knab from Lerwick.

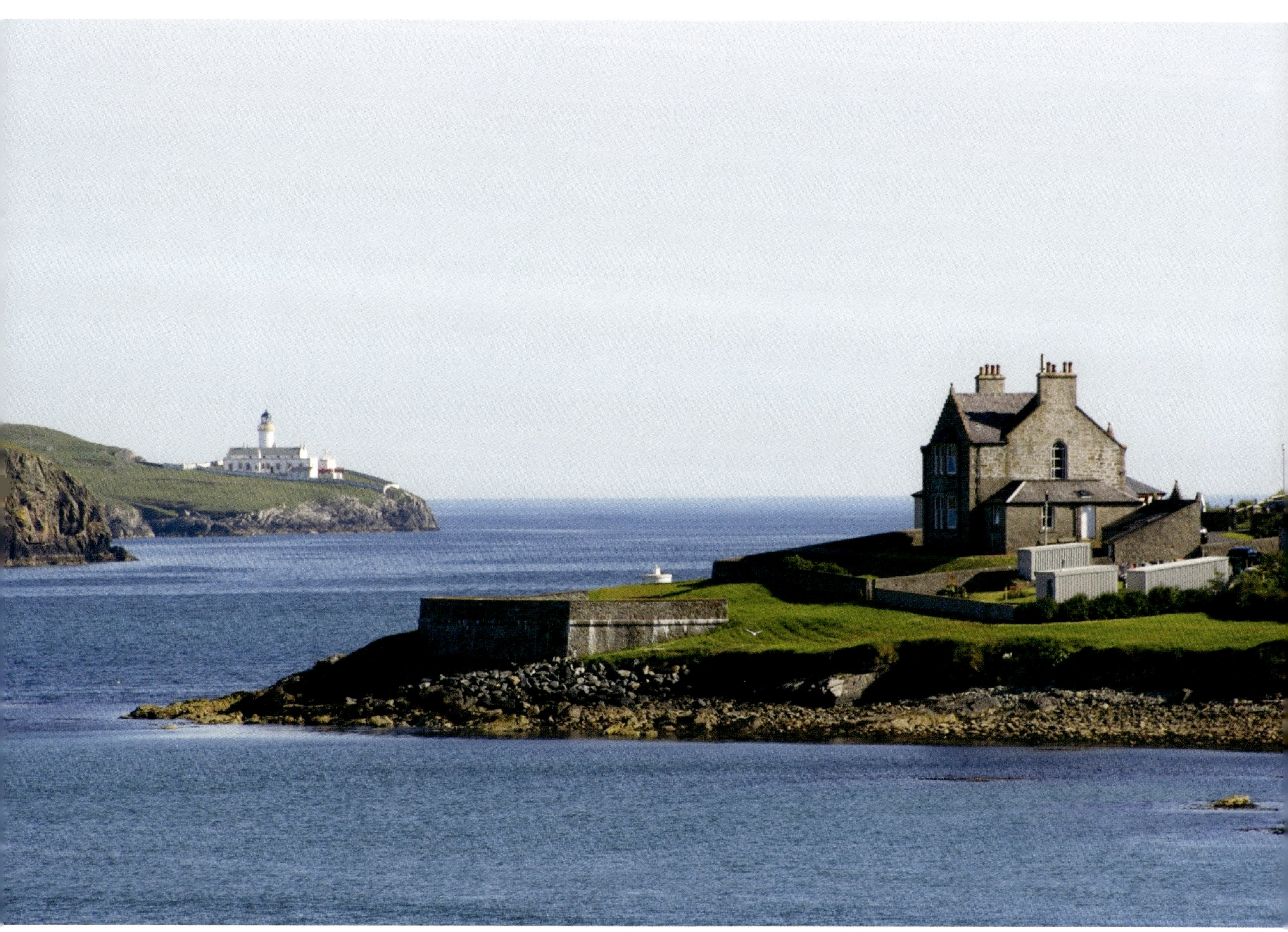

The Bressay Sound with the Kirkabister lighthouse on the island of Bressay.

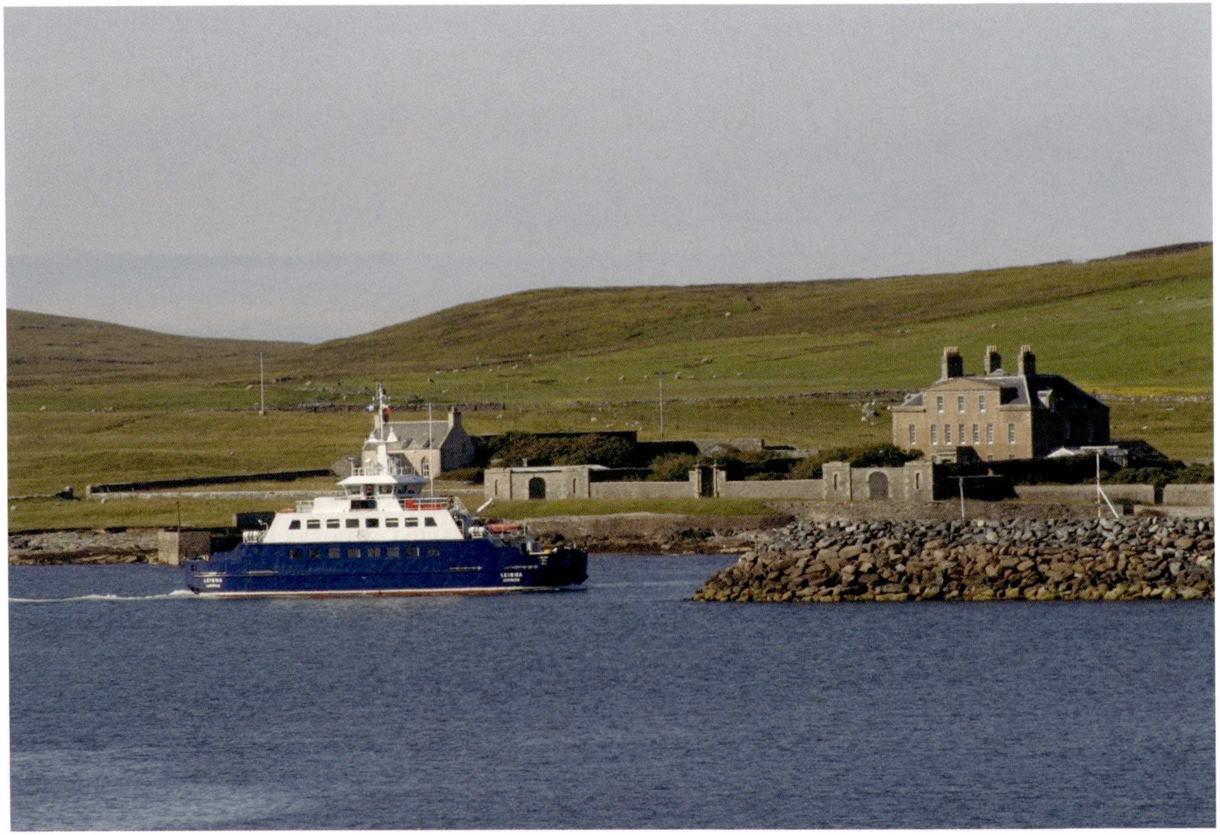

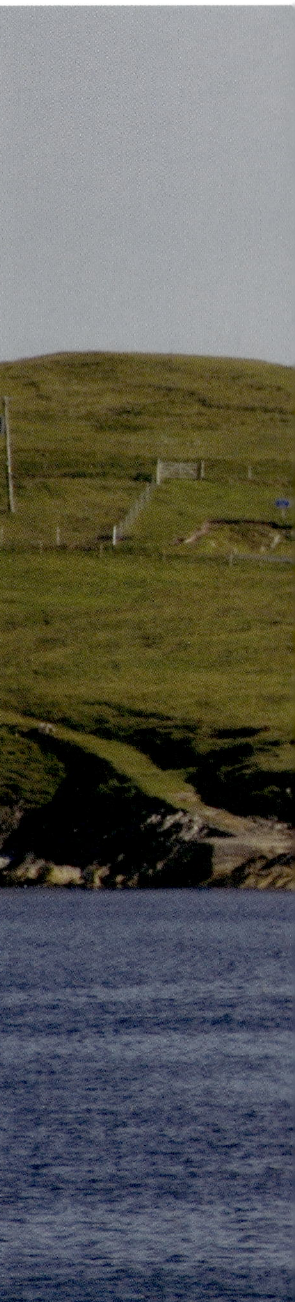

The Liena leaves Bressay to take its passengers back across the Sound to Lerwick.

The Commissioners of the Northern Lighthouses wrote to the Board of Trade in 1854 requesting permission to build a lighthouse on Kirkabister Ness on Bressay, and four years later, on 31 August 1858 the first light was lit. It was automated in 1989, and is monitored remotely from Edinburgh. In 1995 the Shetland Amenity Trust bought the old keepers' cottages, and has now turned them into self catering accommodation.

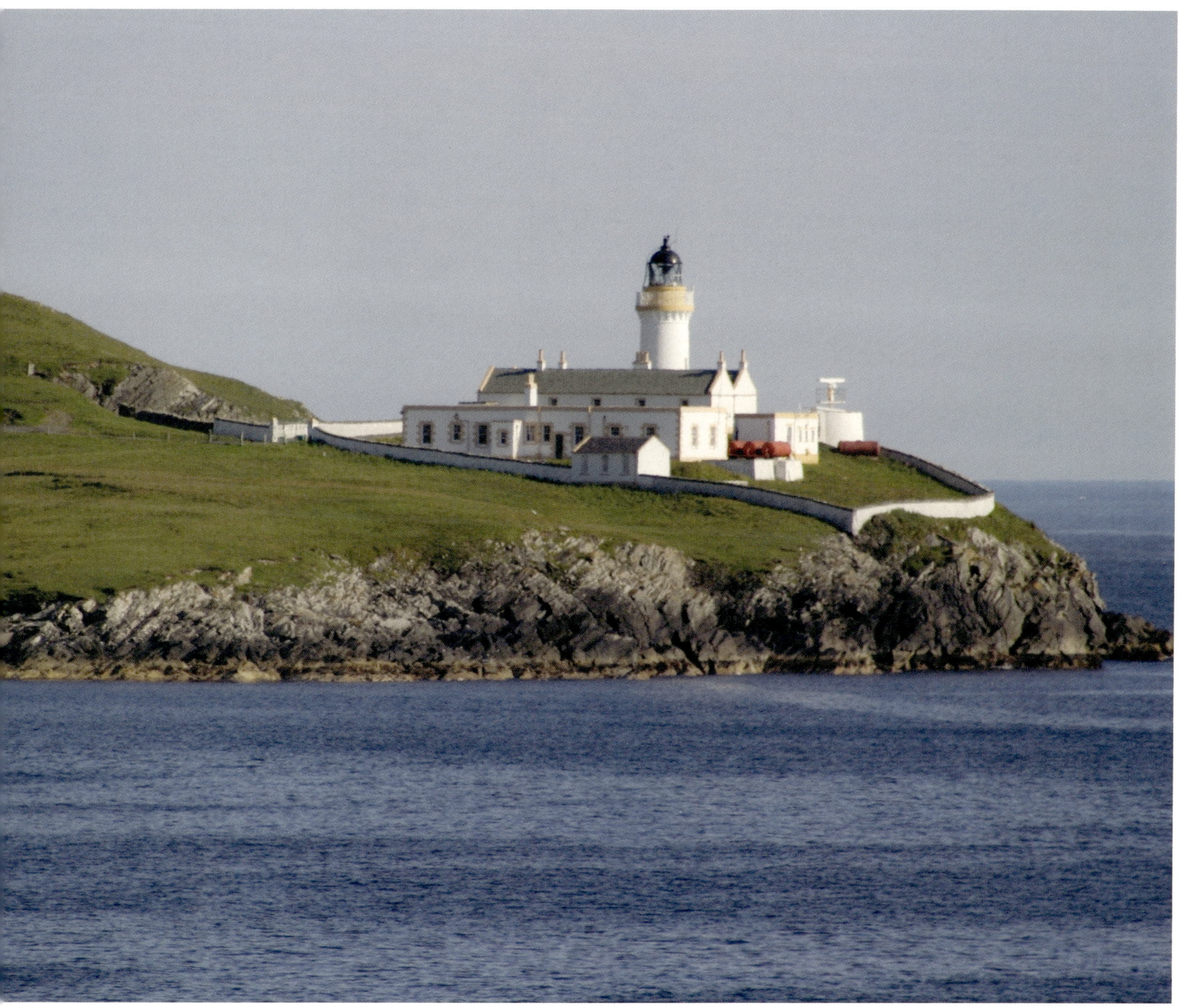

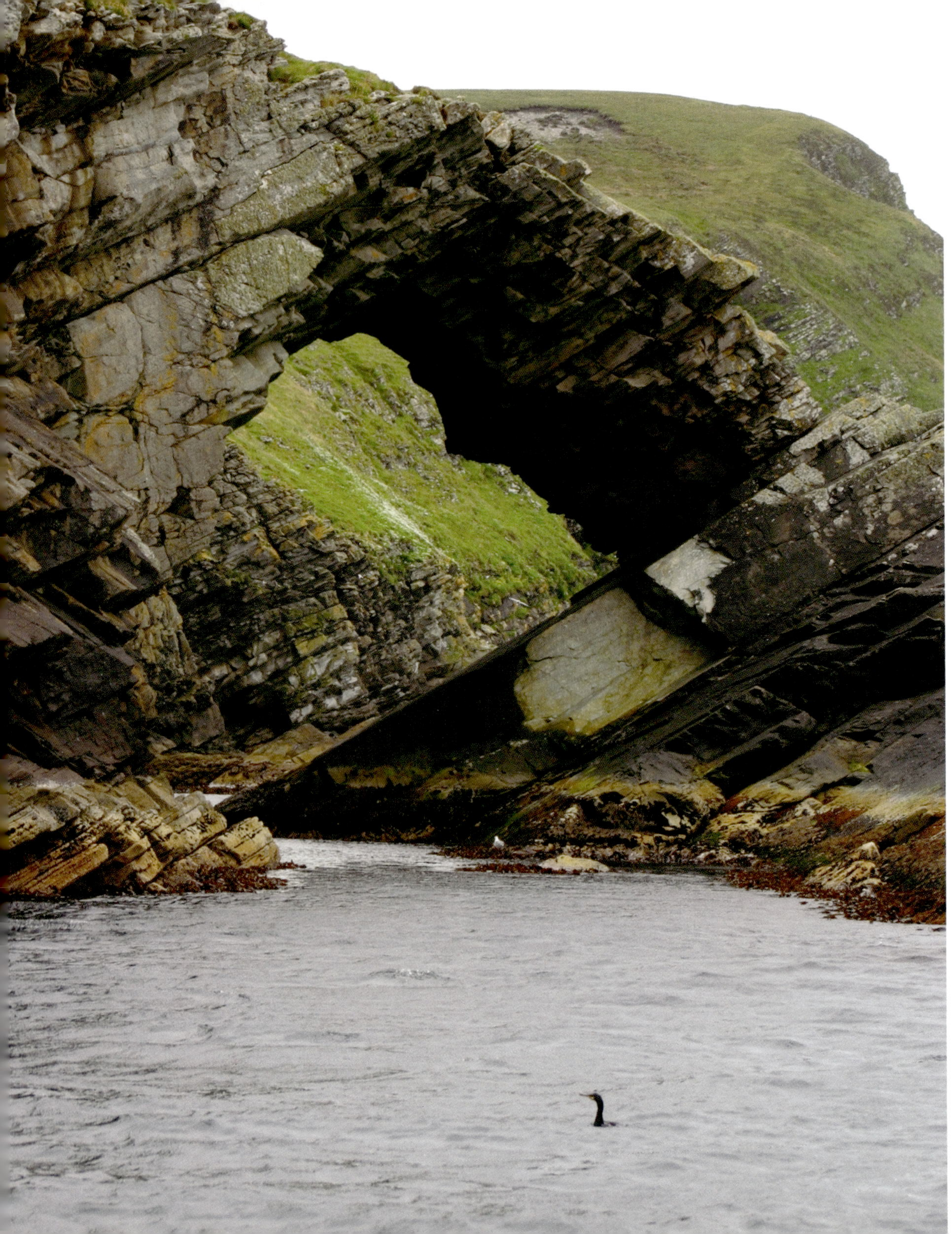

A superb natural stone arch near Kirkabister on Bressay, with a shag swimming in the waters below.

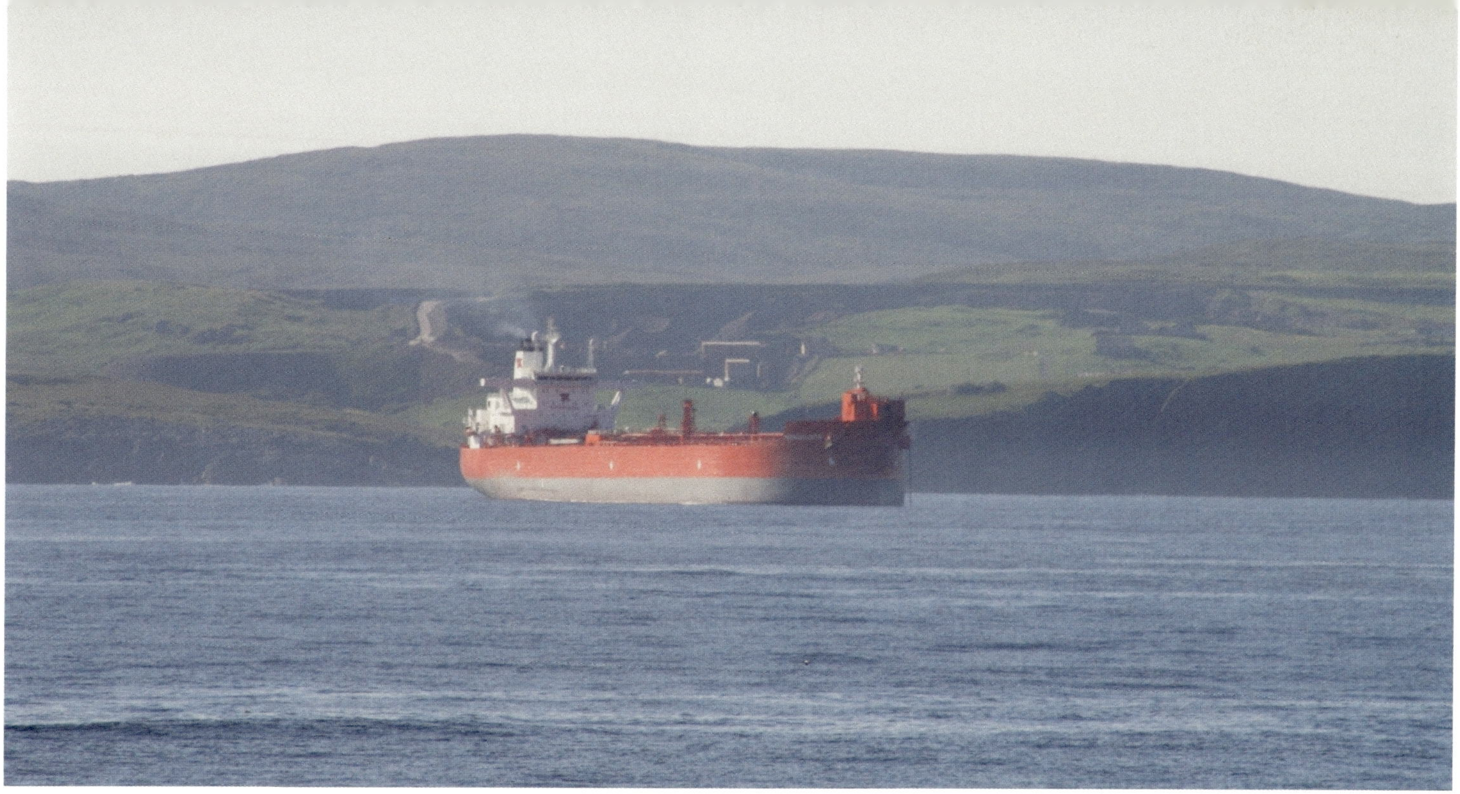

Many ships call in at Lerwick, and often lie at anchor in nearby Gulber Wick for days while they resupply.

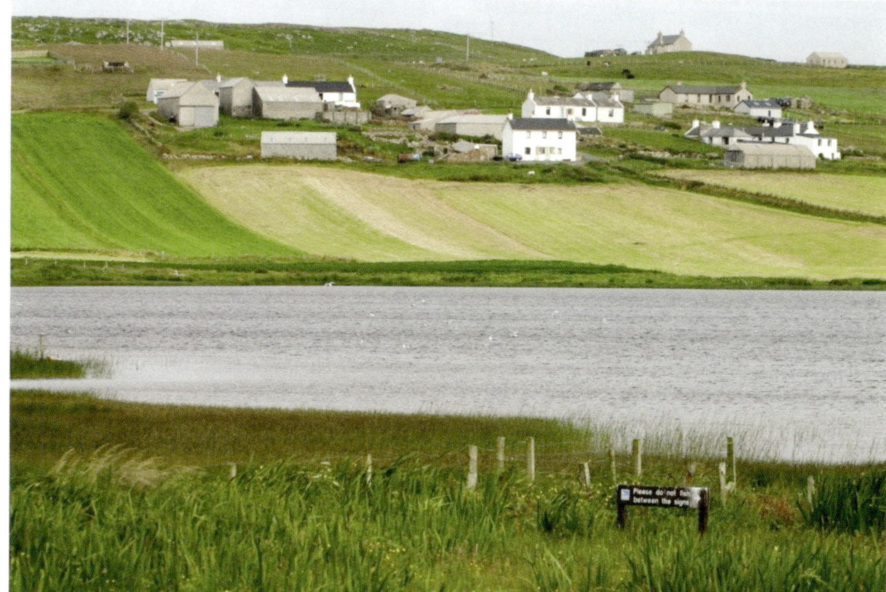


In the south of Shetland Mainland the RSPB have a noticeable presence at the Loch of Spiggie. This is an important breeding ground for waders and wildfowl, and also sees thousands of birds arriving in the autumn as they move south from the Arctic for the winter.

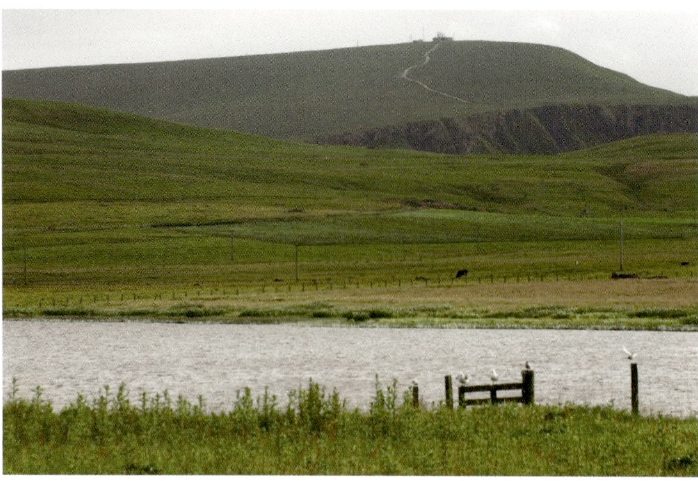

Fitful Head from the Loch of Spiggie.

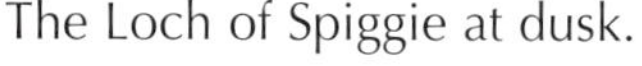

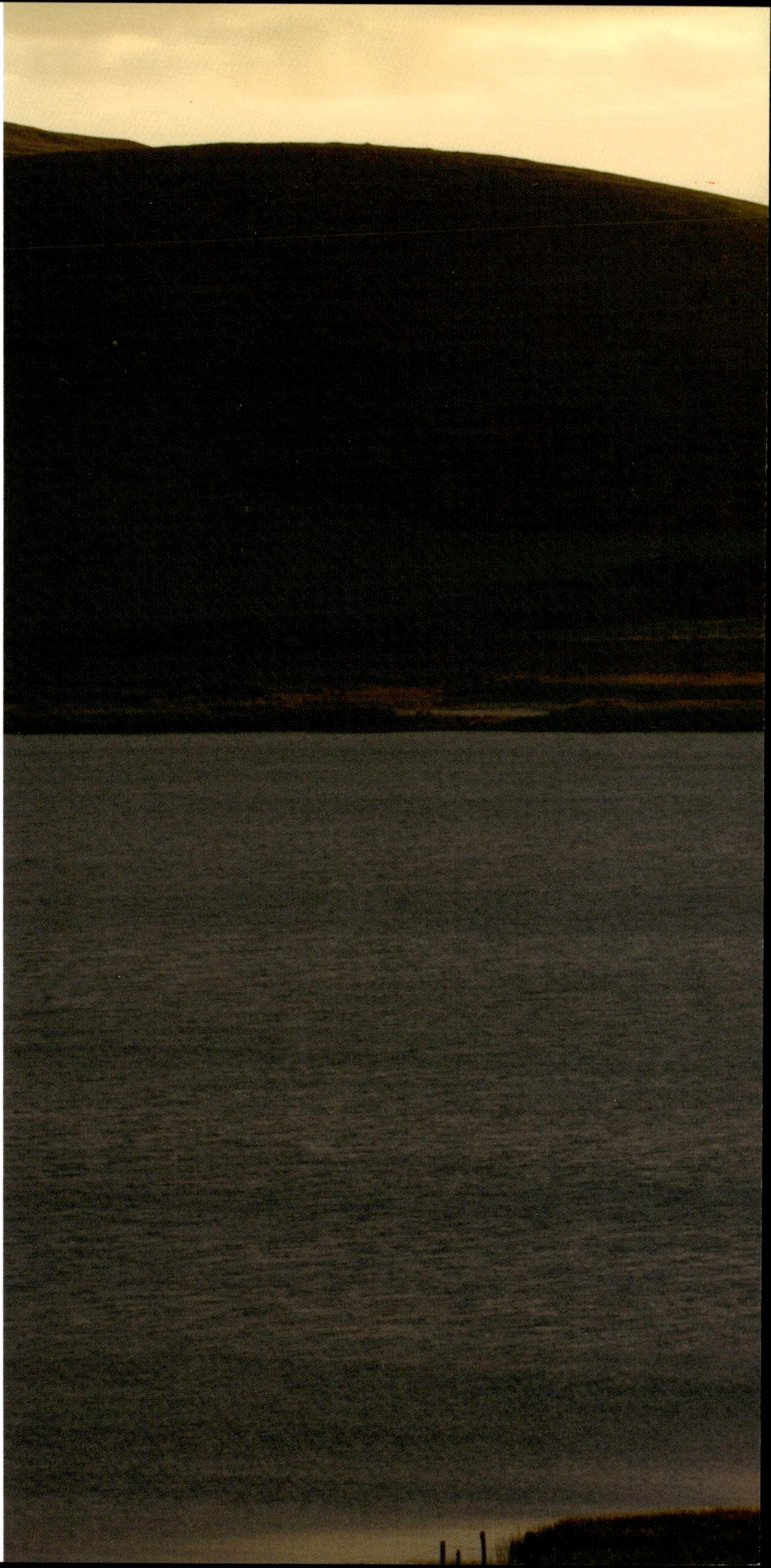

The Loch of Spiggie at dusk.

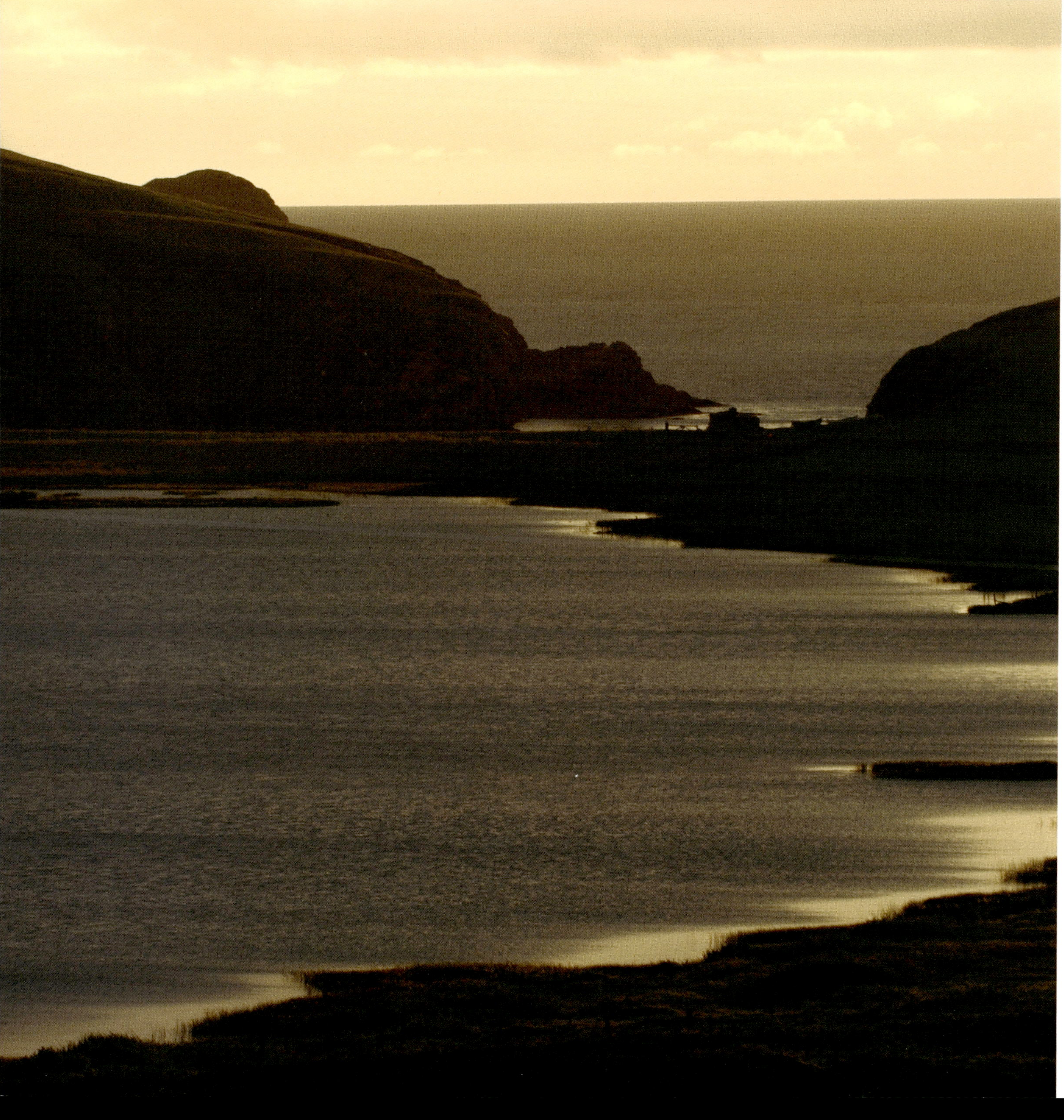

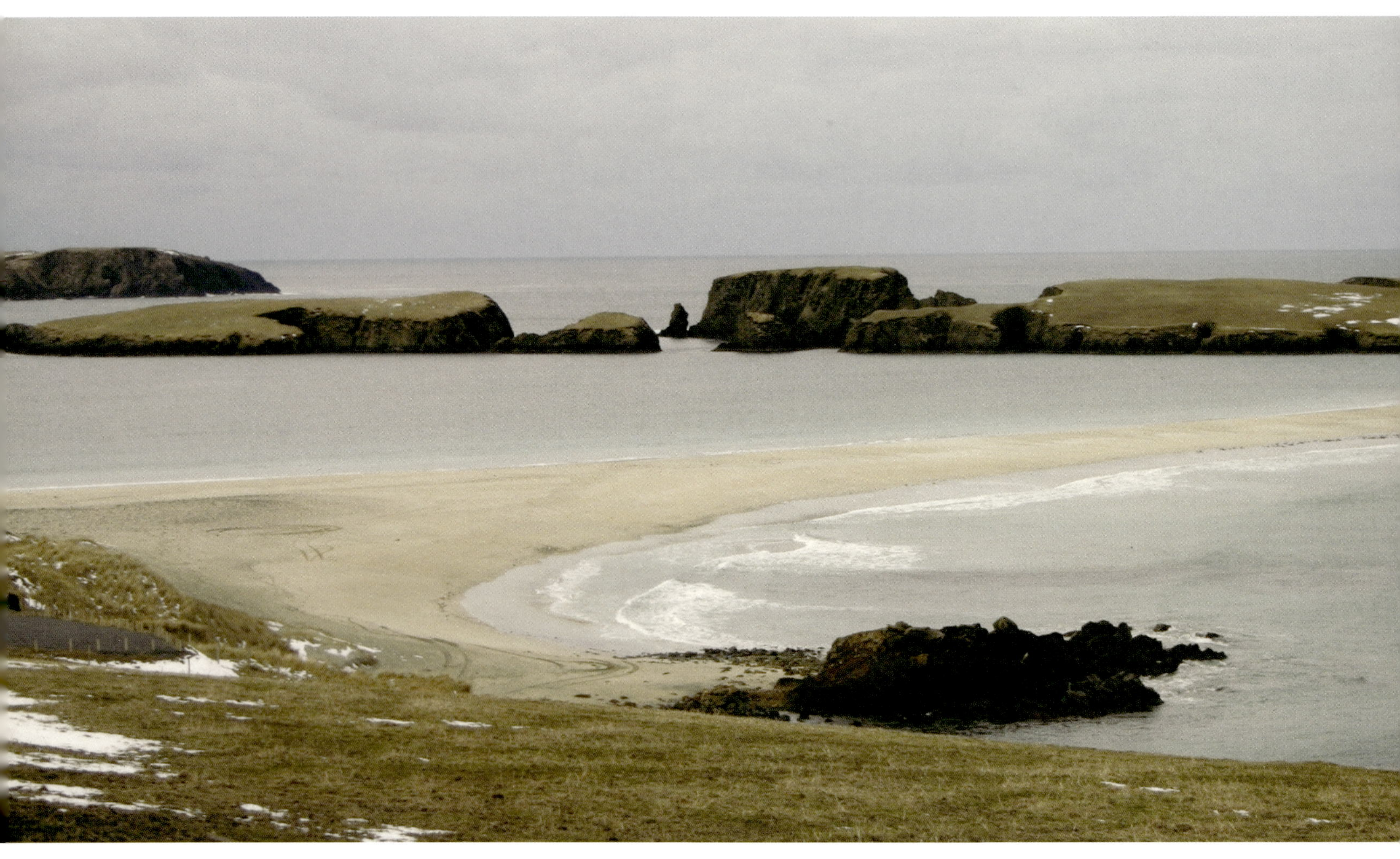

On the west coast of South Mainland lies the wonderful St Ninian's Isle. Many historians believe that the site was used as a domestic residence from the first century BC, and then as a pre-Christian burial ground from the third century AD. The island is connected to Mainland by this sand tombolo, unique in the British Isles. Here, in winter, snow falls right down to sea level.

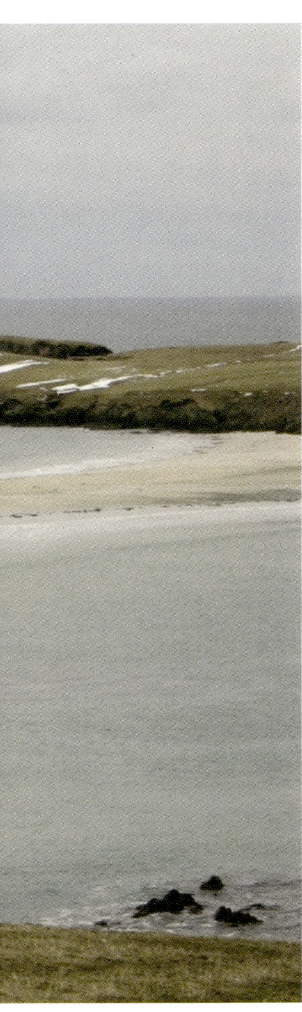

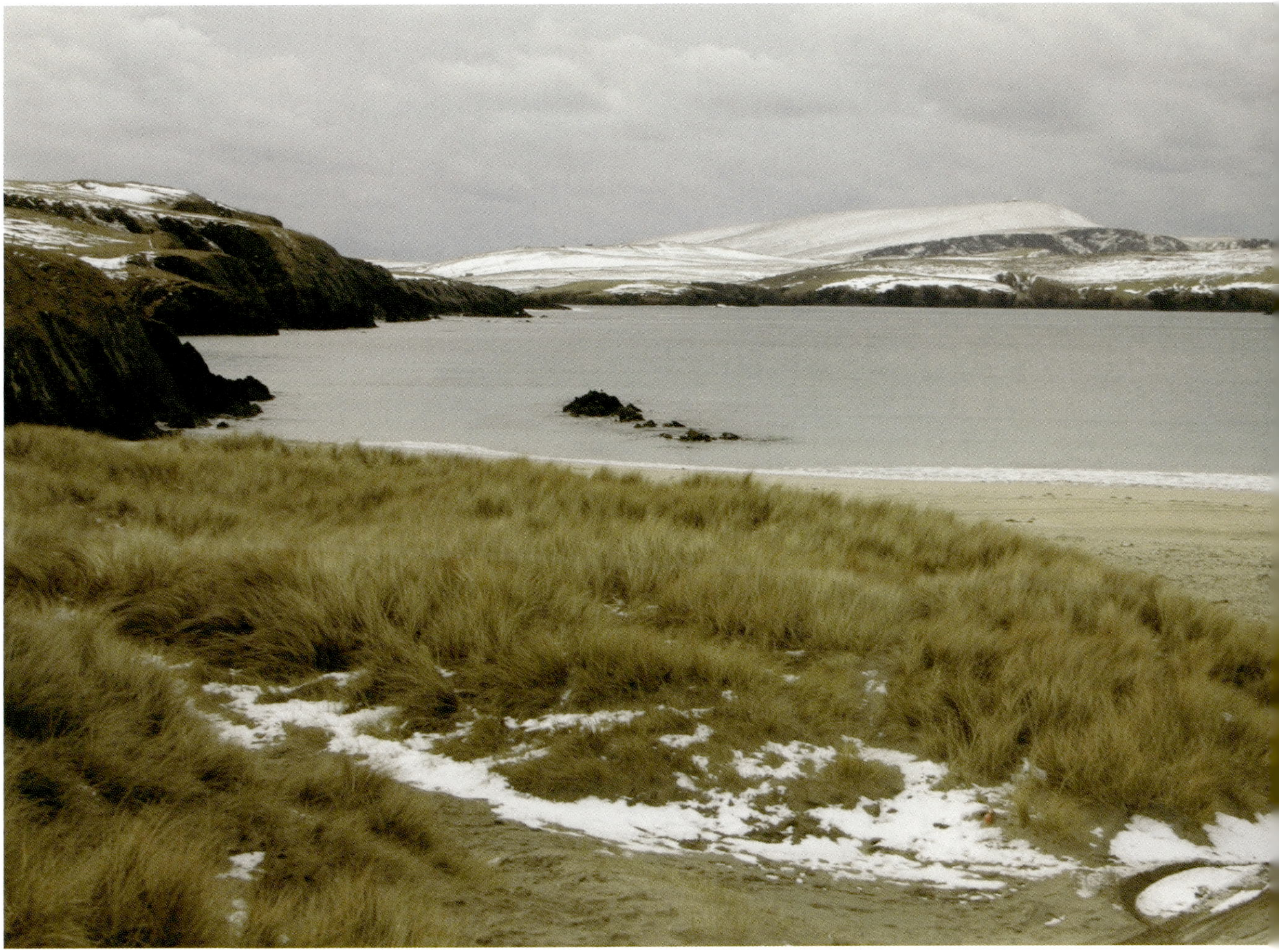

The winter scene at St Ninian's Bay, with Fitful Head in the distance and the island of Colsay away to the right.

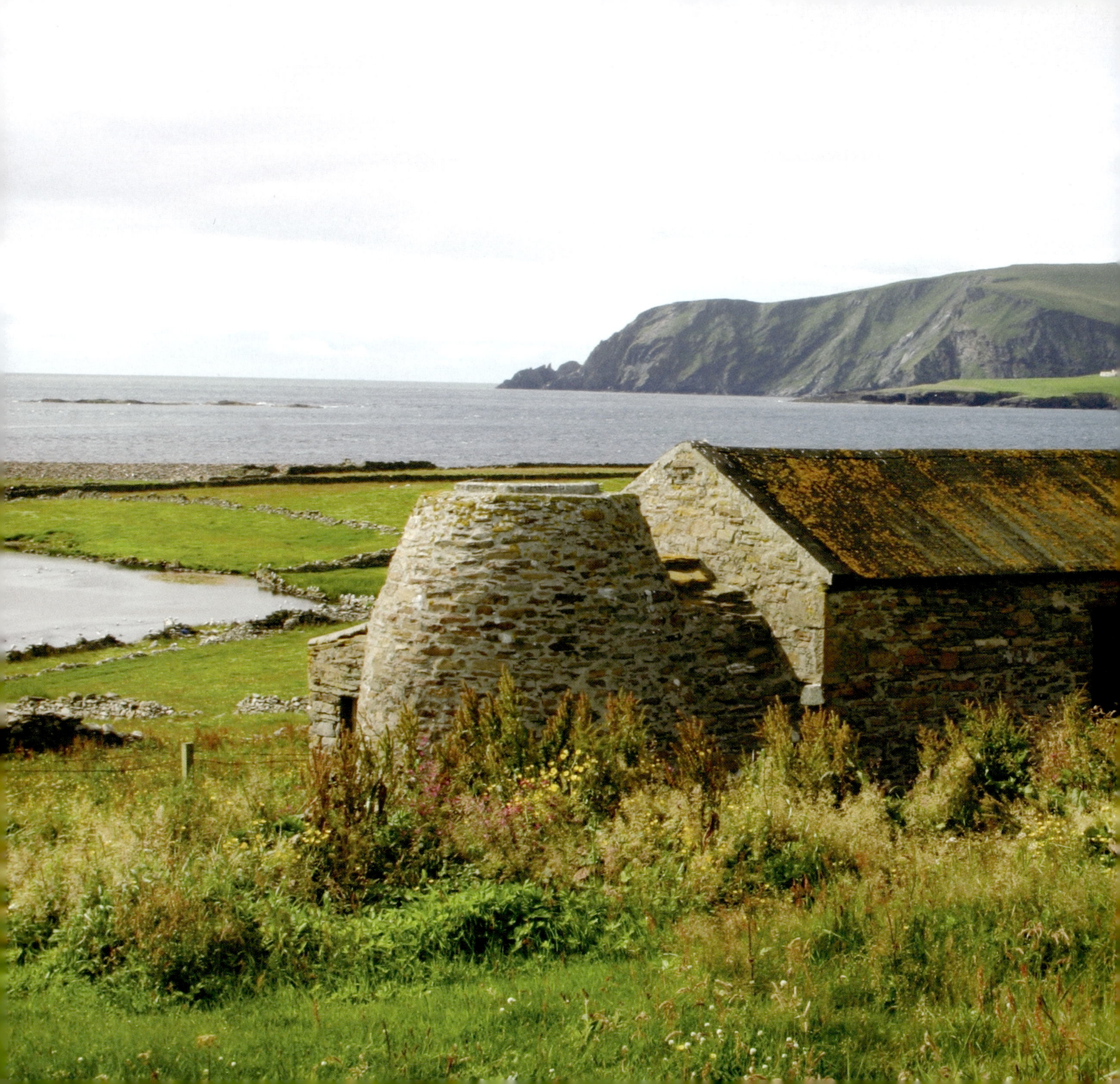

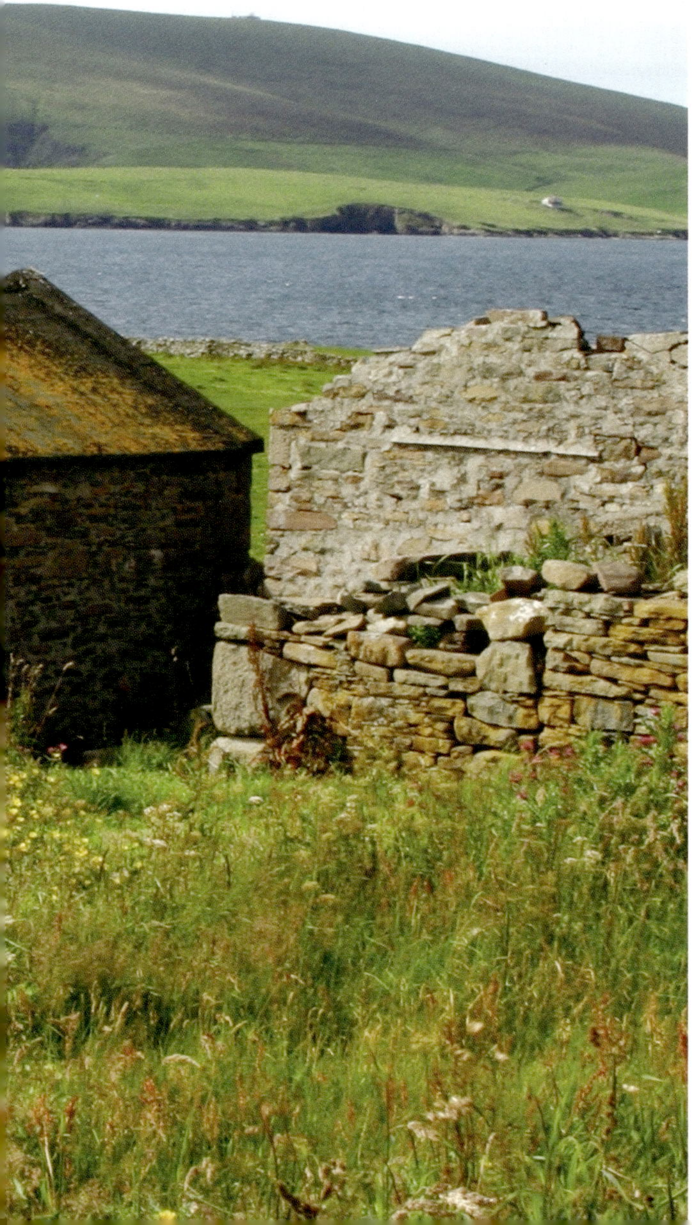

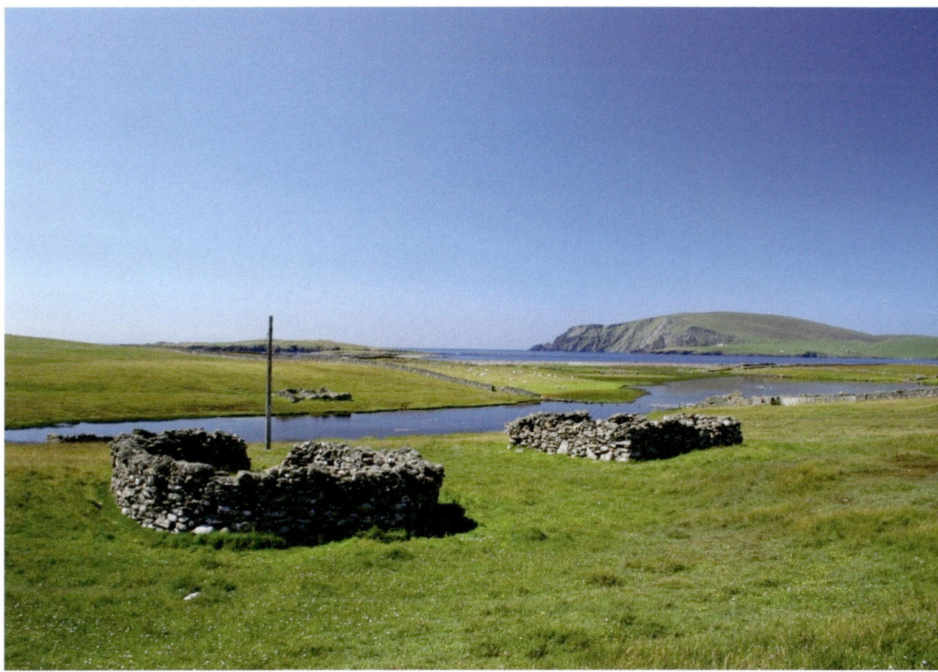

The peninsula of Scatness juts out into the West Voe of Sumburgh, and here on this promontory, there are a number of old settlements. The stone from some of these ancient houses has been reworked into sheep folds.

Fitful Head from an old corn-drying kiln at Scatness.

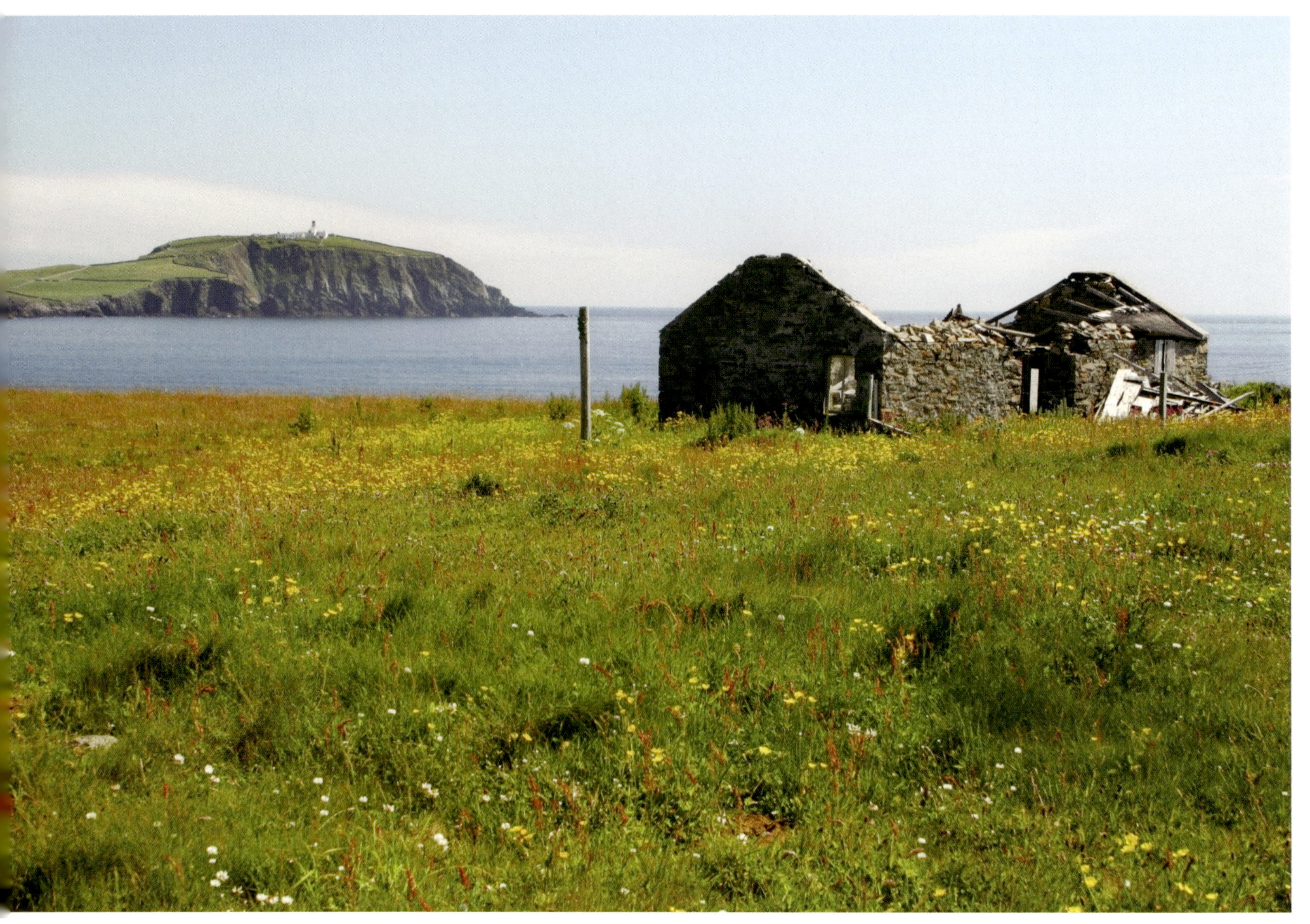

The view across the West Voe of Sumburgh towards Sumburgh Head, from an old cottage at Scatness.

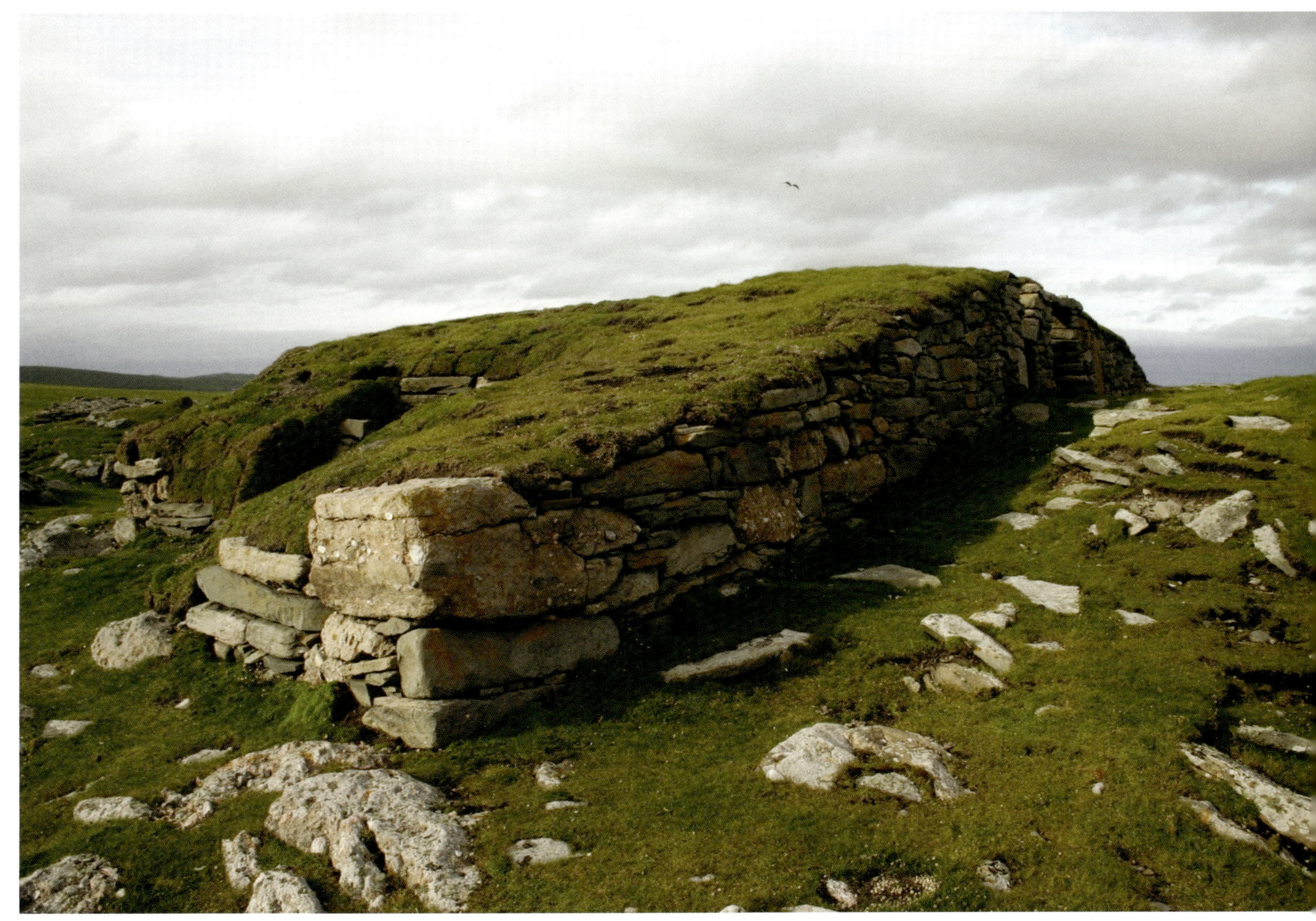

On the southern tip of Scatness, across short-cropped turf and overlooking the West Voe of Sumburgh, lies the Ness of Burgi Iron Age fort. This low, fortified dwelling place stands on a small rocky promontory on the east side of the headland. You can walk through the twin ditches and up to the house, then crawl into the rooms by low doorways.

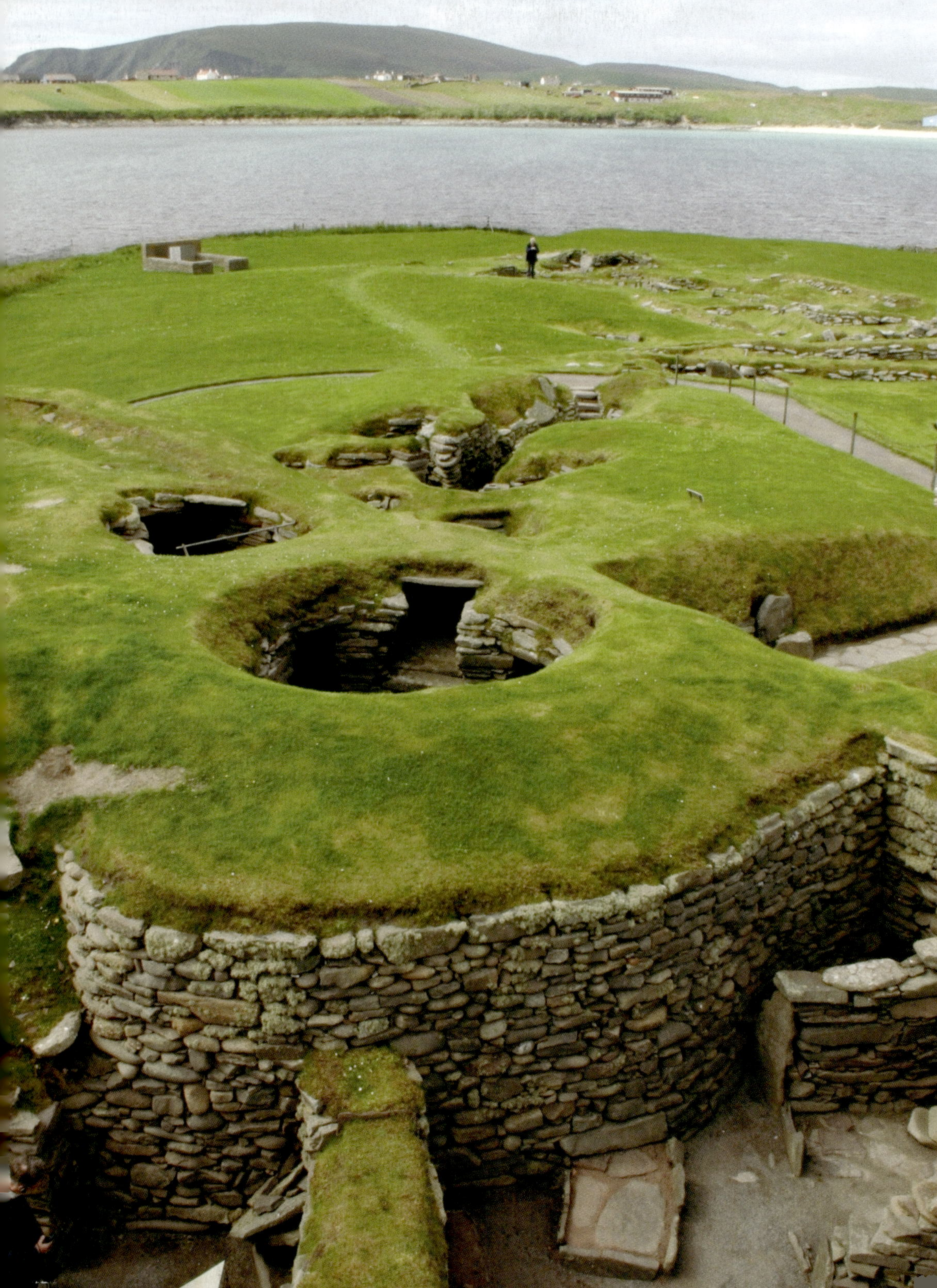

The 4000 year old village of Jarlshof at Sumburgh is the most important archaeological site in Shetland. Viking remains are built on top of Pictish, which in turn are built on top of Iron Age, Bronze Age and Stone Age dwellings. The whole thing is topped by a sixteenth century laird's mansion.

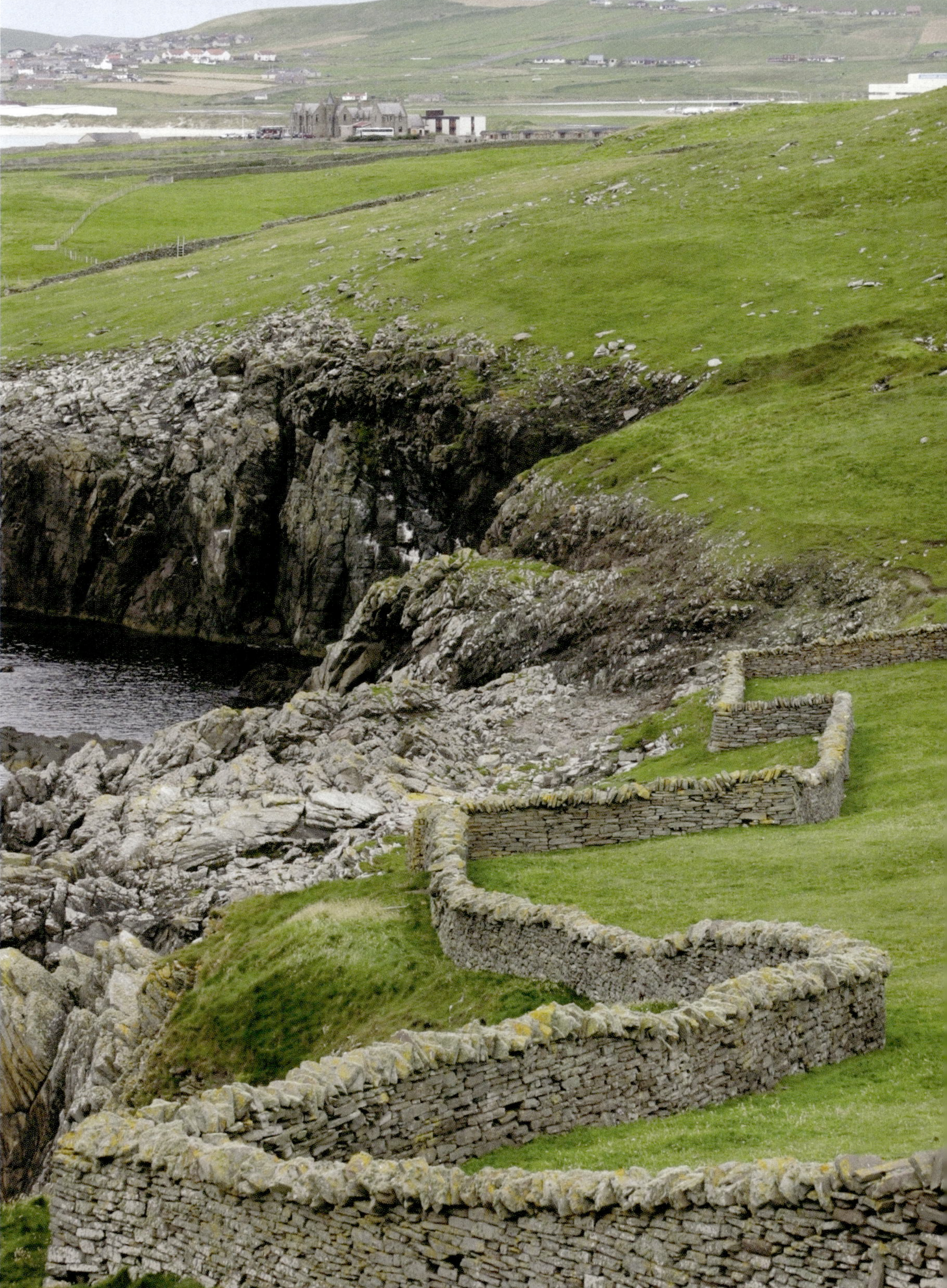

Looking along a line of dry stone walls from Sumburgh Head towards Jarlshof, and Sumburgh Airport.

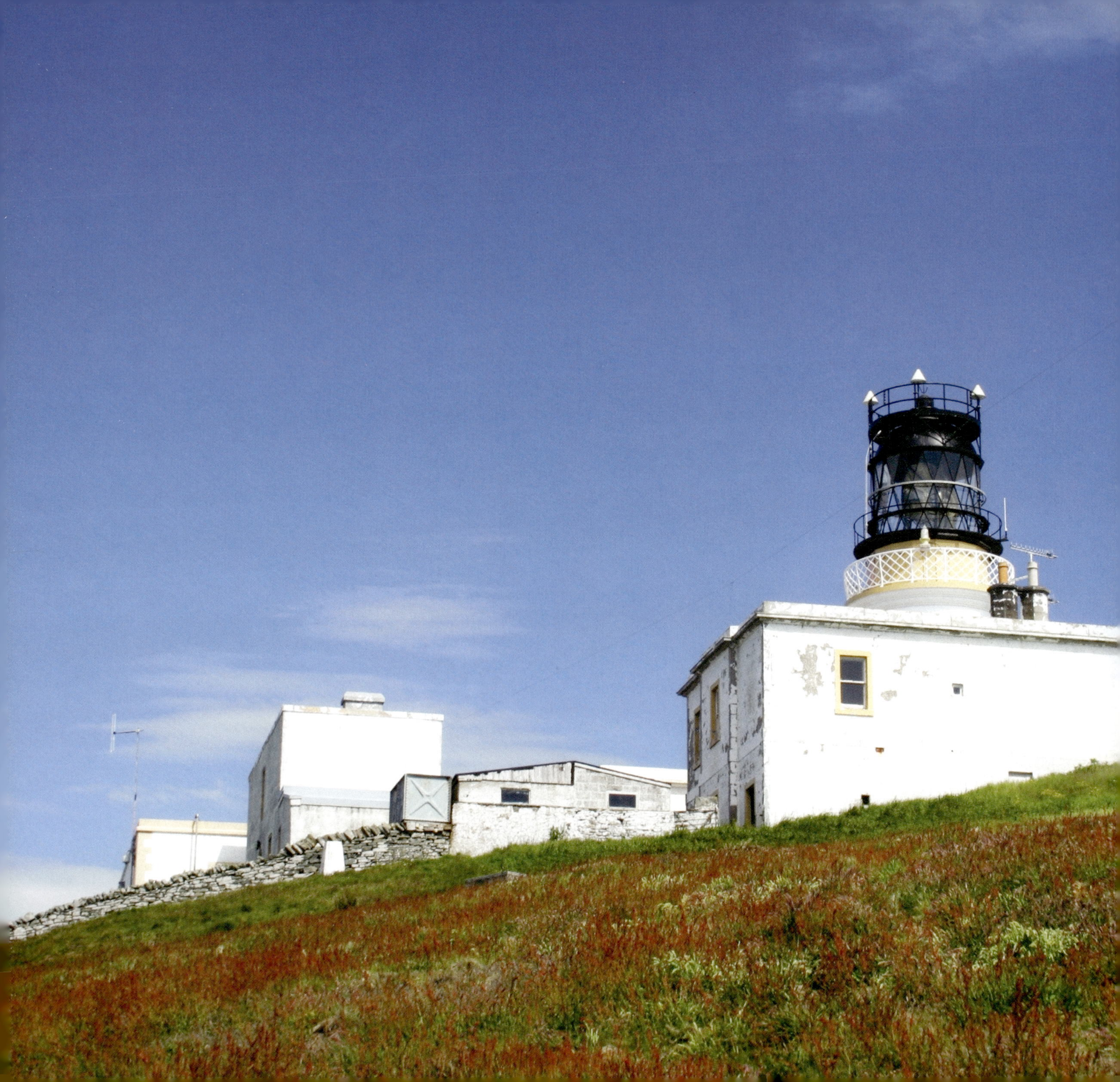

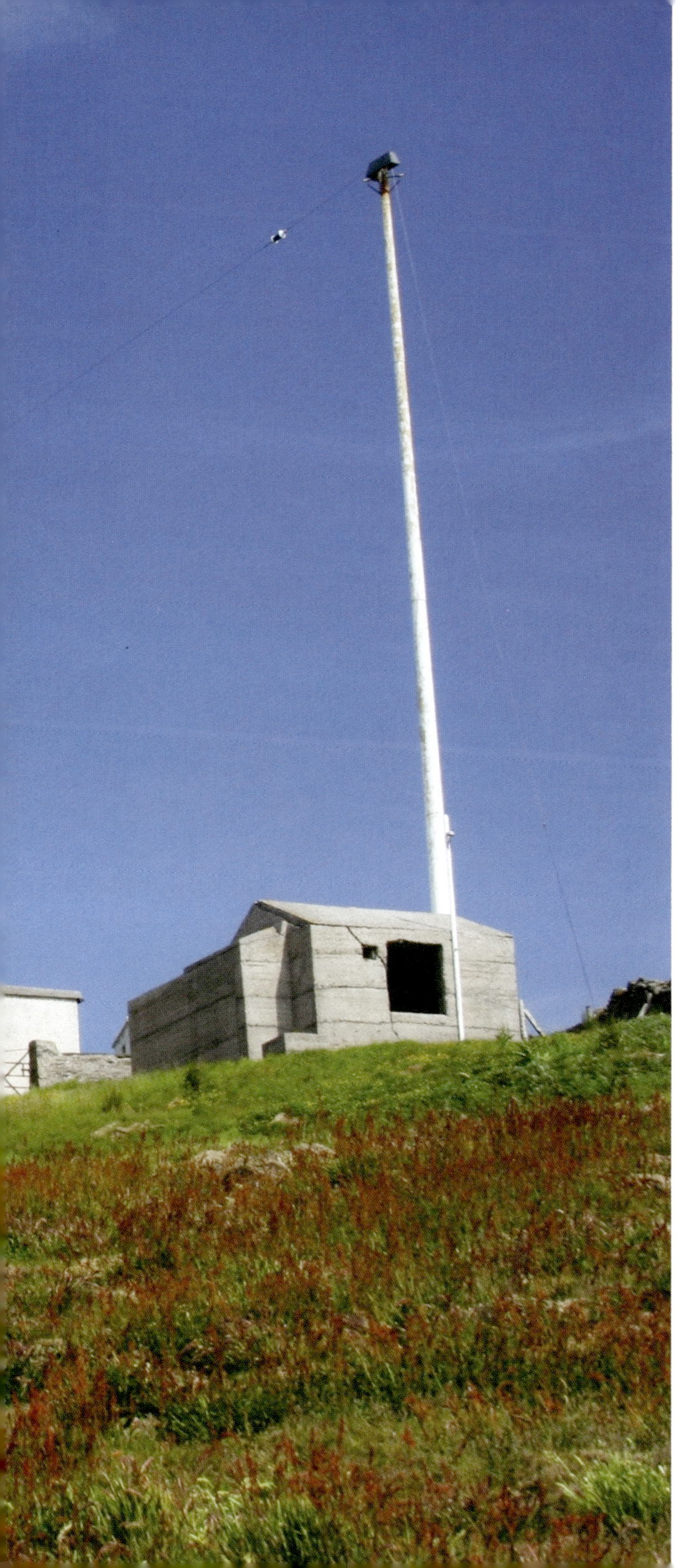

The lighthouse on Sumburgh Head was the first to be built in Shetland. It was constructed by the Stevenson family, with Robert Stevenson in charge. Work began in 1819, and the light was first lit in 1821.

Sumburgh Head today is managed as an RSPB reserve, and here you'll see thousands of seabirds in the summer, including razorbills, guillemots, puffins, kittiwakes, fulmars, great skuas, and Arctic skuas. The stone walls around the headland are also a good place to spot the tiny Shetland wren – a species unique to these islands. It looks very similar to the common wren, but is a little bit bigger!

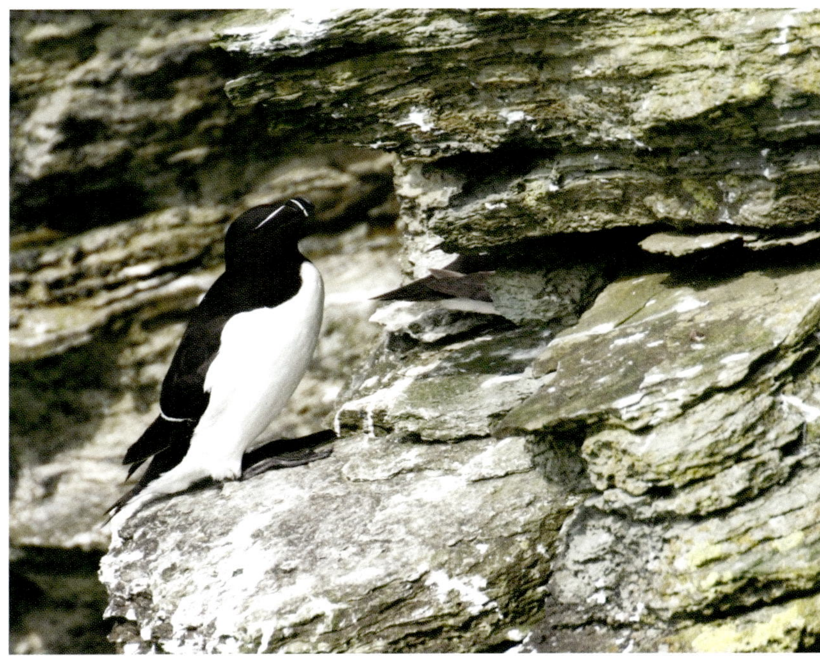

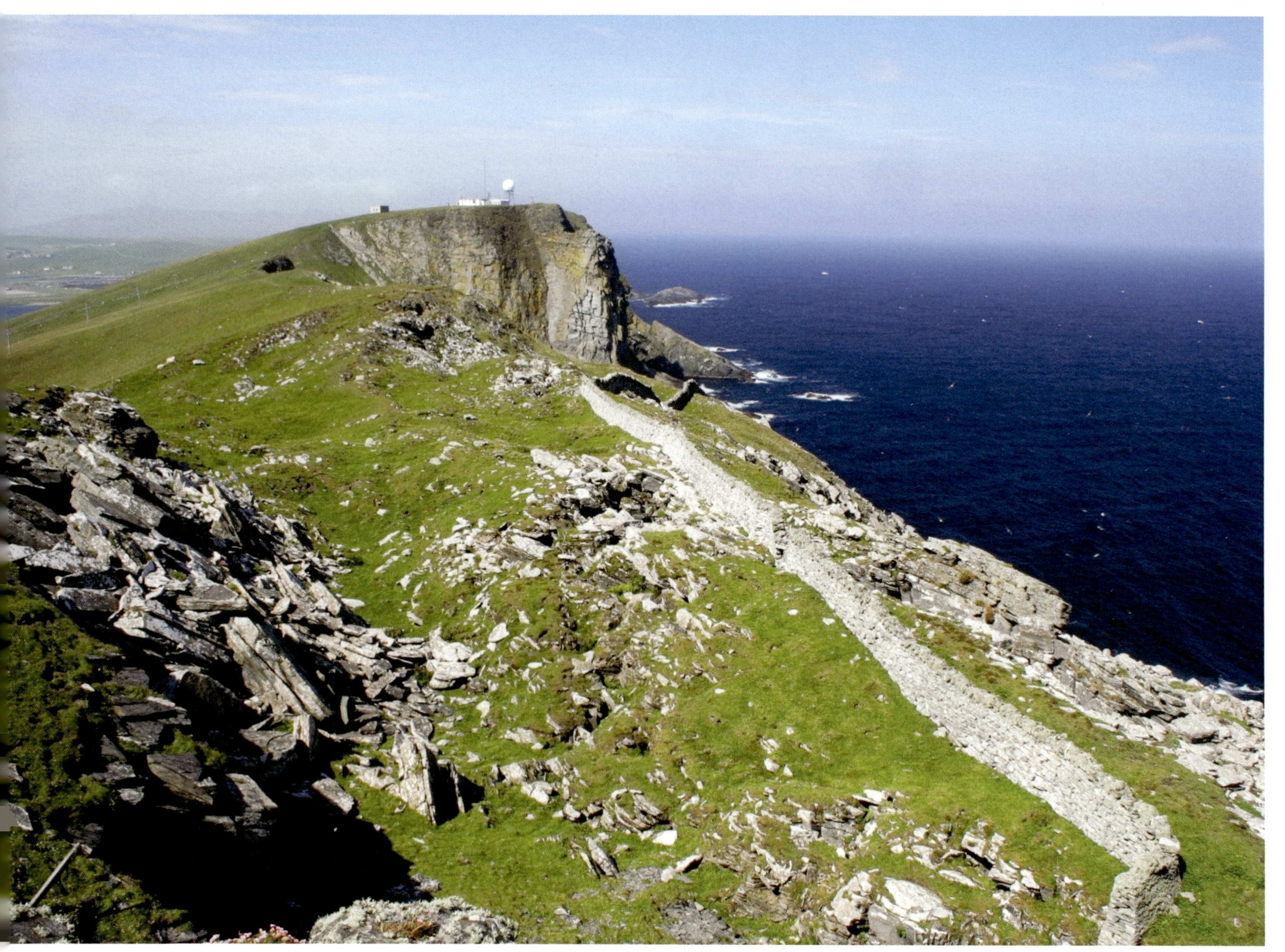

Compass Hill's summit.

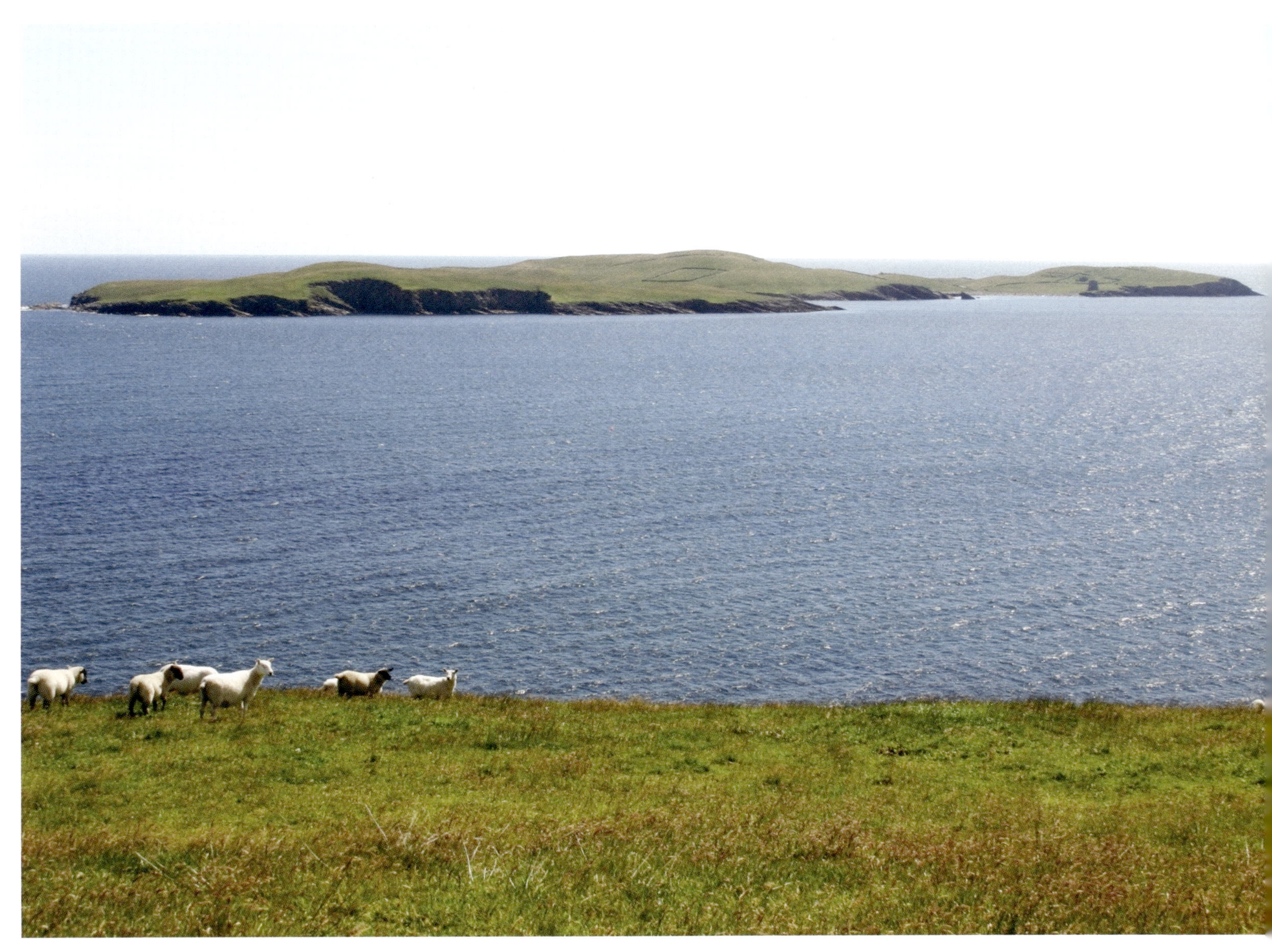

The island of Mousa, off the east coast of south Mainland.

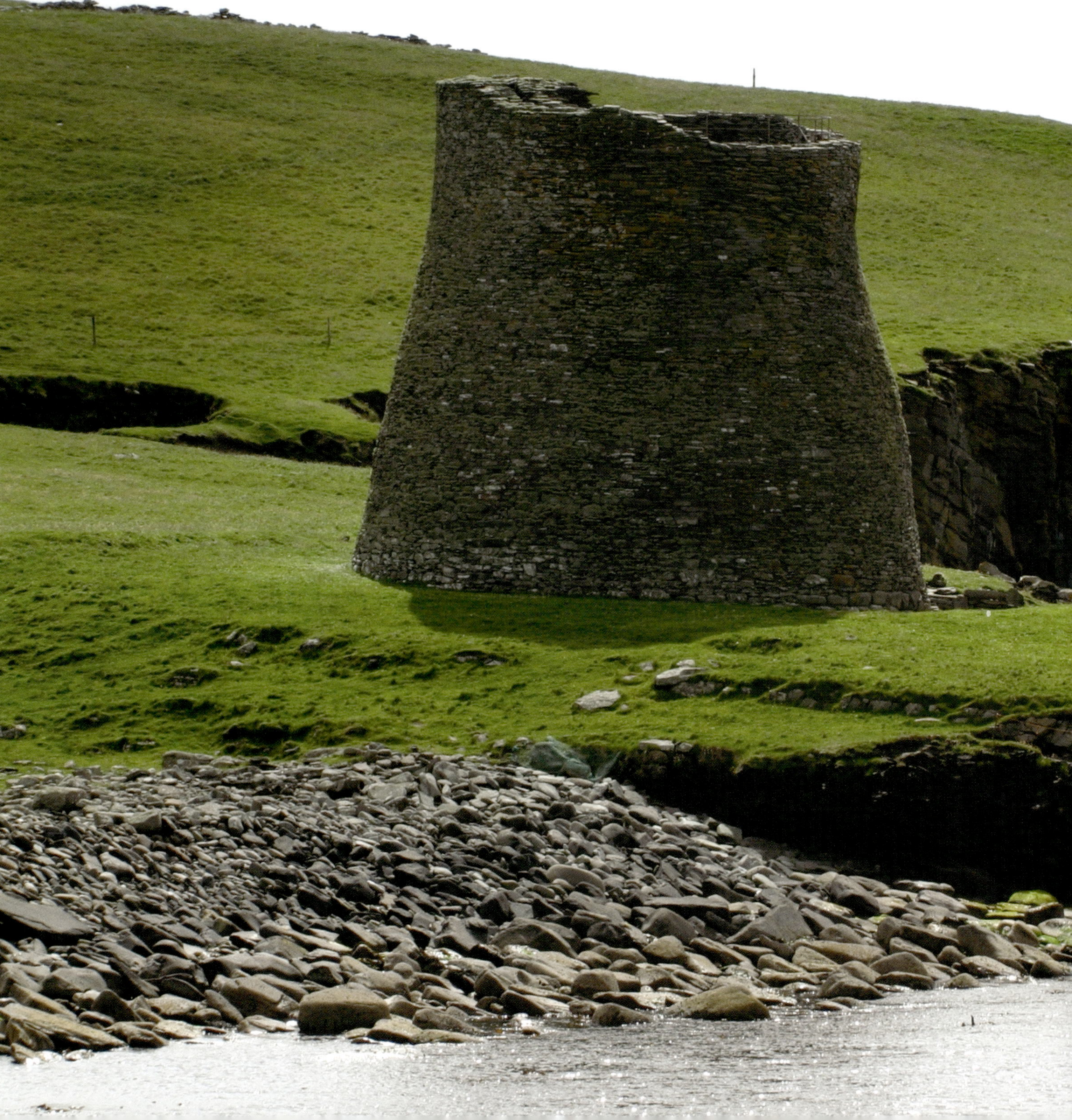

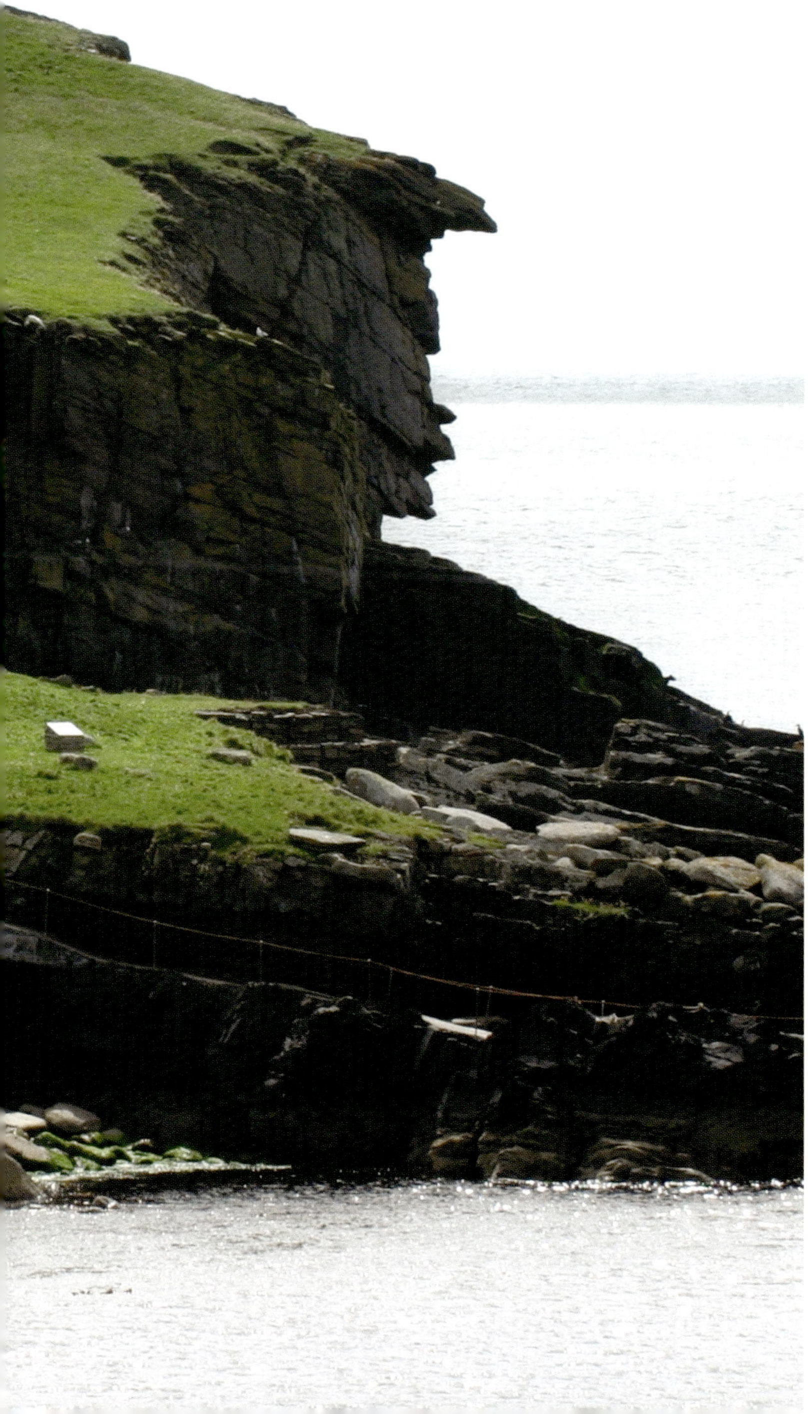

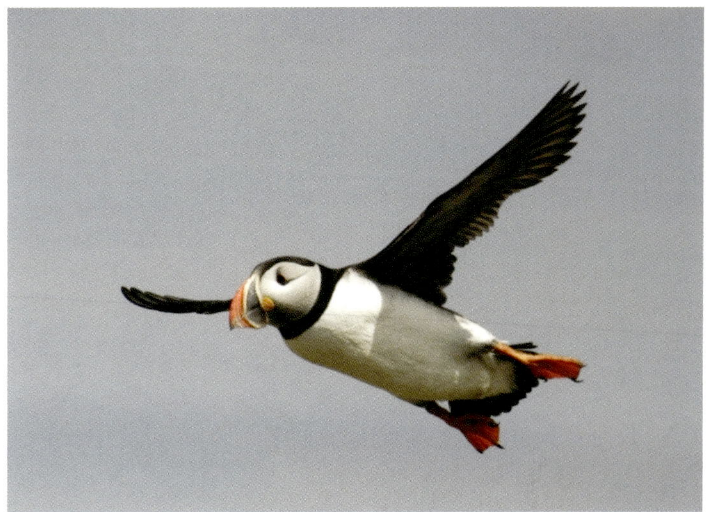

Mousa is also managed as an RSPB reserve, and is an important nesting site for a host of sea birds, including puffins. Common and grey seals also come here to pup, and if you're lucky, you might spot an otter too! During the summer one of the most amazing wildlife spectacles occurs at the broch on Mousa. Thousands of tiny storm petrels return to their nest site within the broch and nearby stone walls, and you can take a night-time boat trip out to see them coming in off the sea.

Mousa is famous for its 2000 year old broch. The Mousa Broch is the finest preserved example in Scotland (brochs are unique to Scotland) and rises to 40 feet. You can still climb up to the highest level, making a walk to the broch here a memorable experience.

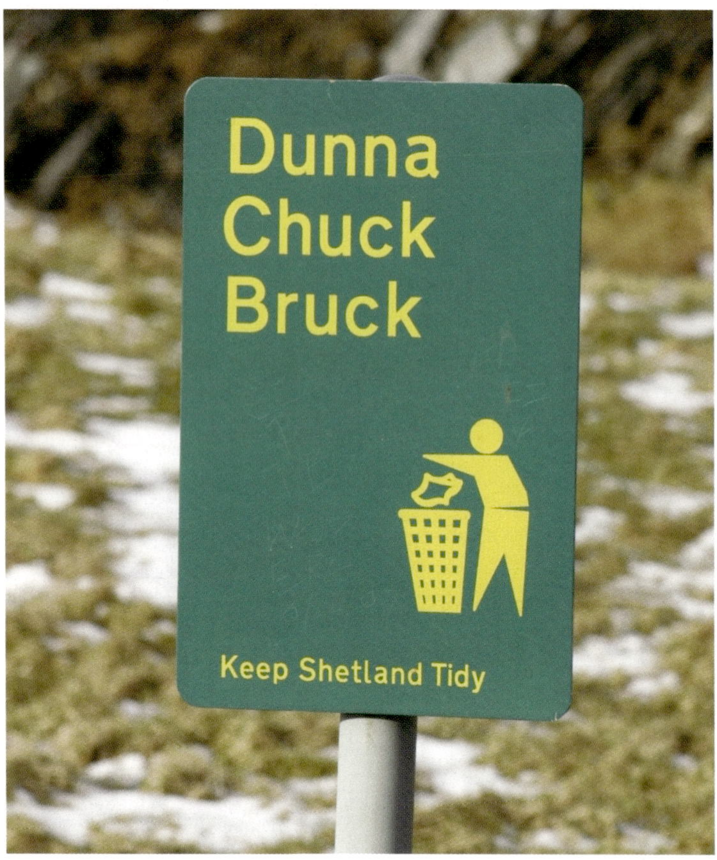


A typically light-hearted sign on Shetland. Better than 'Keep Britain Tidy'!

Scalloway was once the capital of Shetland. The castle here was built by forced labour in 1600. Patrick Stewart, Earl of Orkney and Lord of Shetland, had it built as his Shetland residence, and it is said that the mortar for holding the stones together was mixed with blood and eggs. Stewart was a half brother of Mary Queen of Scots. He was executed in 1615, and in 1653 his castle at Scalloway became a temporary garrison for Cromwell's troops. Soon after it became disused, and fell into ruins.

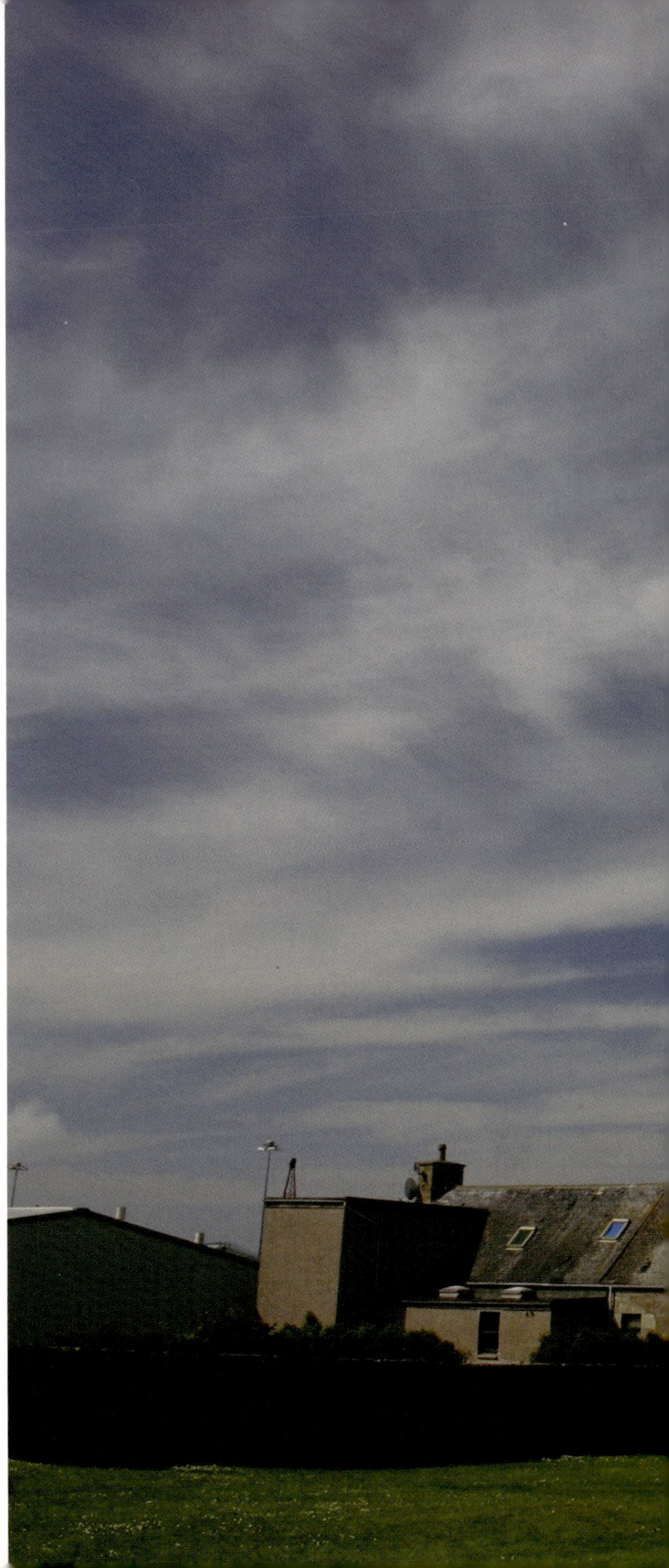

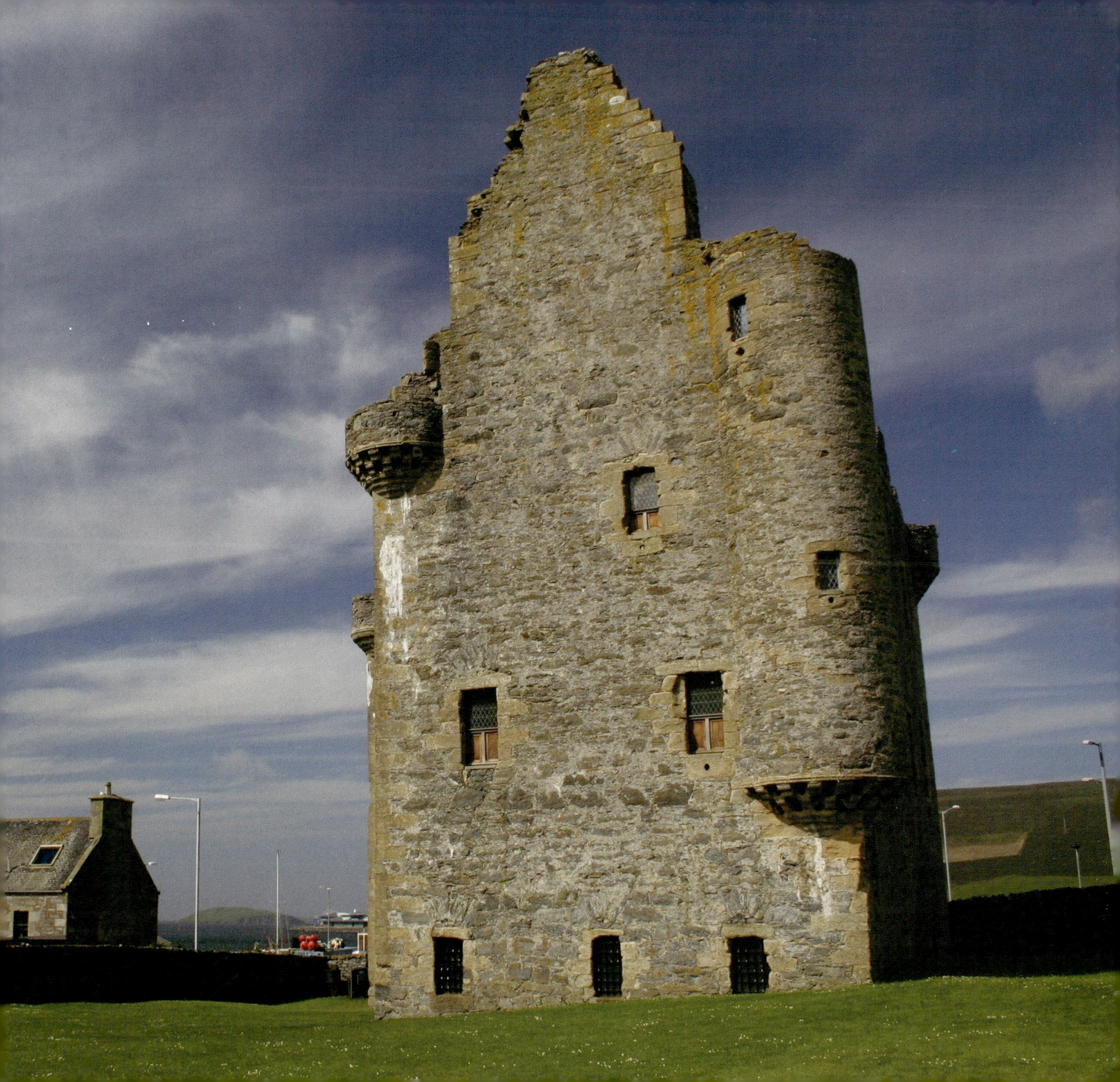

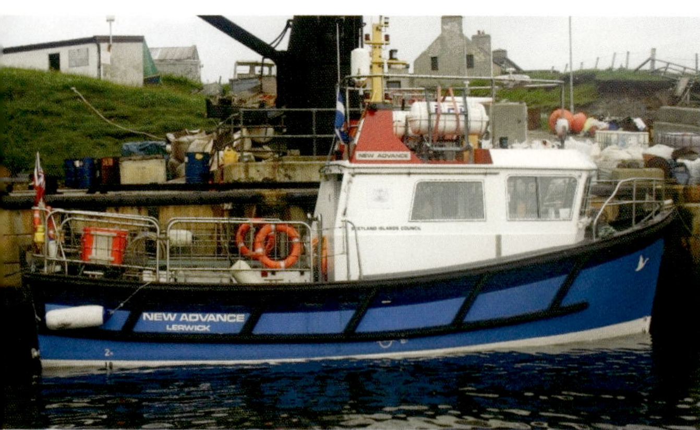


Foula is the most remote inhabited island in Britain. It lies off the west coast of Shetland, way out in the Atlantic, and takes three and a half hours to get there on the *New Advance* ferry from Scalloway.

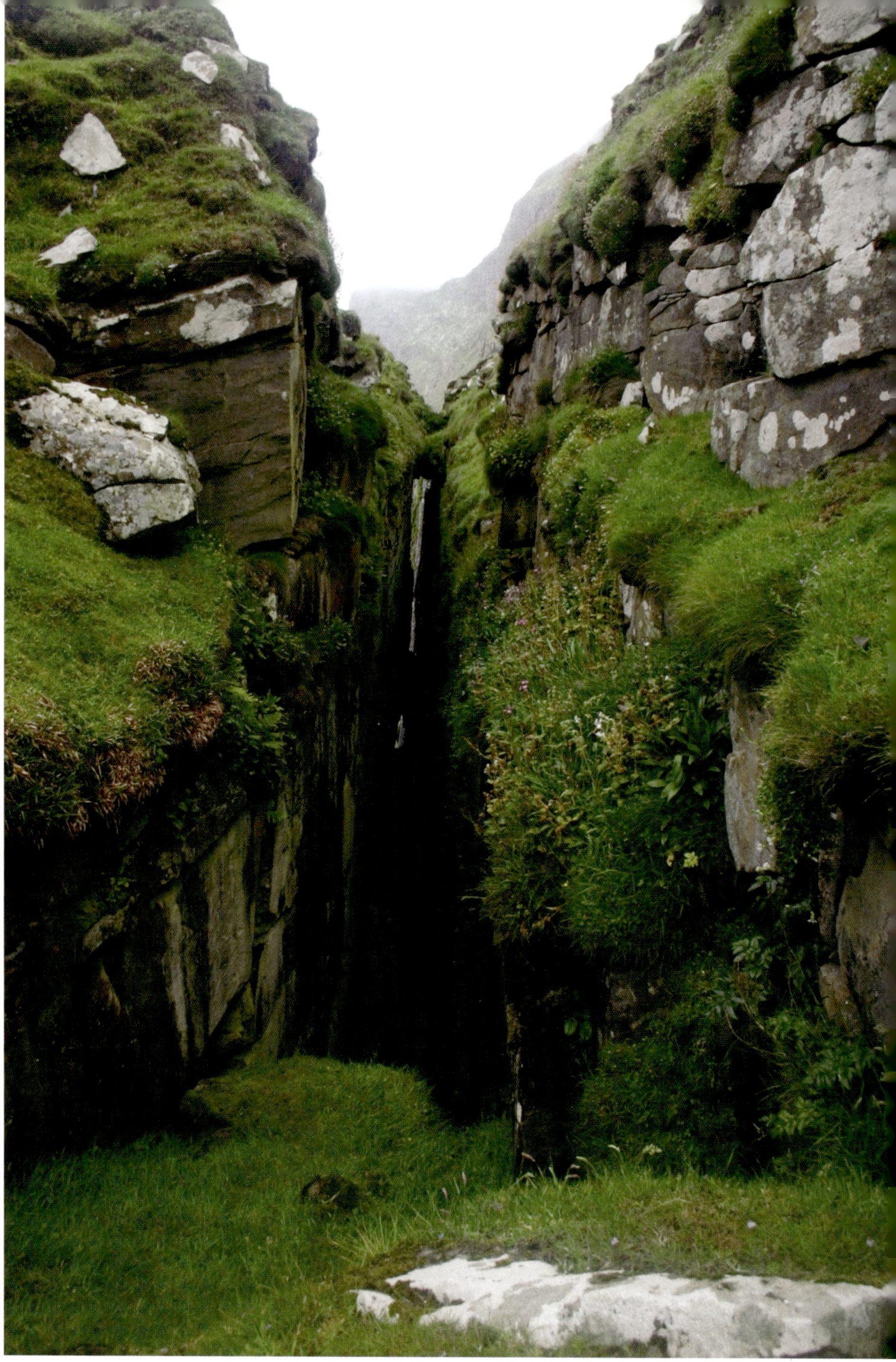

Da Sneck o da Smaalie on Foula. Local legend has it that this is where the trows, or small people, brew up trouble and bad weather!

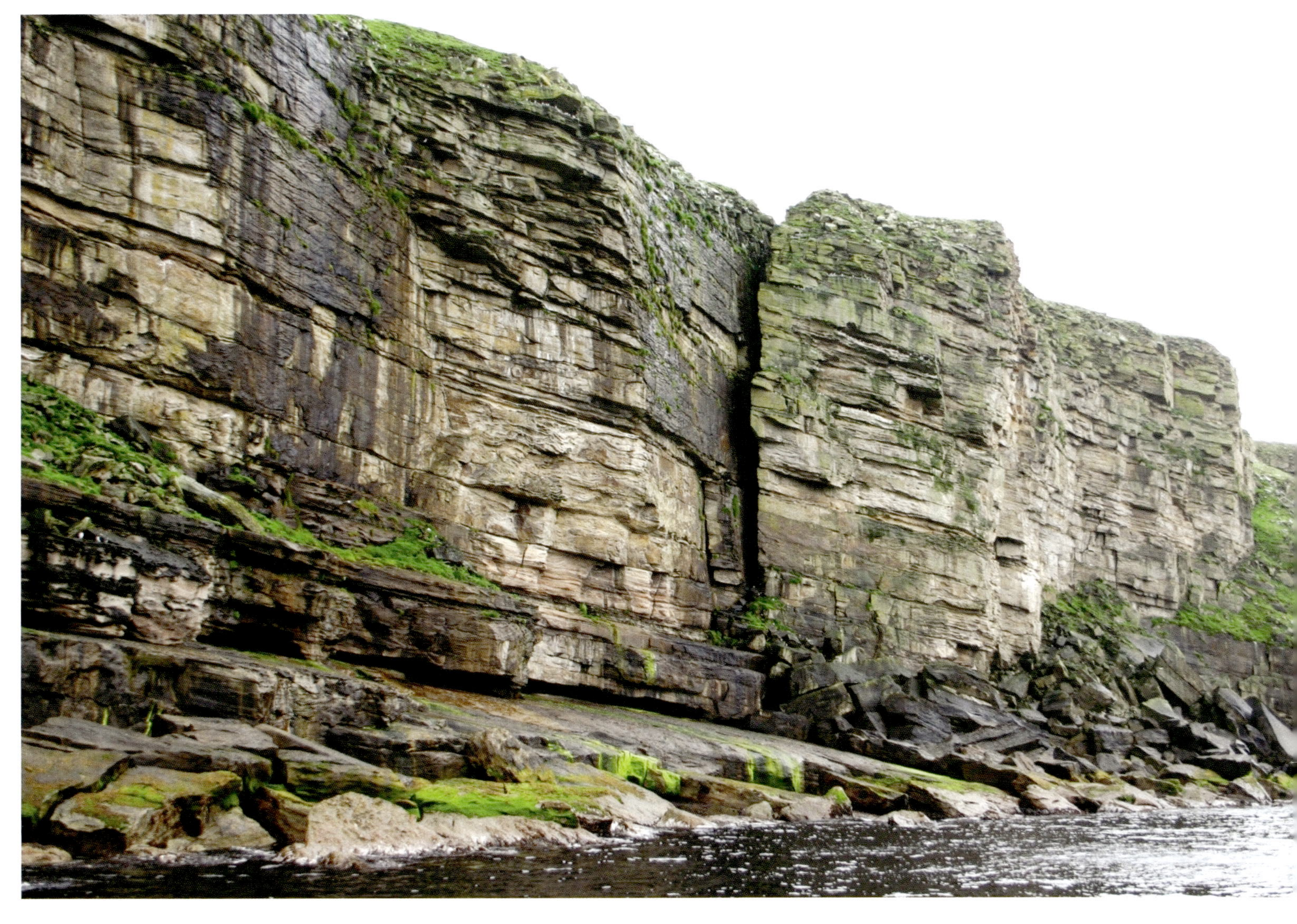

Da Sneck o da Smaalie is a huge slit in the cliff face off the west coast of Foula.
It is possible, with great care, to scramble down the sneck.

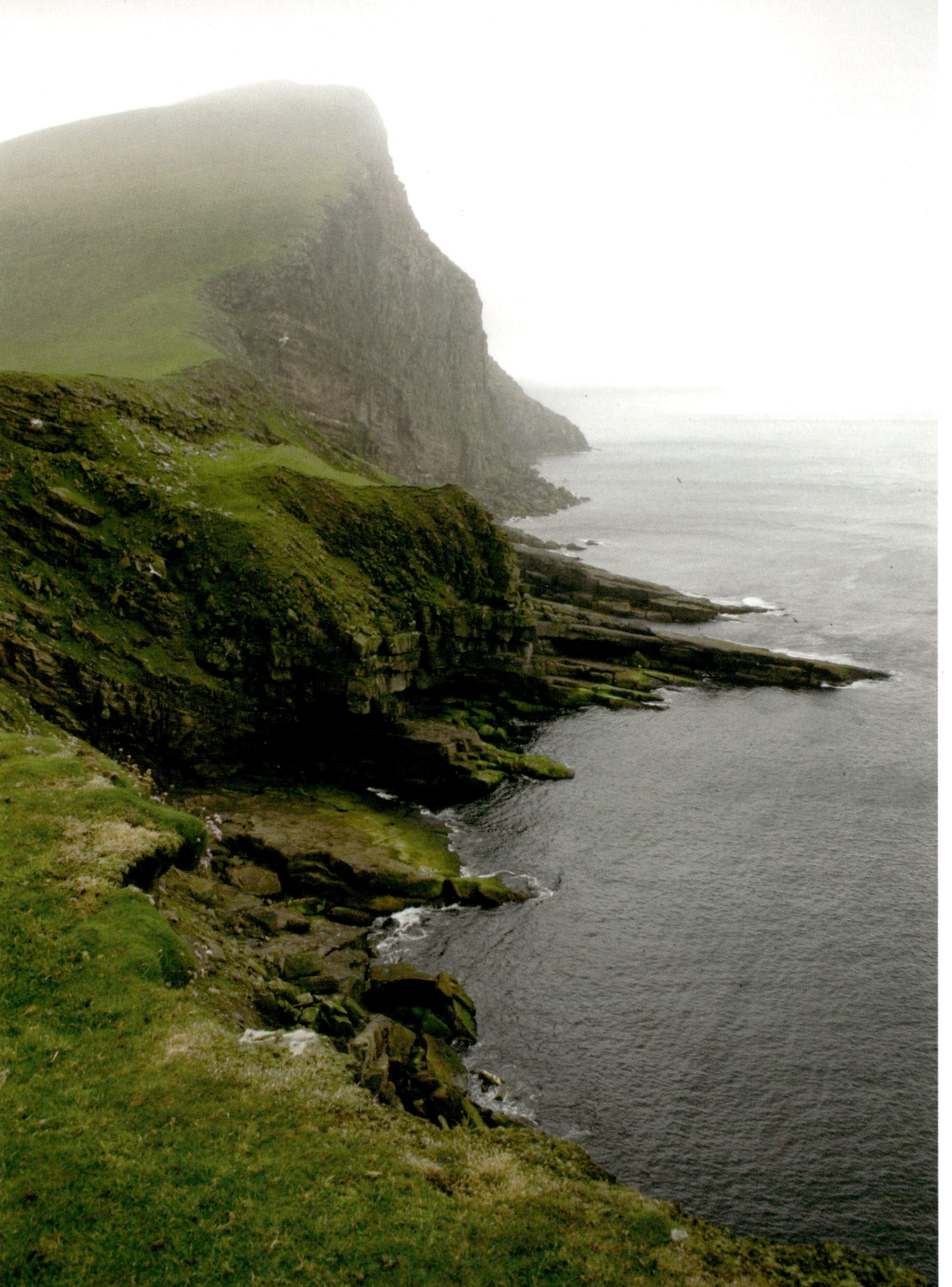

The wonderful little hill of Da Noup on the southern tip of Foula.

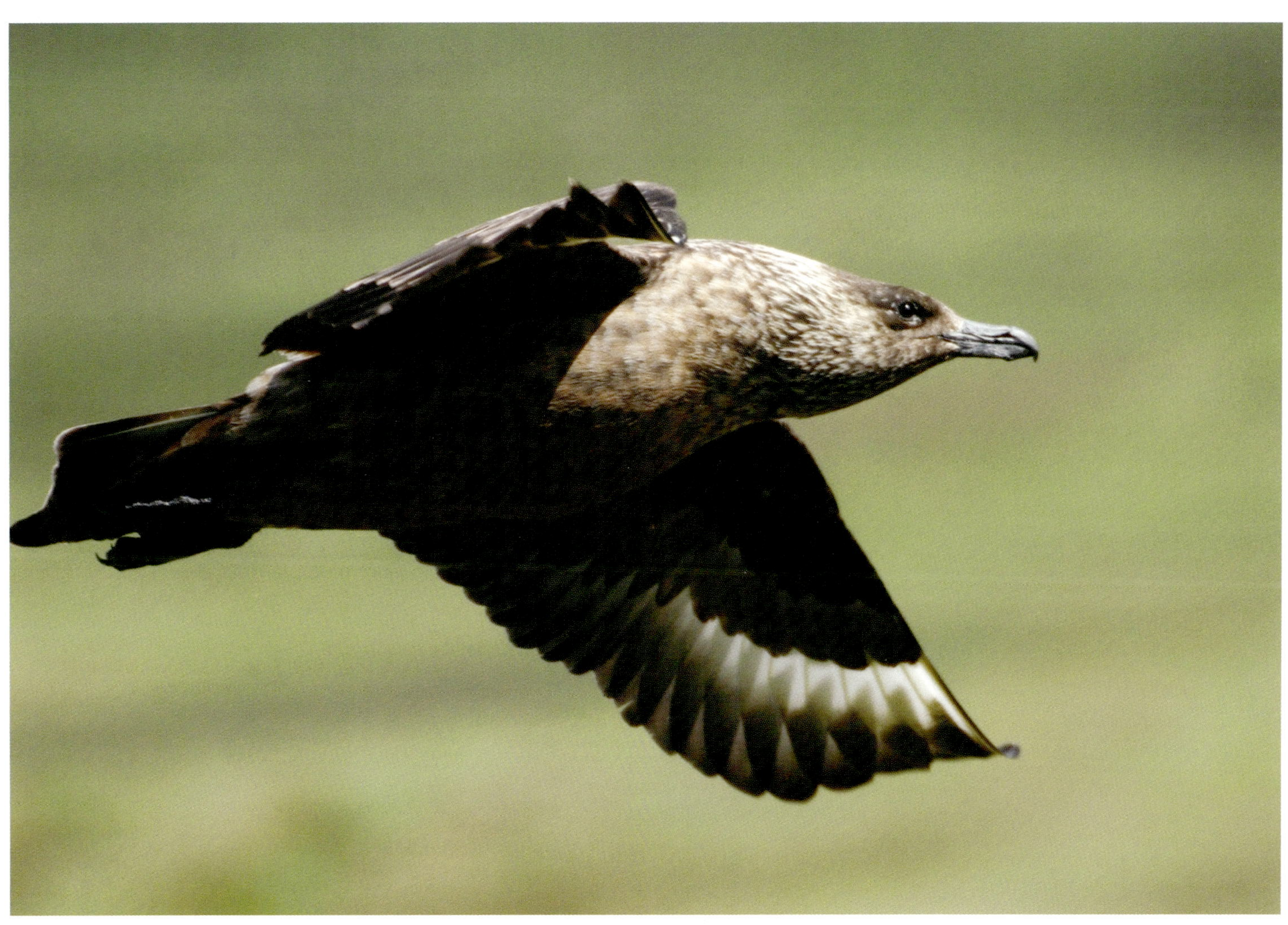

Crossing the moor to the top of Da Sneck o da Smaalie, through Da Daal, scores of great skuas are found nesting in the summer months. Locally, great skuas are known as bonxies. They make a living by chasing other seabirds to force them to regurgitate their last meal, which the bonxie then eats. They are not averse to dive-bombing people either!

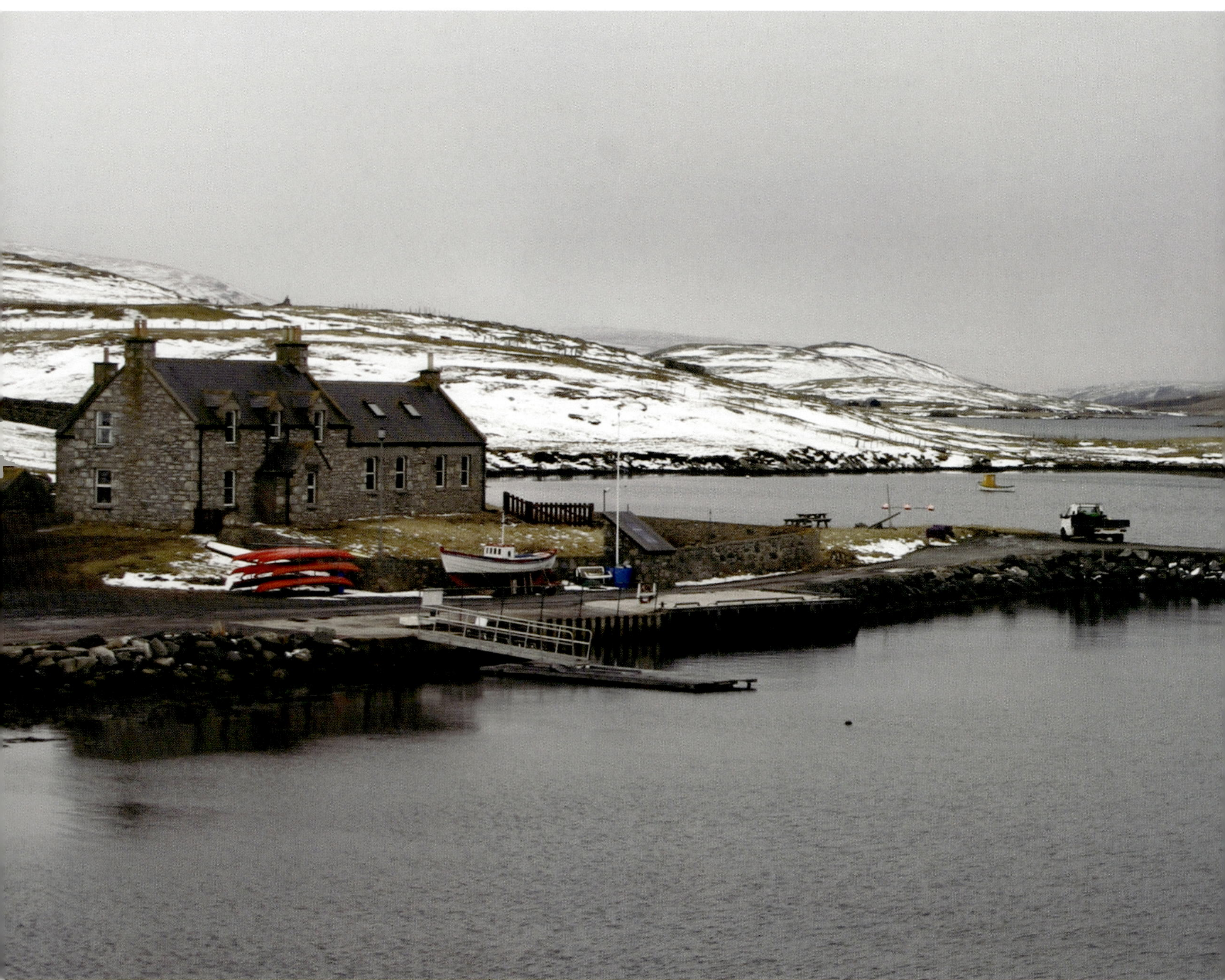

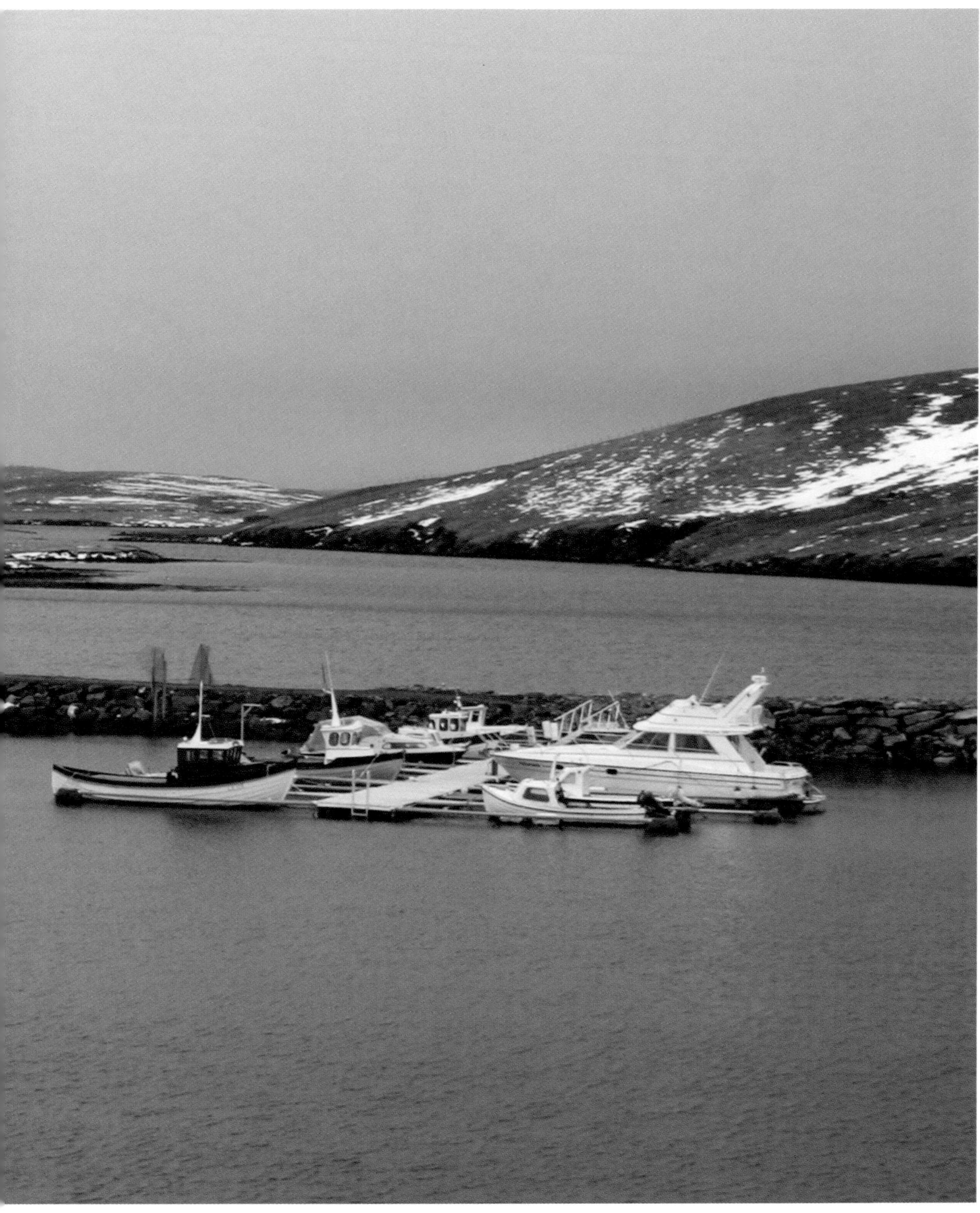

Winter can be cold and grey on Shetland, and with few daylight hours many people find it a harsh place to visit. Cloud hangs low here over Grunasound, between the islands of West and East Burra.

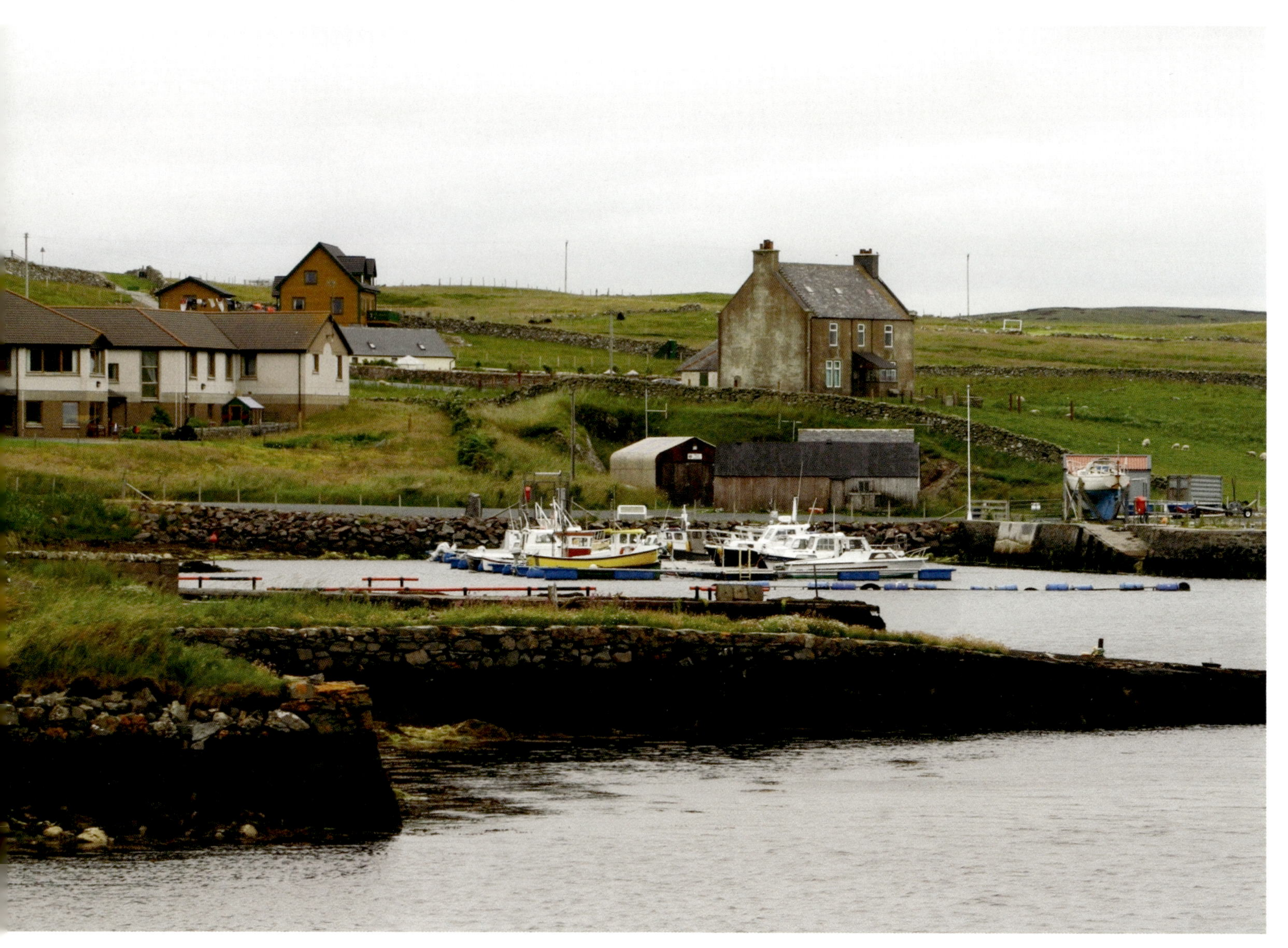

Westside forms a large chunk of Mainland. Here, at Walls (pronounced 'waas' locally) life is very laid-back.

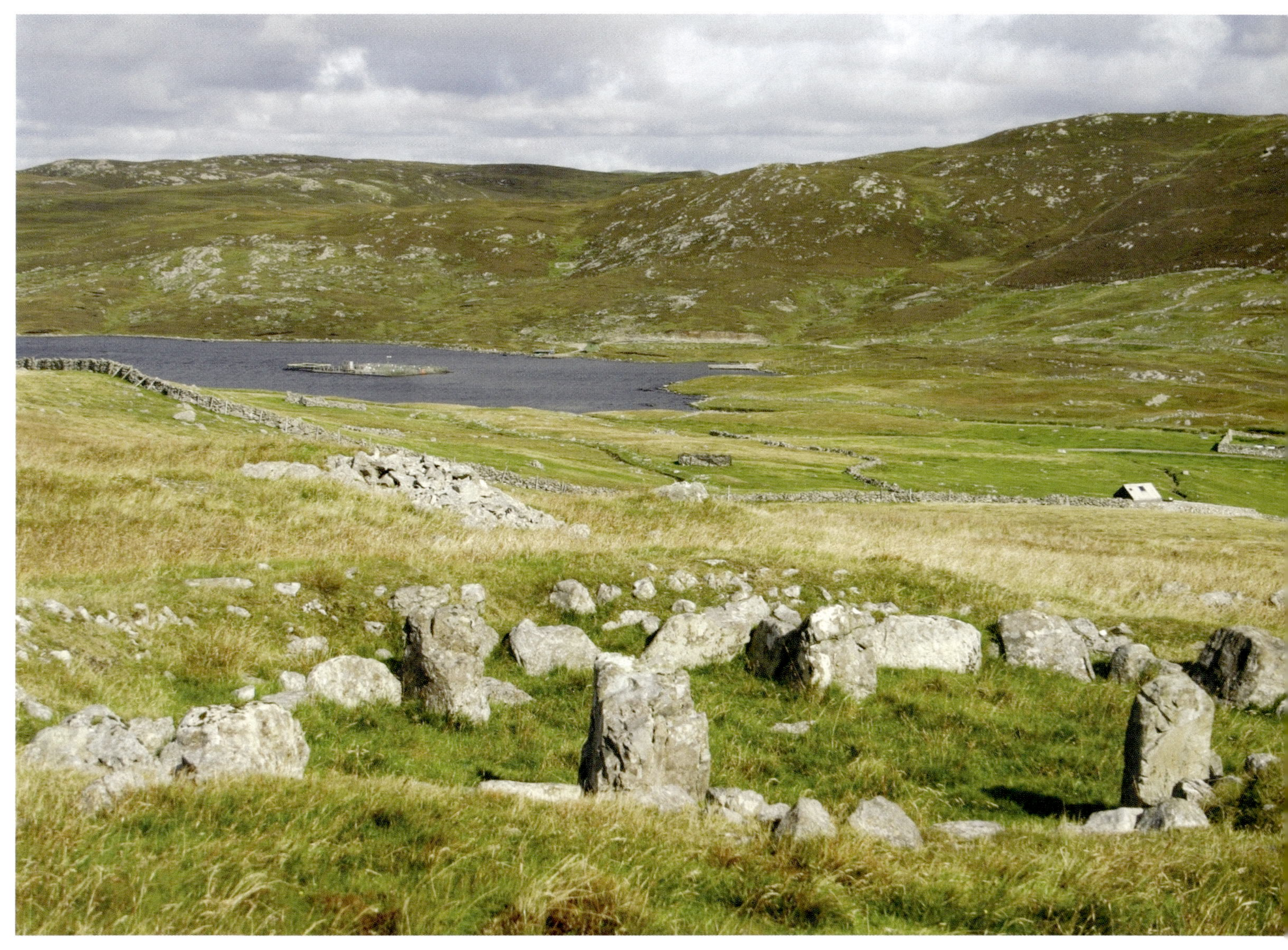

The Scord of Brouster is an open hillside archaeological site overlooking the Lochs of the Brouster on Westside. The site is littered with the remains of what was once an extensive Neolithic settlement. Oval houses and interlinking field systems can be seen, all dating from around 2000BC. There is also a perfectly circular kerbed cairn, and a large oblong stone enclosure, all from the same period.

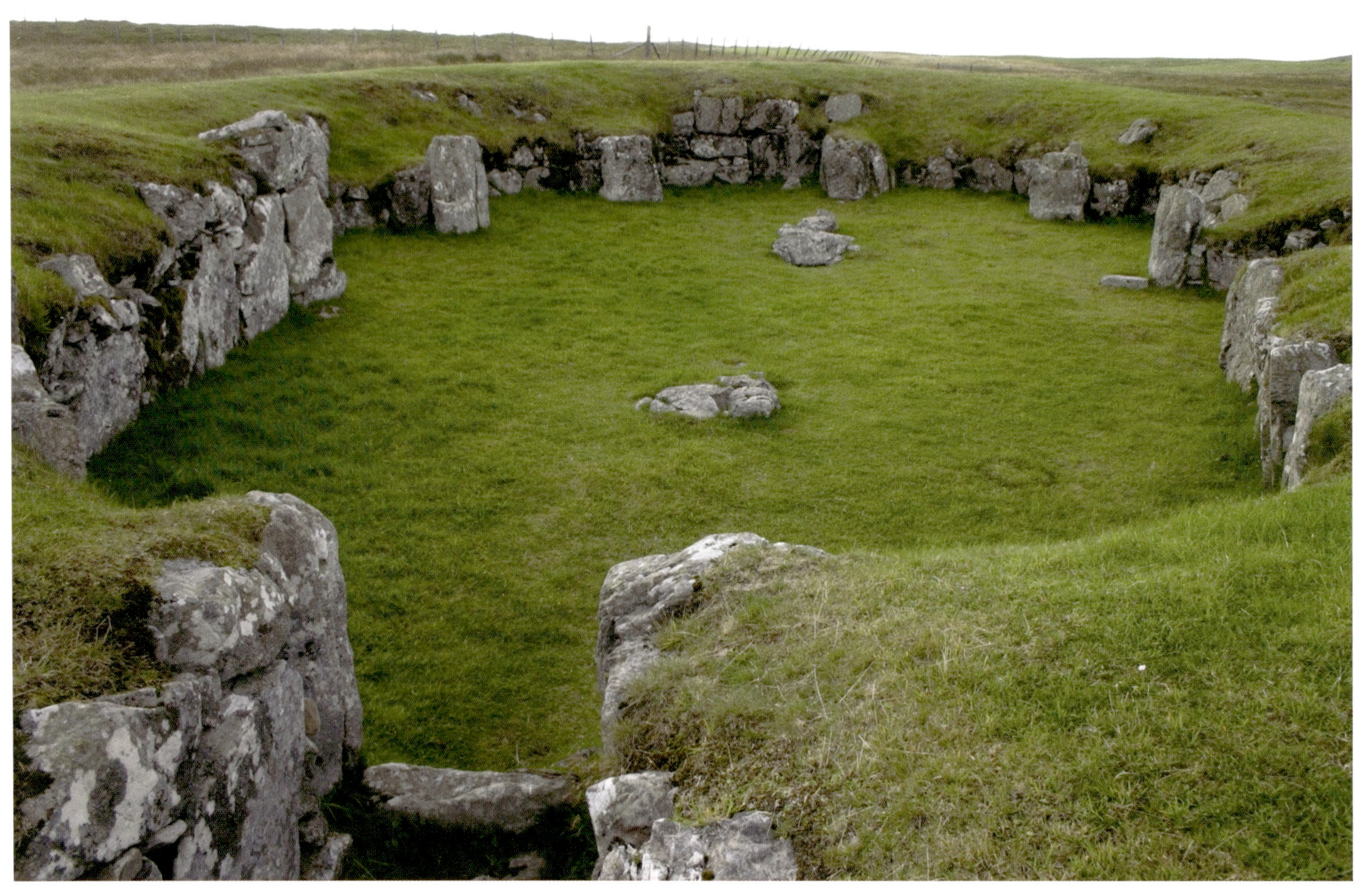

Staneydale Temple is a Neolithic site dating back to around 3000BC. The main feature on the site is an oval structure with a single entrance passage leading into the large hall. There are half a dozen alcoves leading off the main hall, each separated by huge stone pillars, and it is thought that such a substantial building was probably the chieftain's house. It almost certainly wasn't a 'temple'.

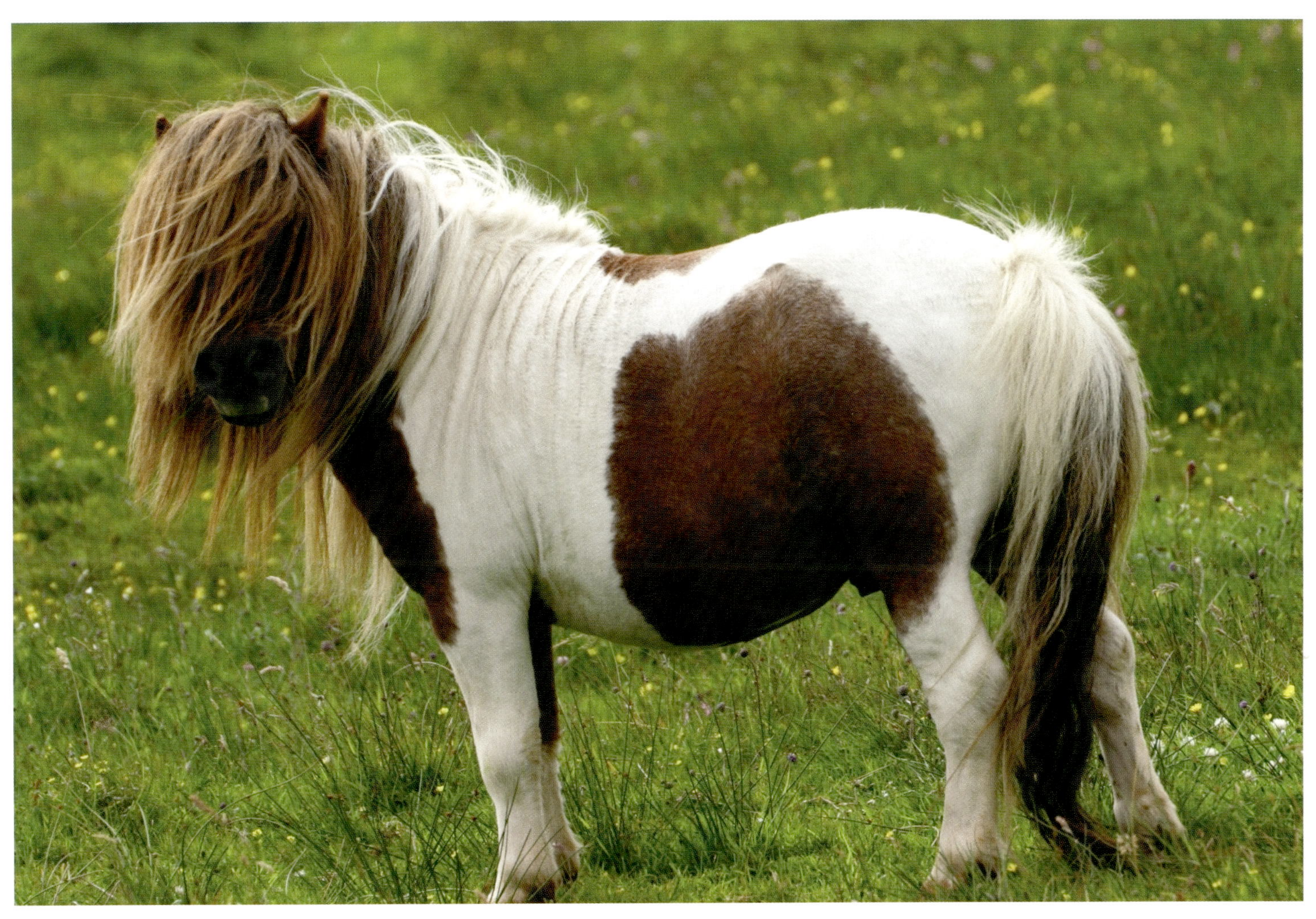

The diminutive Shetland pony – full of character, and hardy enough to withstand the harsh Shetland winters.

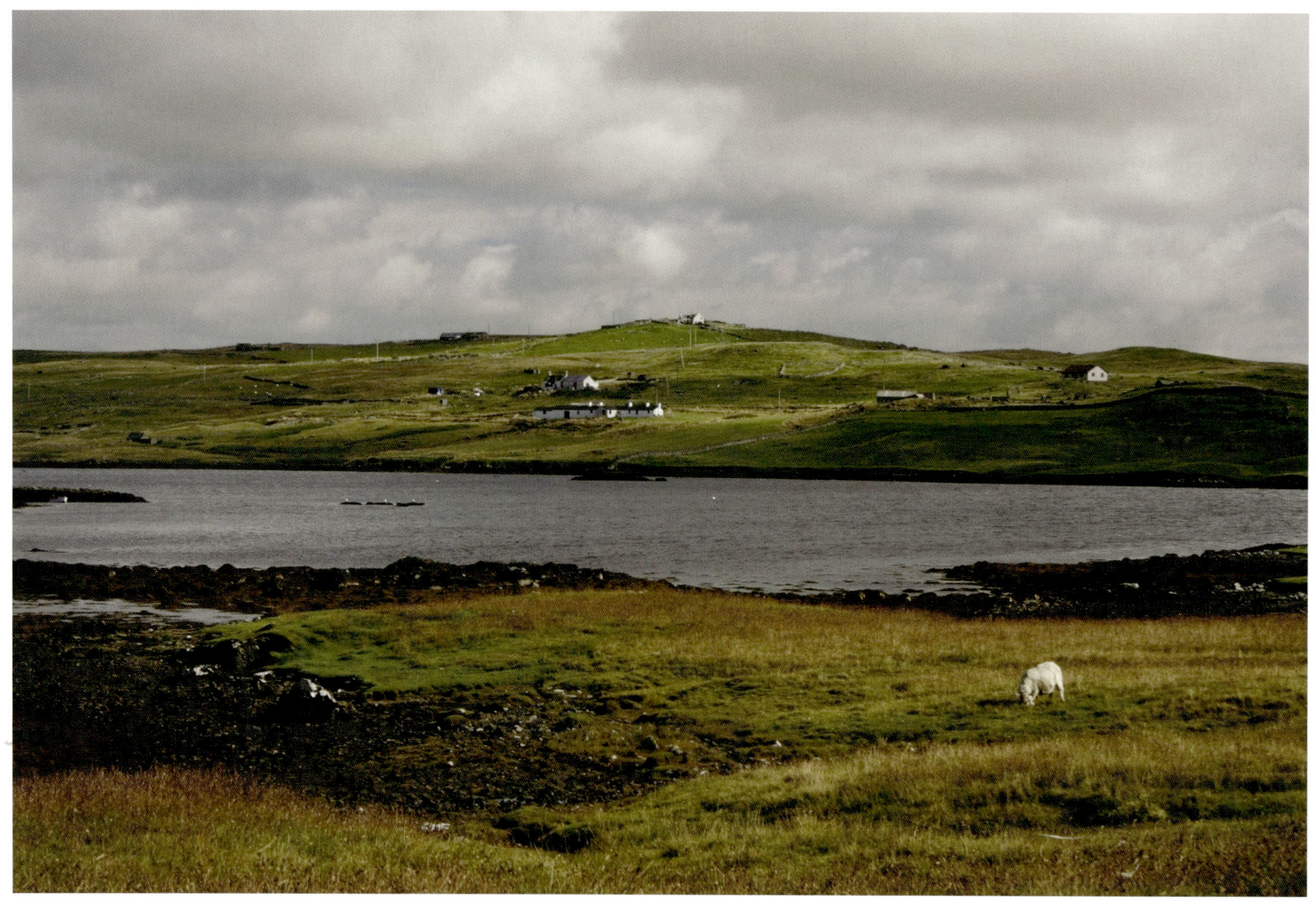

Above: The Voe of Browland on Westside.

Right: At Noonsborough the old pier stanchions lie piled on the meadowsides, barnacles still clinging to their once submerged uprights.

Far right: The view from the Ness of Noonsborough across the tranquil waters of Voe of Clousta to the Ness of Clousta.

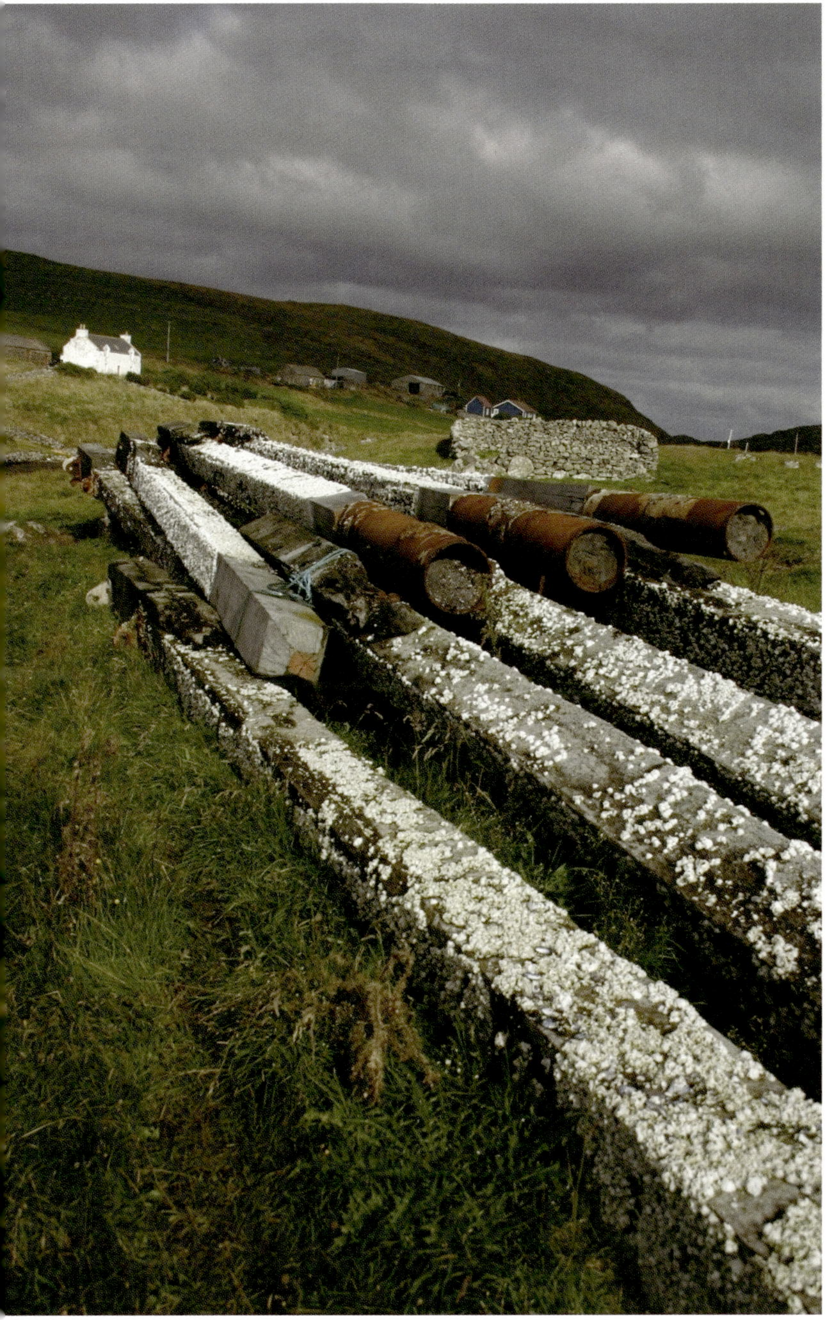

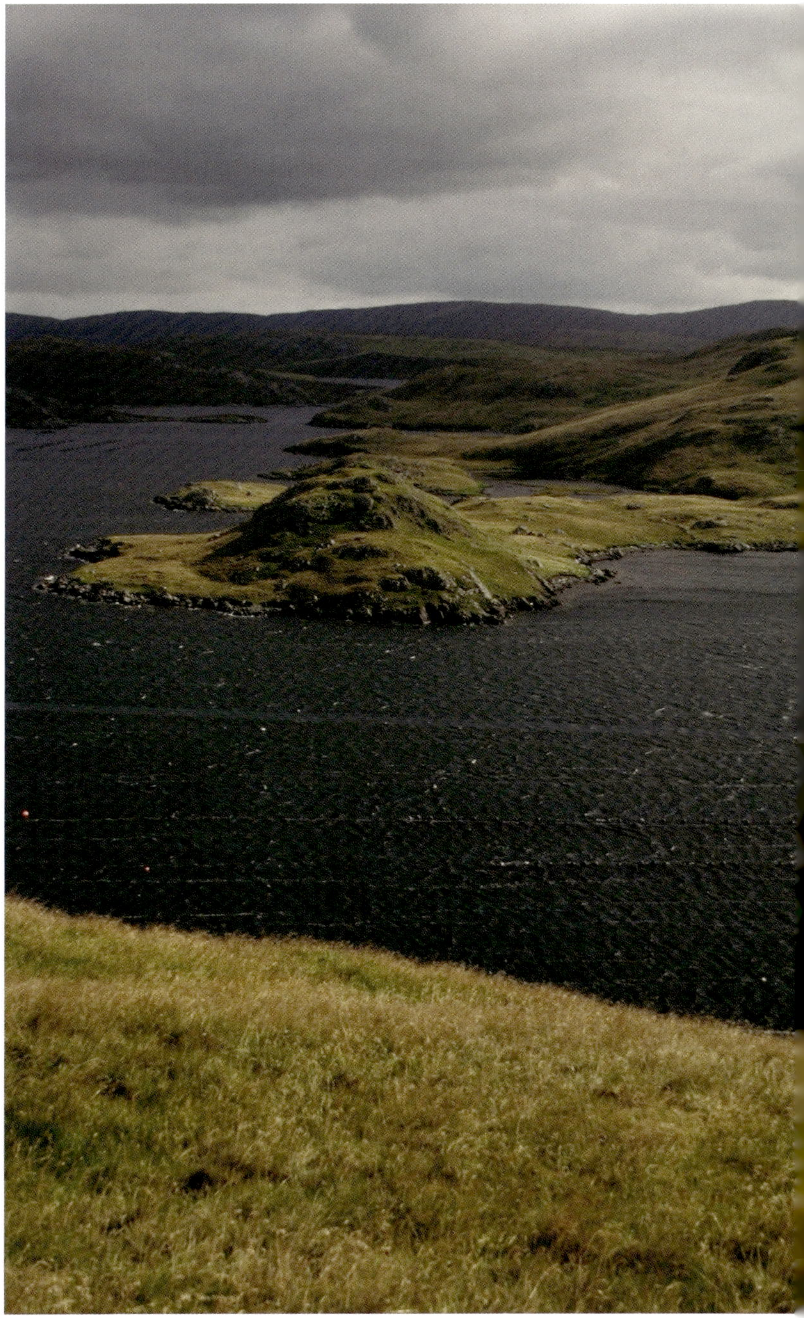

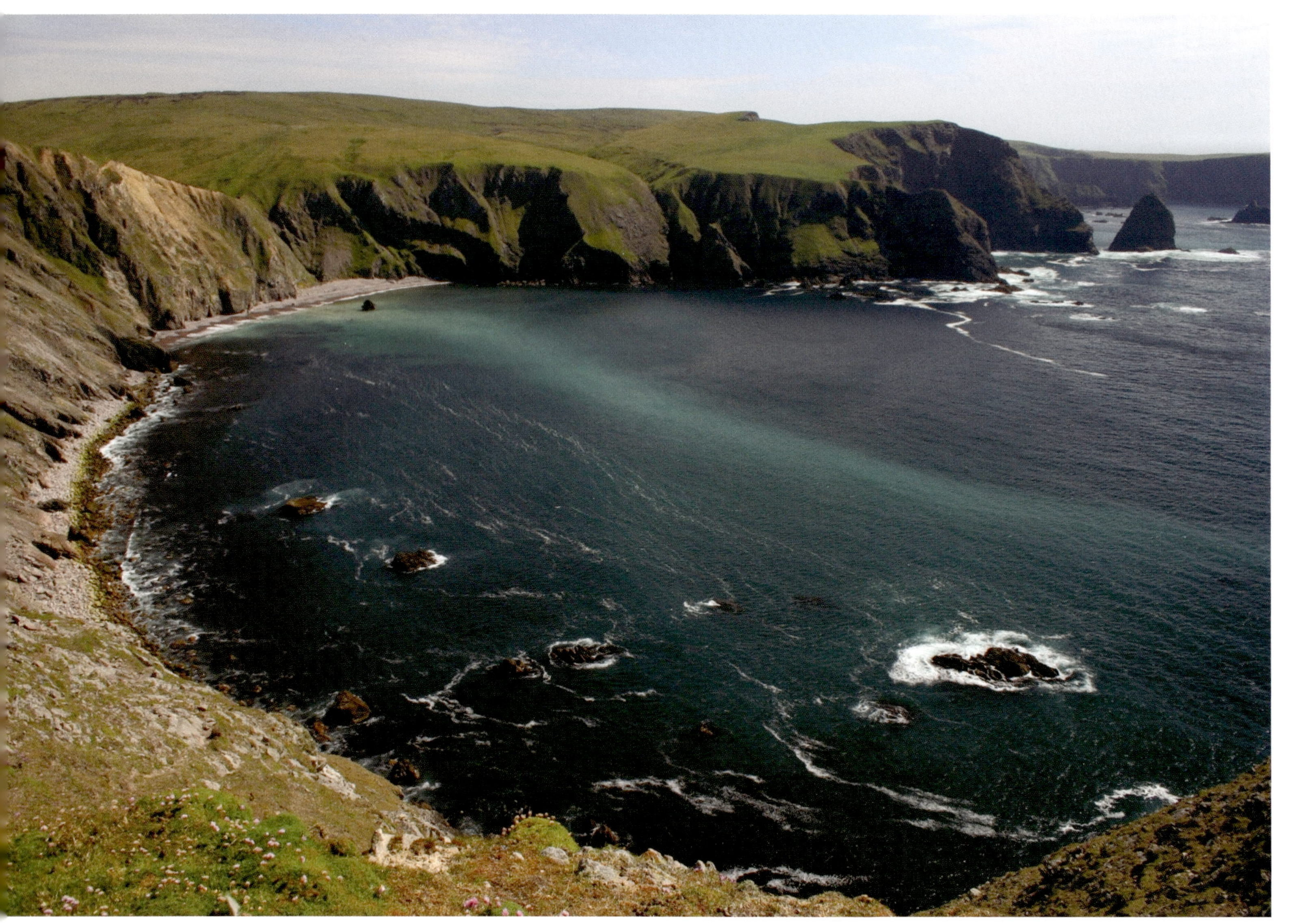

The spectacular sweep of Bay of Deepdale, just beneath the summit of Sandness Hill on Westside.

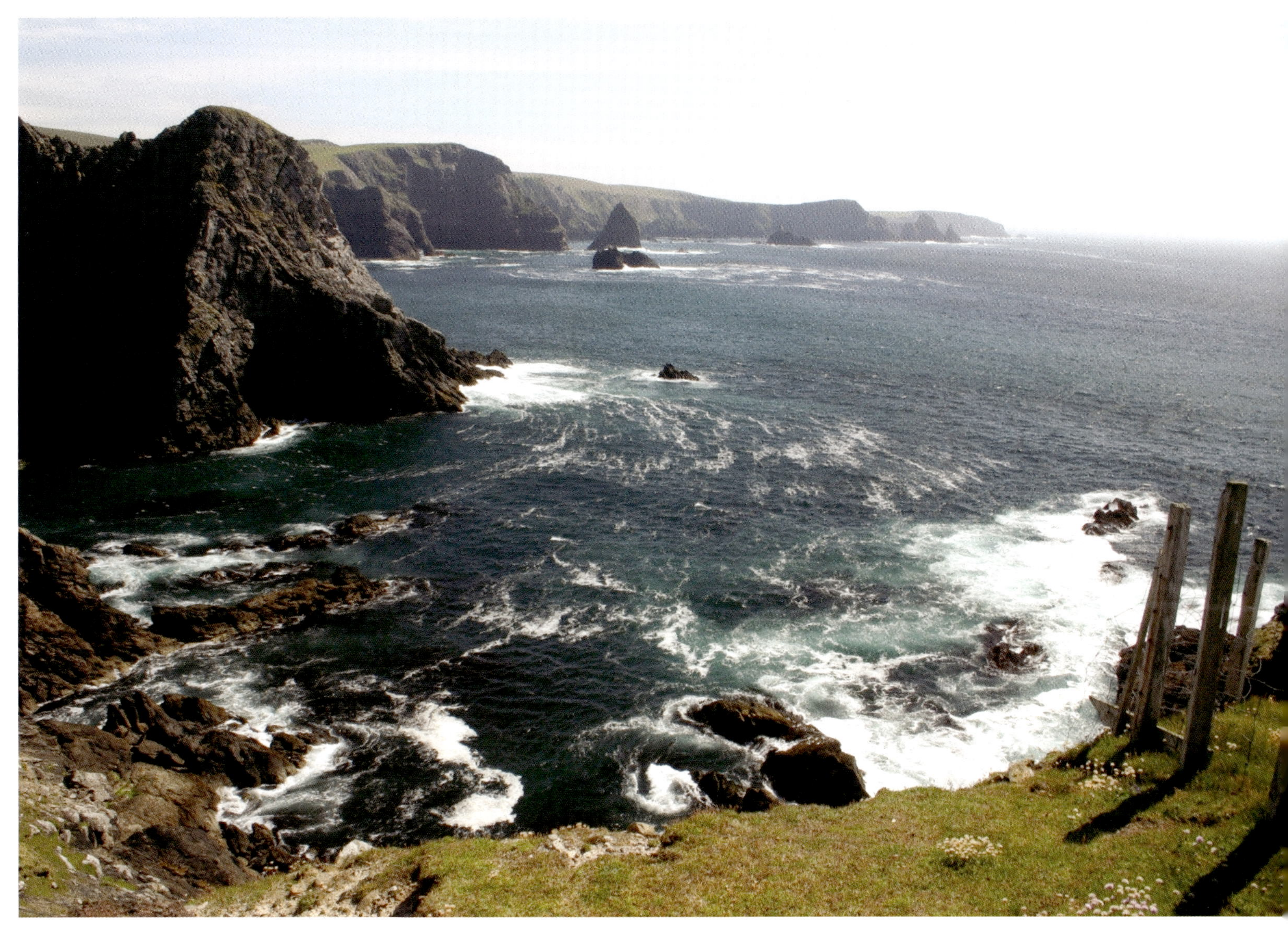

Looking down the coast of Westside from Hesti Geo, beyond Bay of Deepdale to distant Mu Ness.

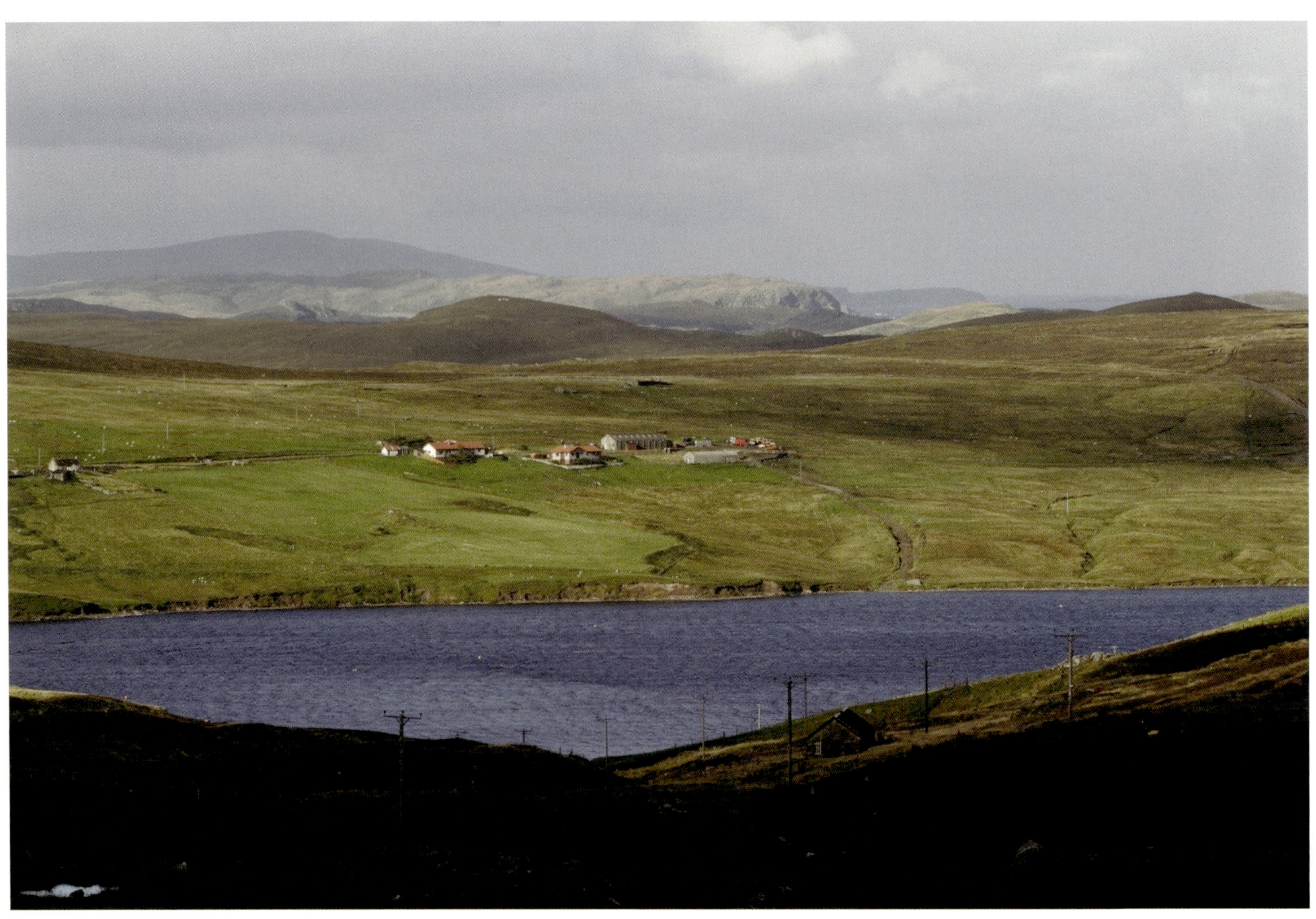

The view into Westside from Aith Voe.

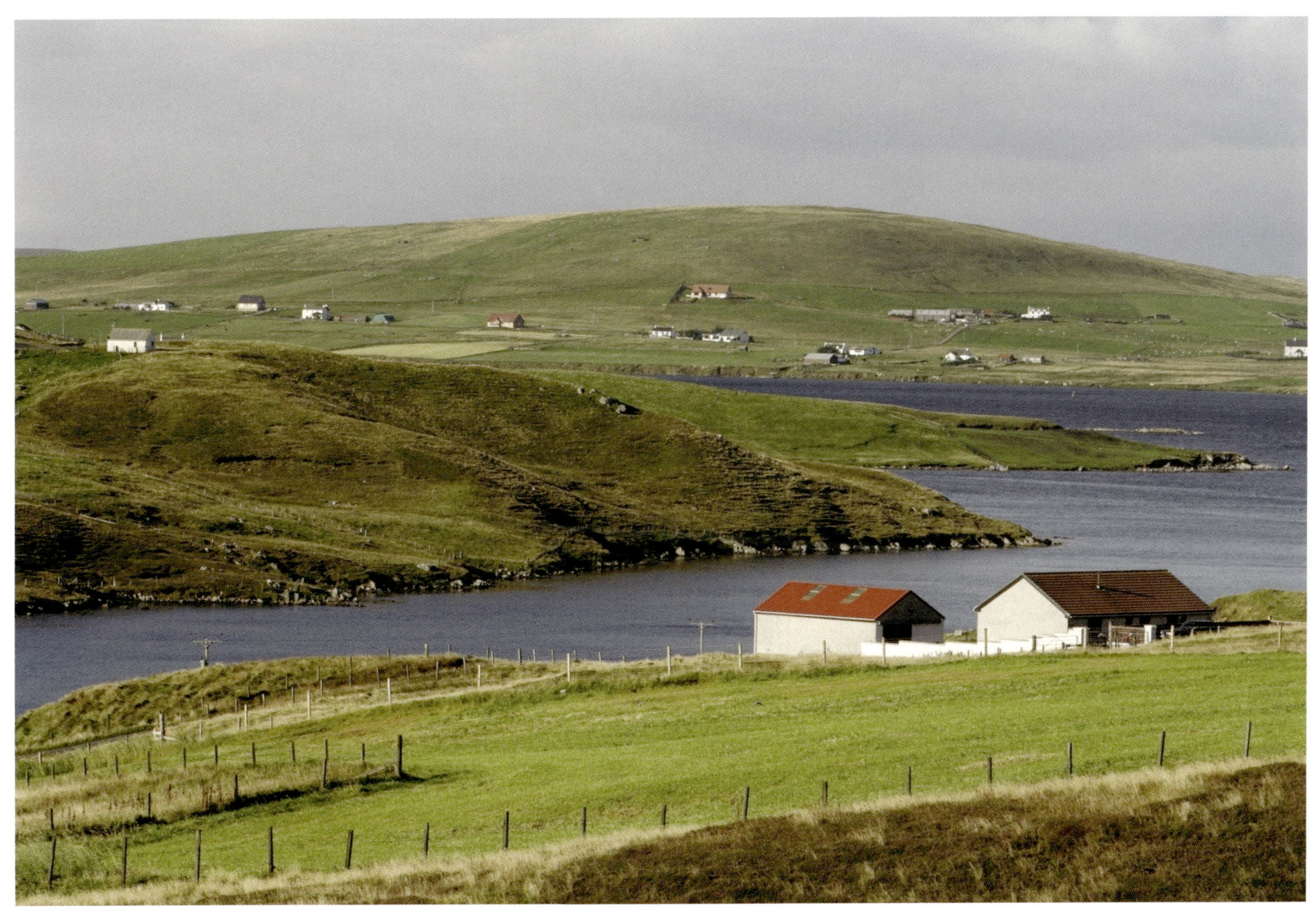

Scattered crofts and cottages dot the landscape on Westside.

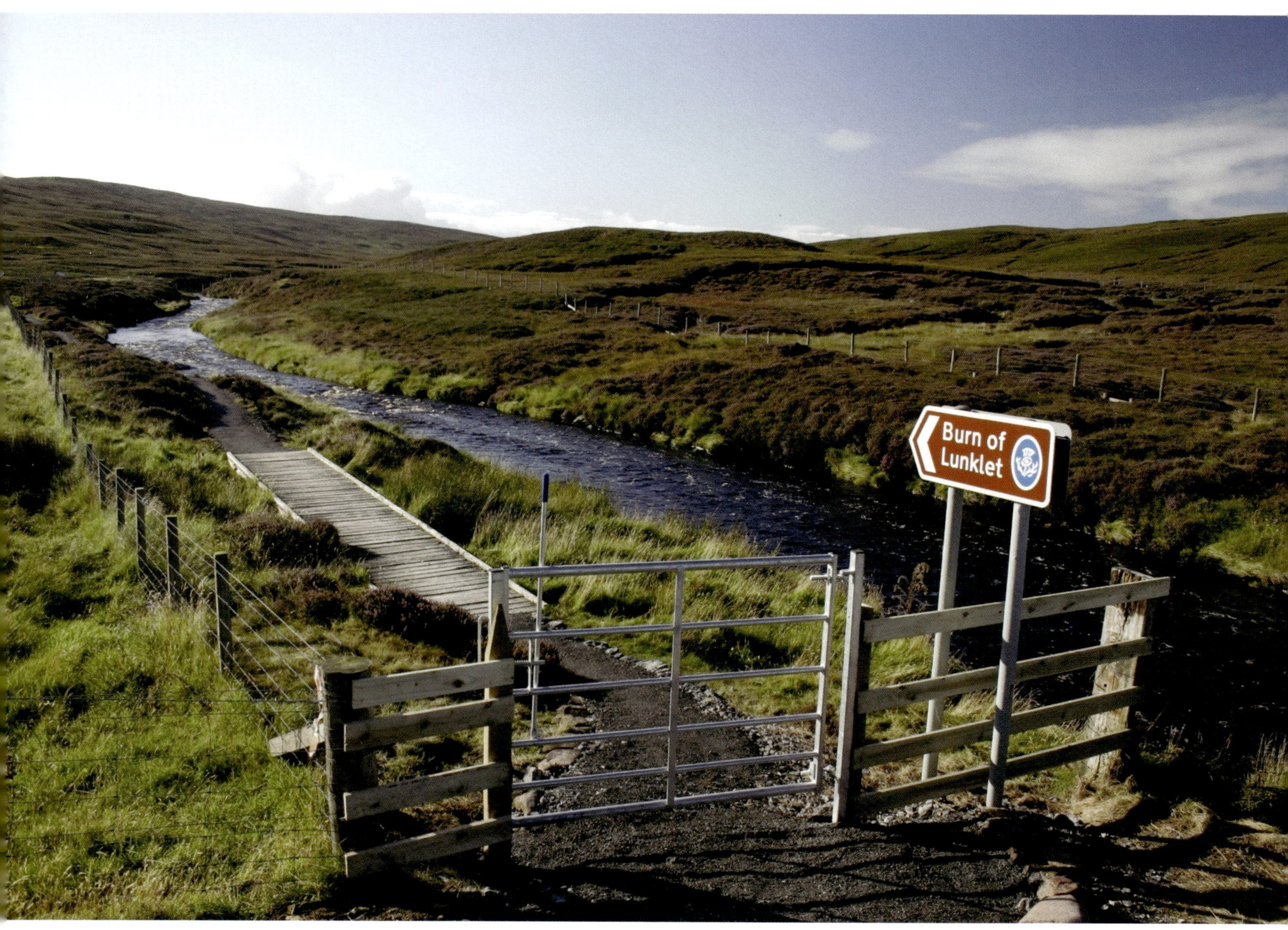


The start of a lovely moorland walk along the Burn of Lunklet near East Burrafirth.

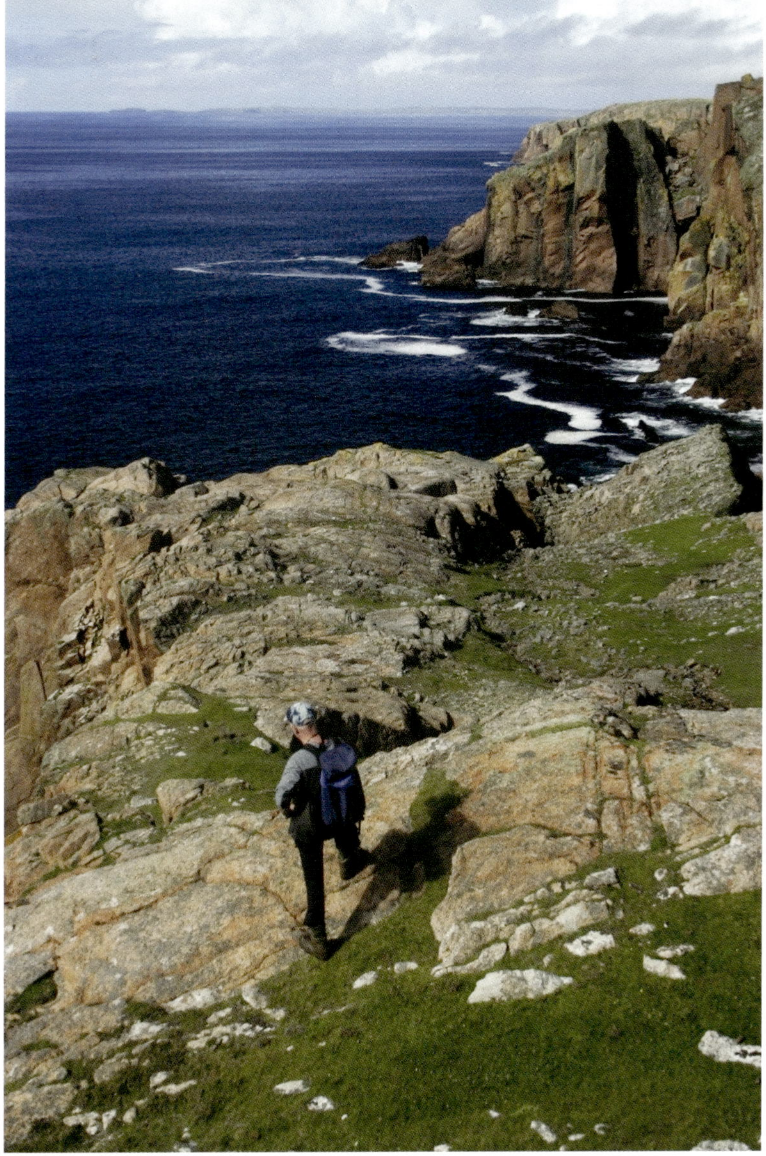

One of the finest islands for scenery in Shetland is Muckle Roe, just off the coast of north Mainland. Muckle Roe is connected to Mainland via a bridge, and from the end of the public road you can walk out to the Hams, where spectacular coastal scenery awaits.

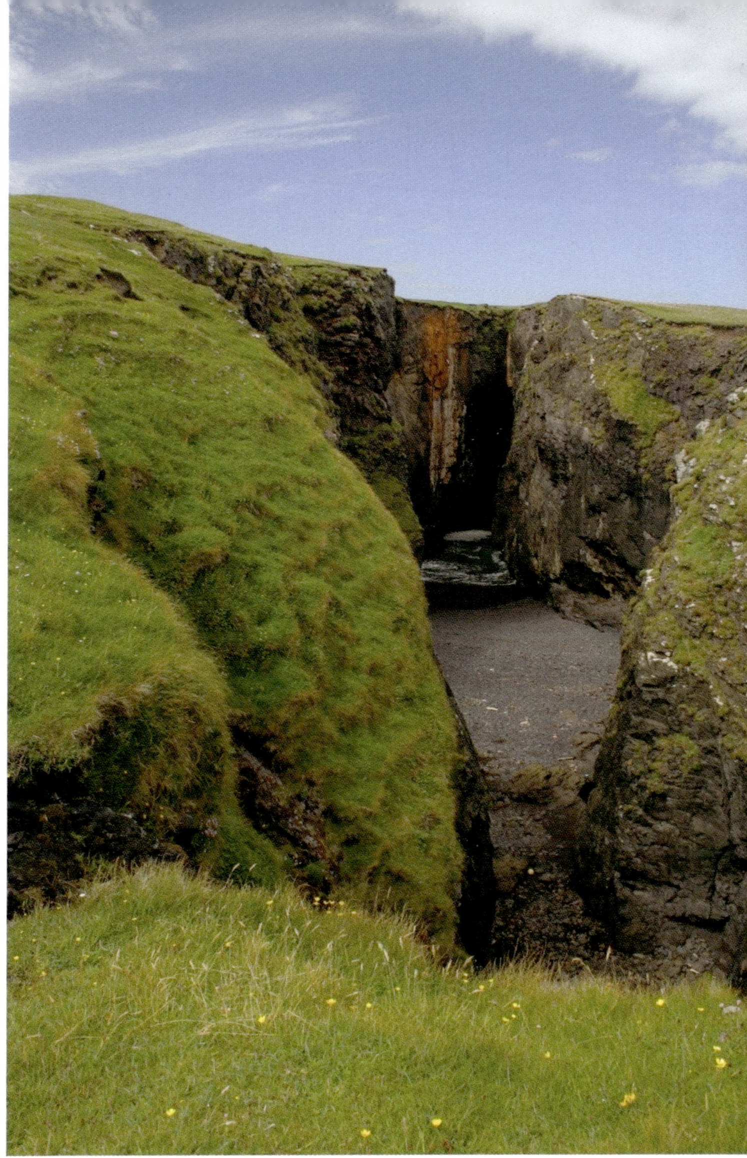

Eshaness means 'headland of volcanic rock', and it is well named. Great sea cliffs fall into the waves, and here, at the Holes of Scraada, a long subterranean passage connects this blow hole to sea, a good hundred yards back from the cliff edge.

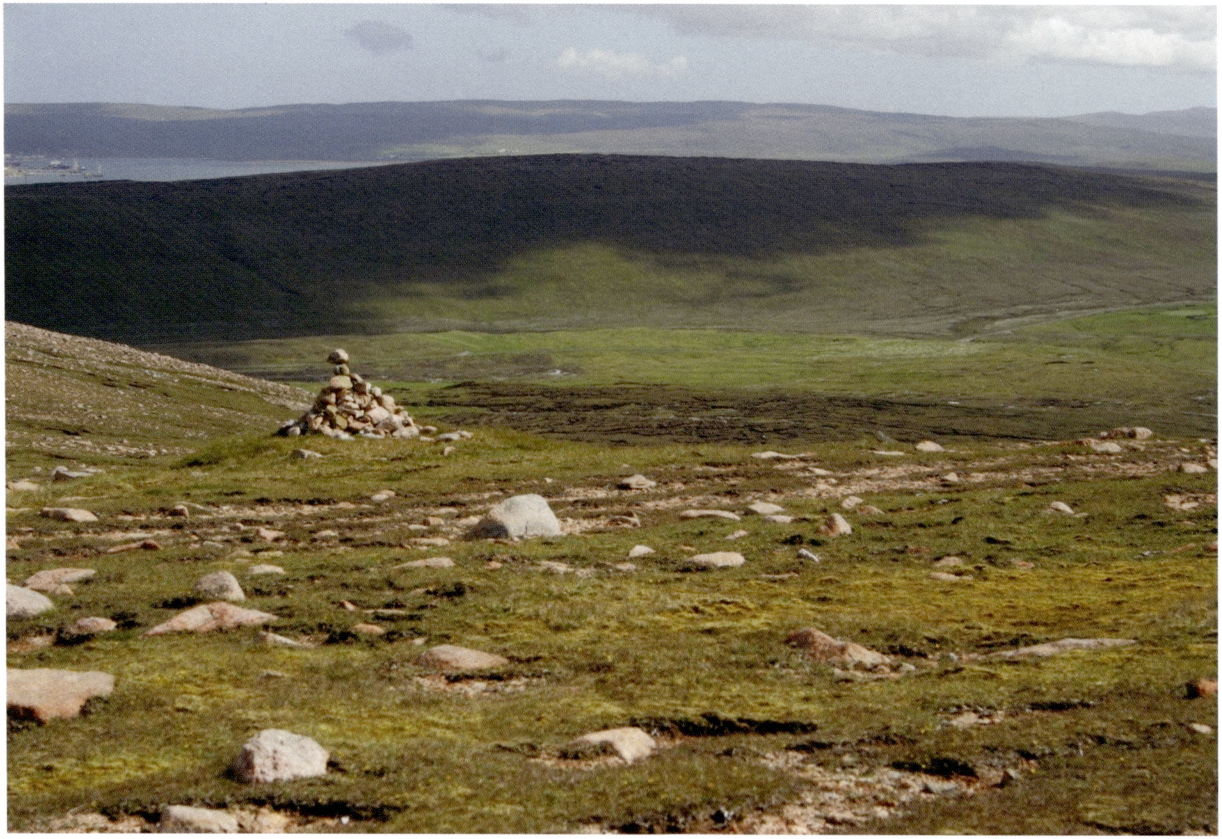

Shetland's highest hill is Ronas Hill, in North Mavine.

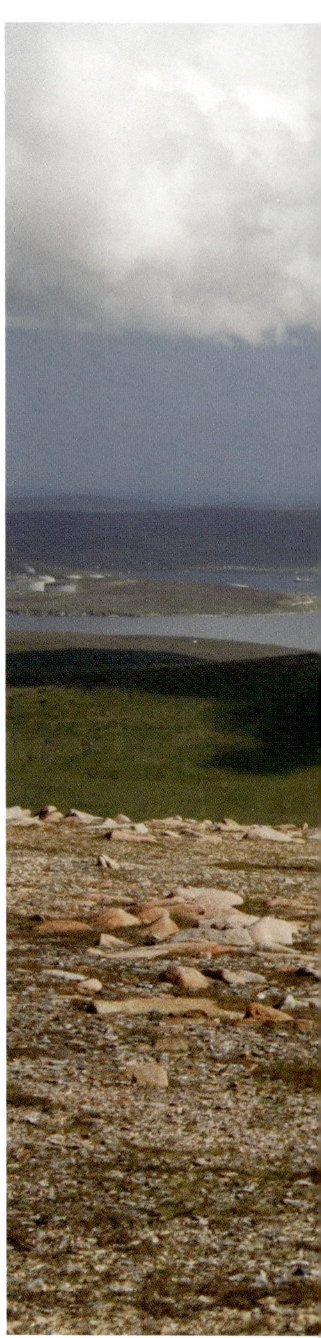

A walker climbing the granite boulder slopes of Ronas Hill.

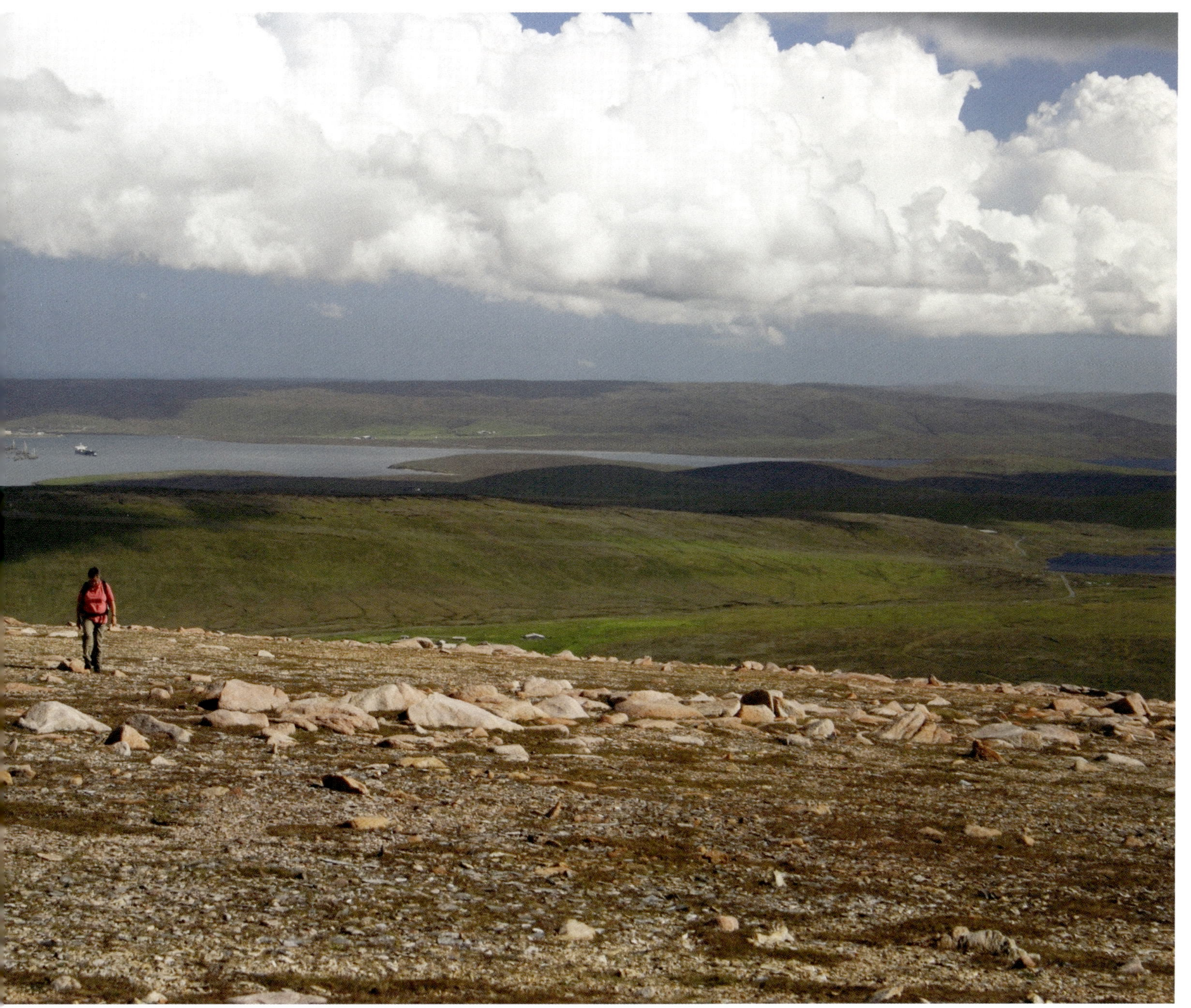

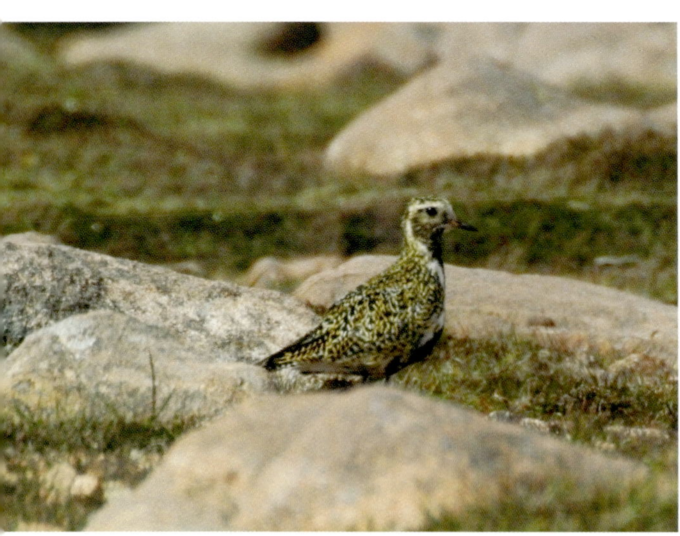

There are many birds associated with high mountains that nest on lowly Ronas Hill, including golden plover.

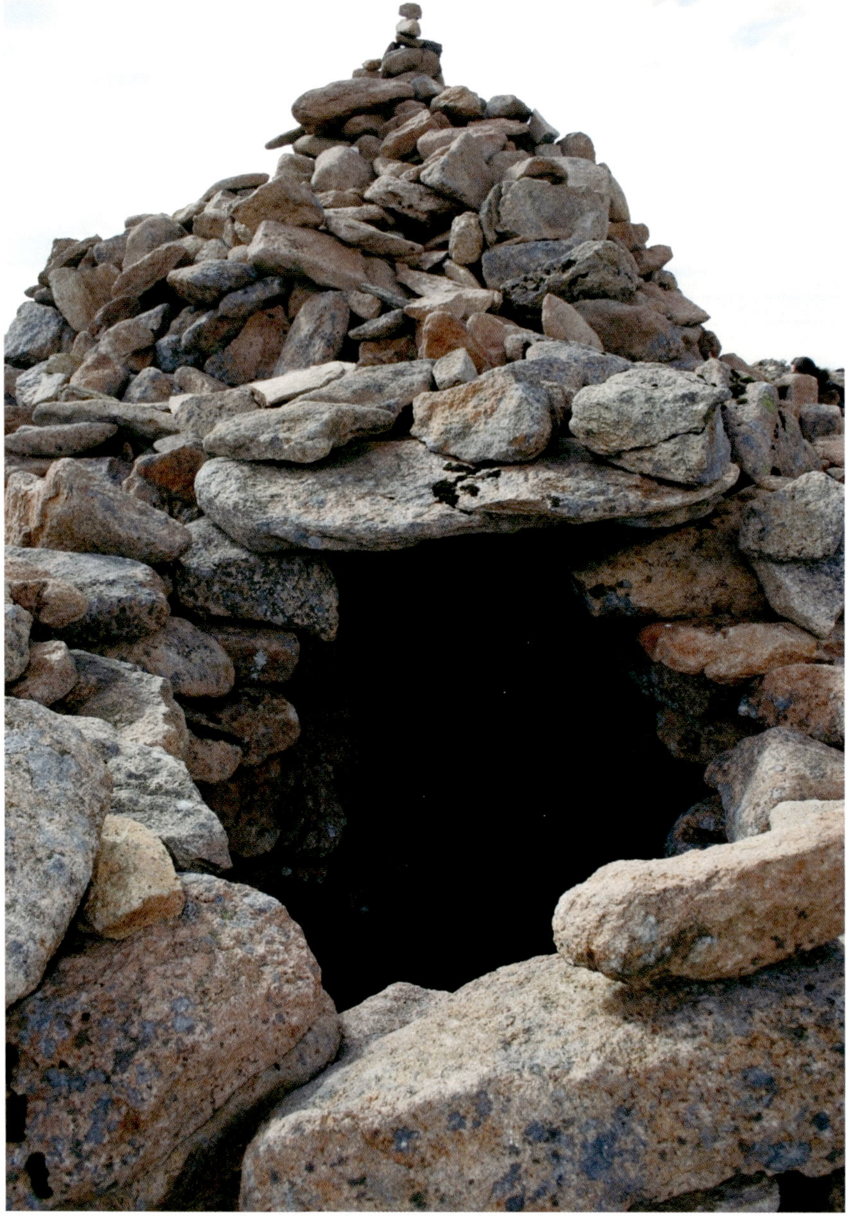

The summit of Ronas Hill is marked by a large burial cairn.

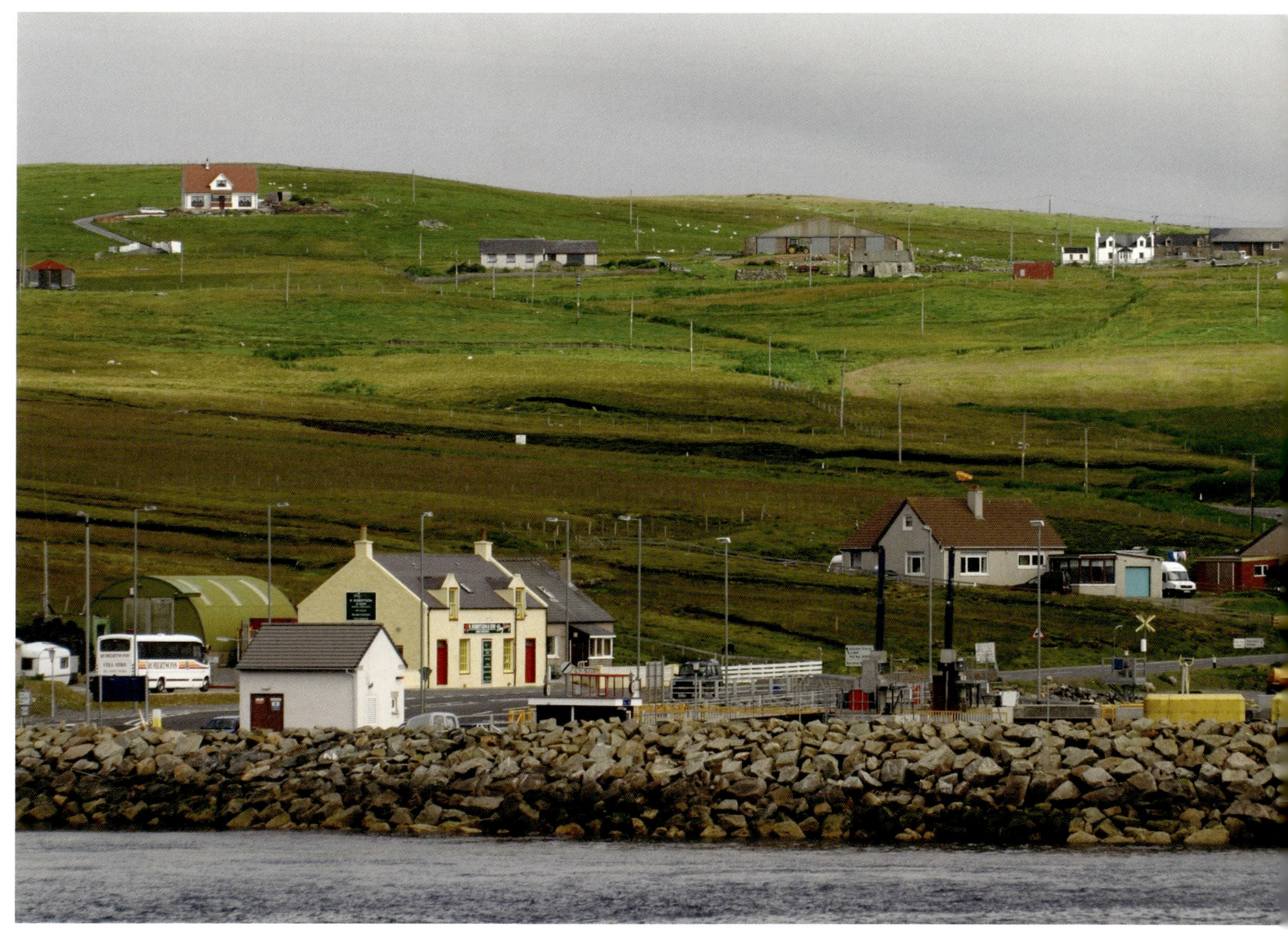

Hop on a ferry from Toft on the Mainland in Shetland and you'll find yourself heading across the Sound to Ulsta on the island of Yell.

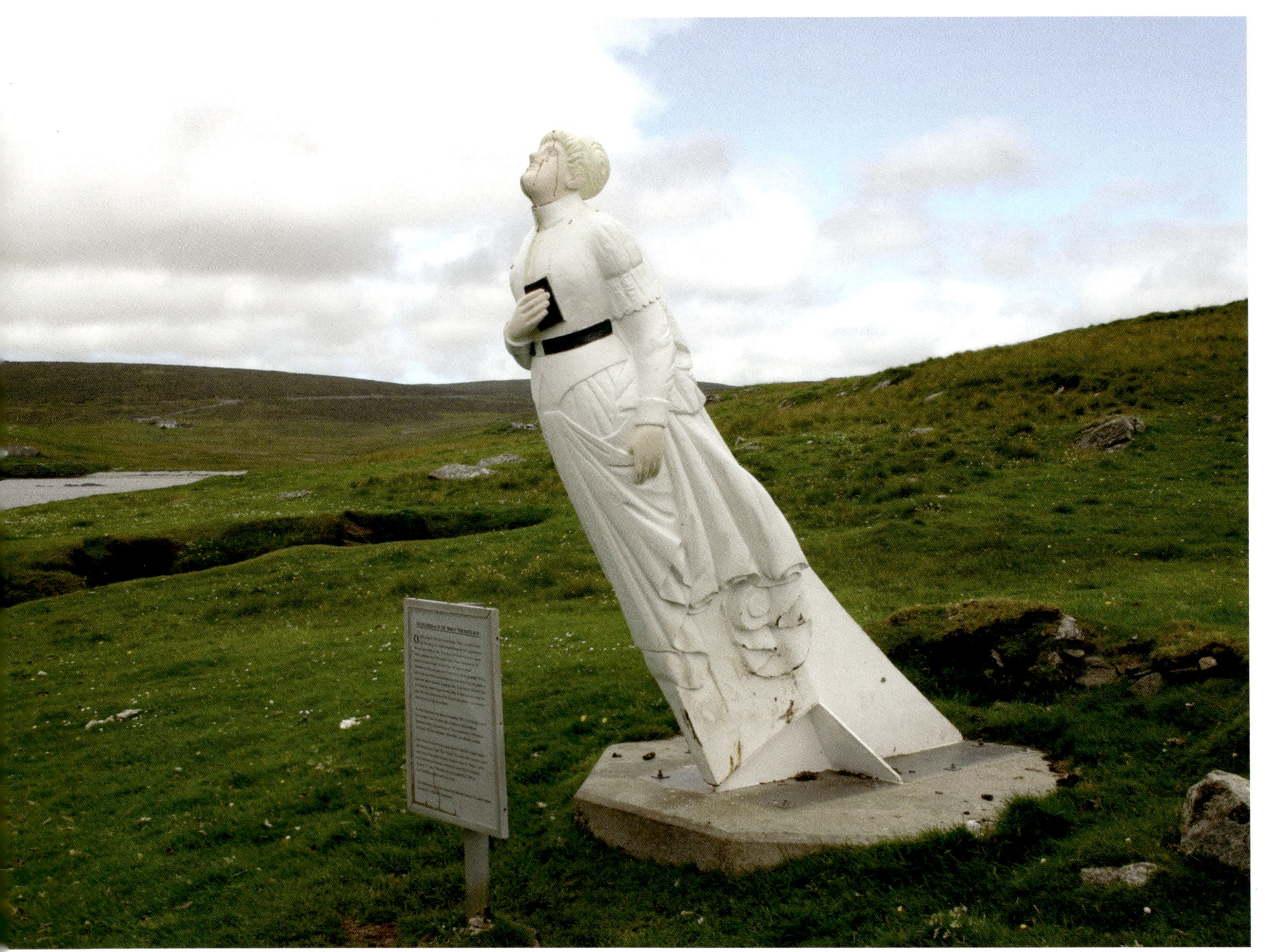

On the east coast of Yell at Otterswick, there is a prominent figurehead known as the White Wife. She was the figurehead from the steel barque *Bohus*, built in 1892. On 26 April 1924, she sailed under Captain Huge Ferdinand Blume around the east side of Yell, and was caught in a terrific storm off Otters Wick. The ship ran aground on the rocks, and three young sailors died as the she broke apart.

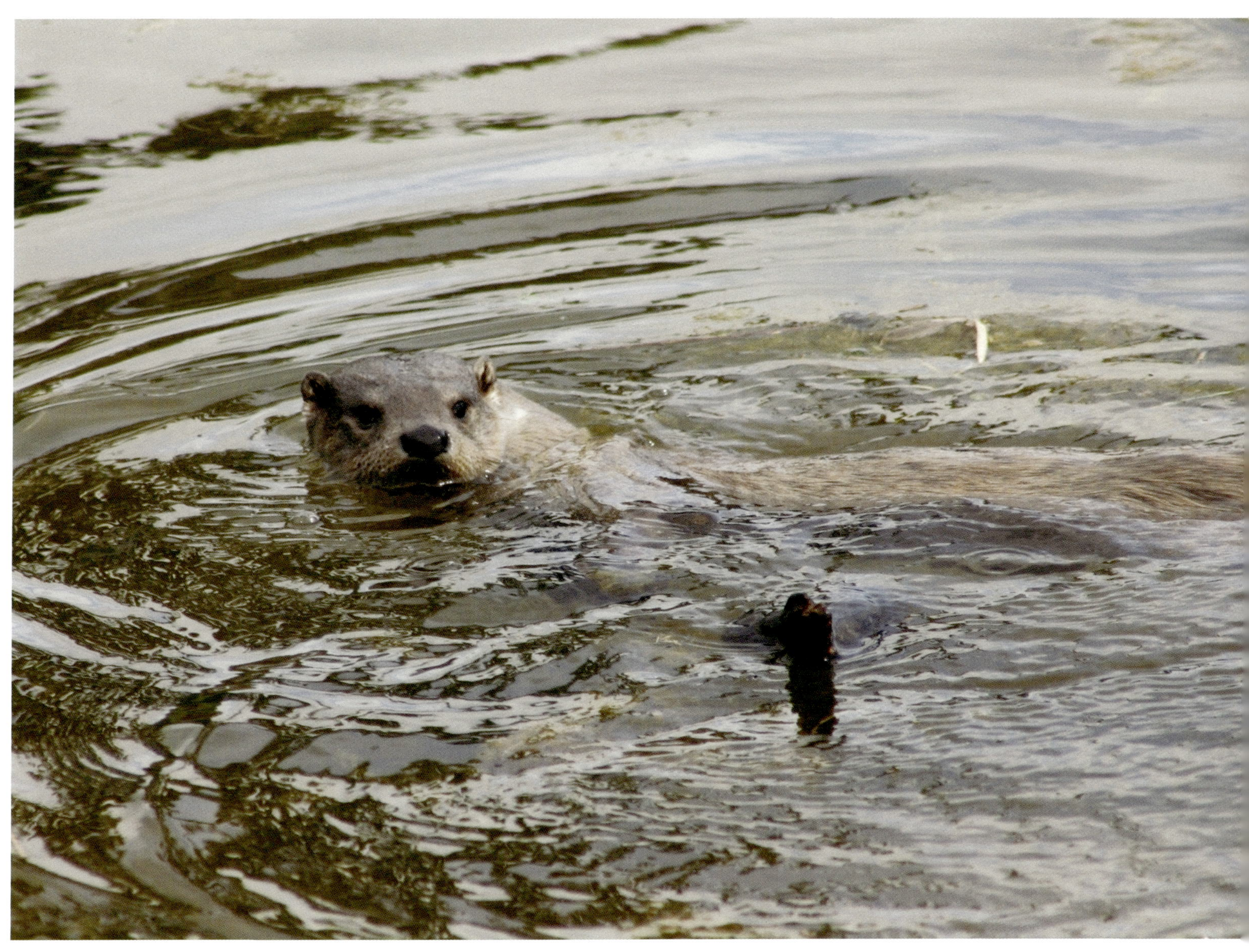

Shetland is one of the best places in Britain to see wild otters. In Britain we have only one species of otter, the Eurasian otter, or *Lutra lutra* to give it its Latin name. While many otters live on rivers, and tend to be largely nocturnal, others choose to live by the sea. These prefer to hunt on a rising tide, and so can be spotted at any time of day.

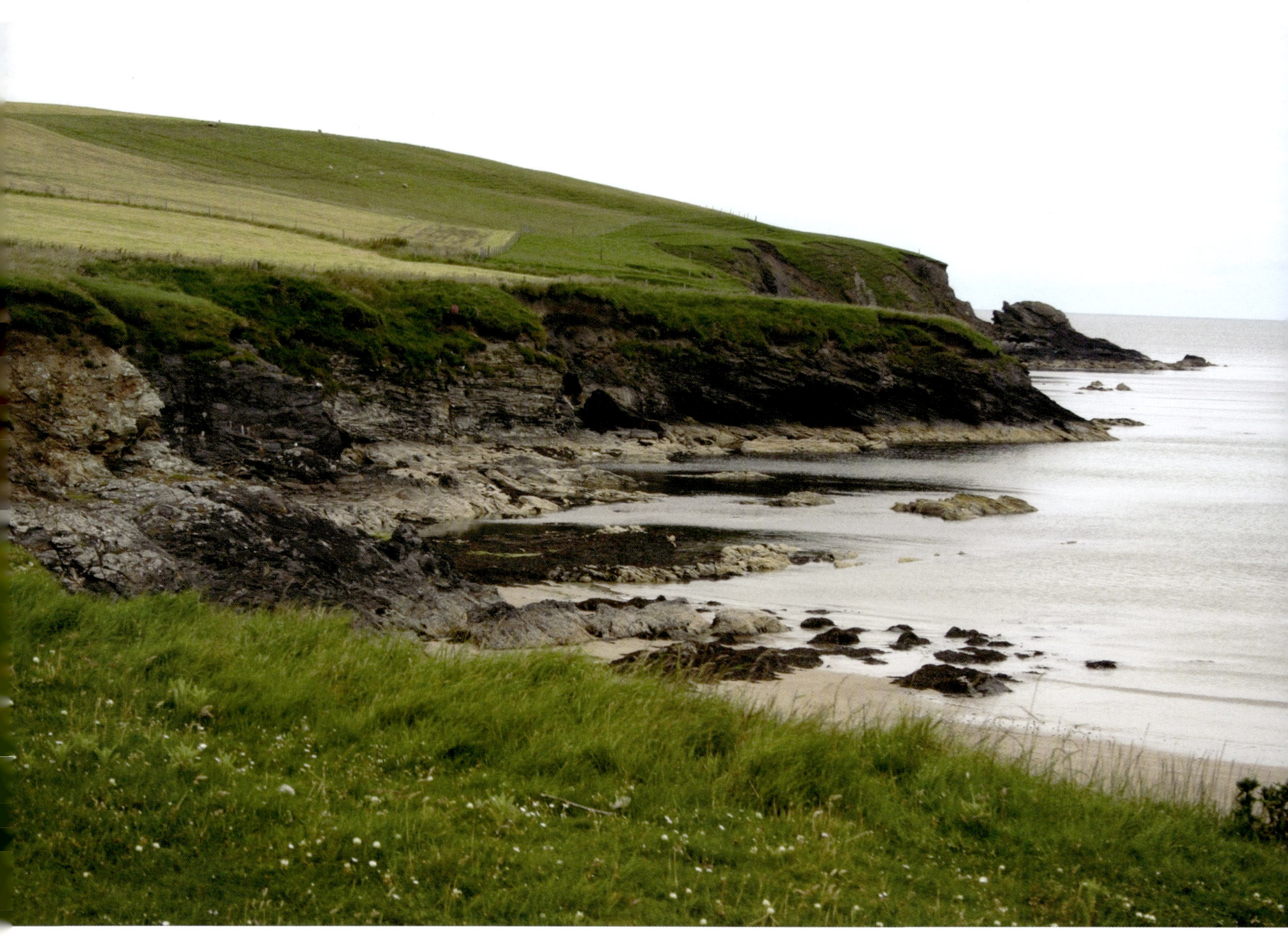

The Fetlar coast near Aith.

On the nearby island of Fetlar an old boat rots on the shore at Ugasta below Brough Lodge.

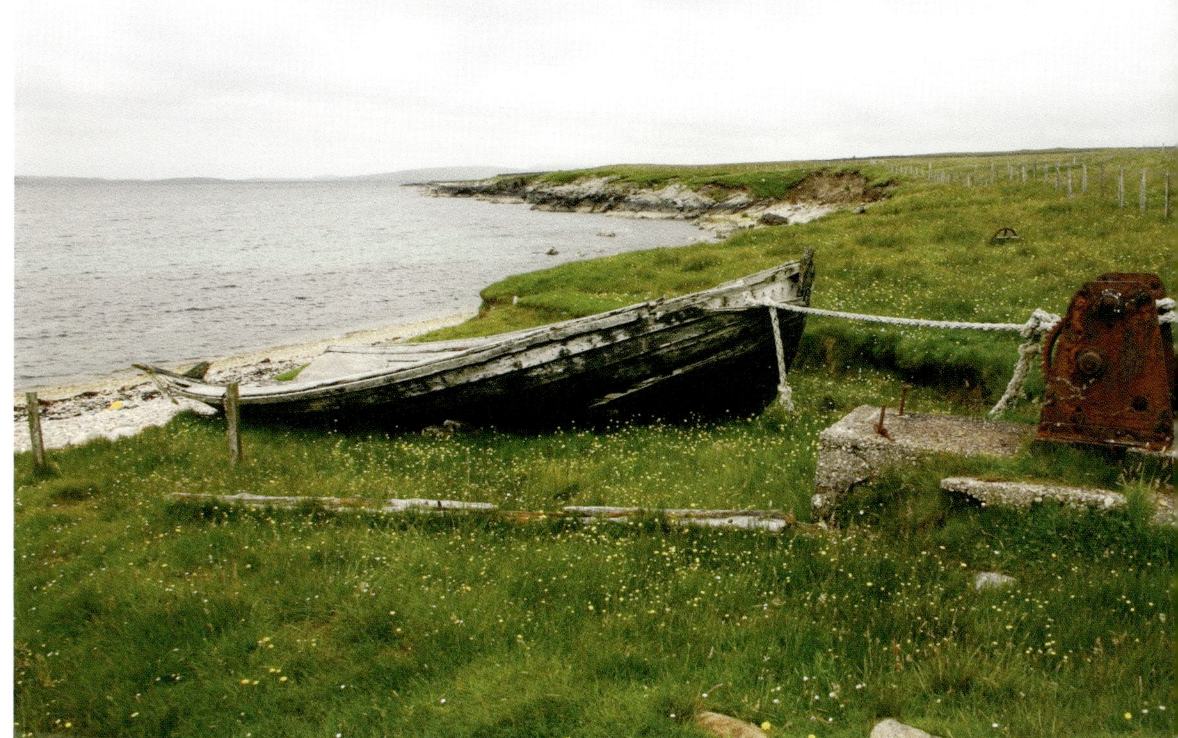

Peat cutting for fuel is still a way of life on the Northern Isles. The peat is cut during the spring and summer and piled in a stook to dry, then flitted to the houses for burning during the winter months. It is all done on a small scale, and is hard manual labour, making it sustainable on these islands where few trees grow for alternative fuel supplies.

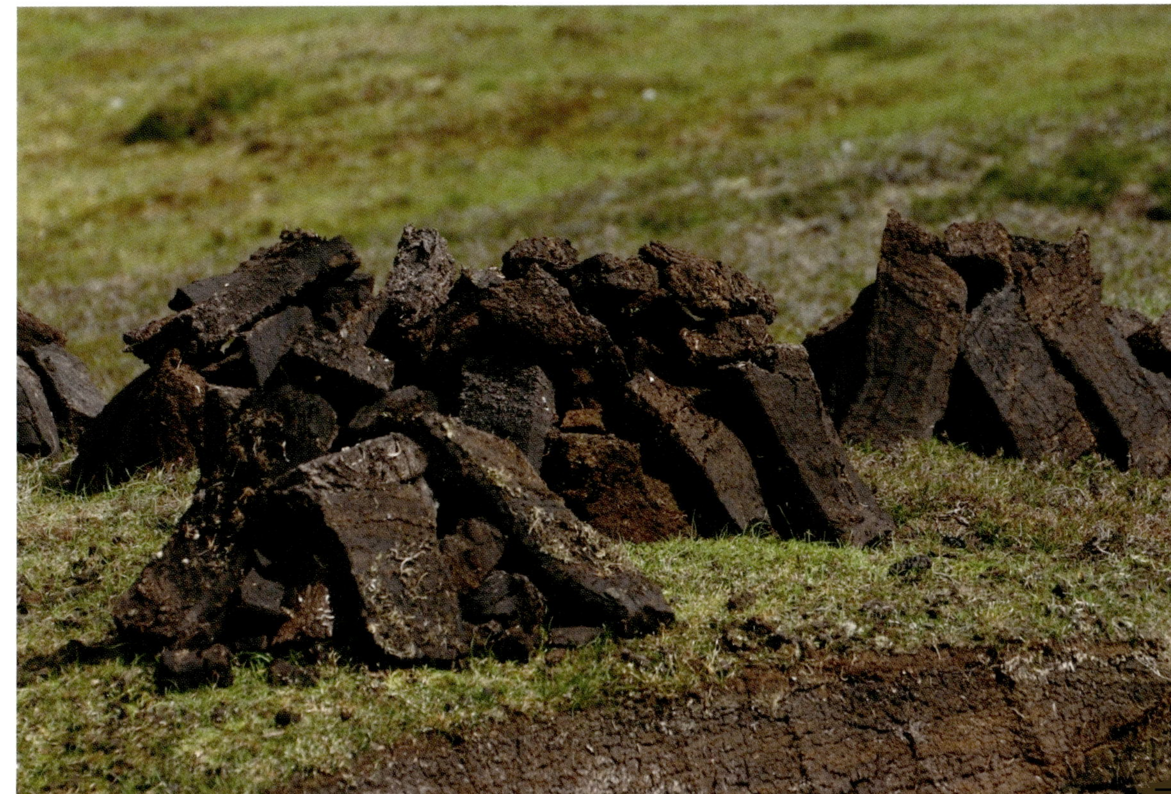

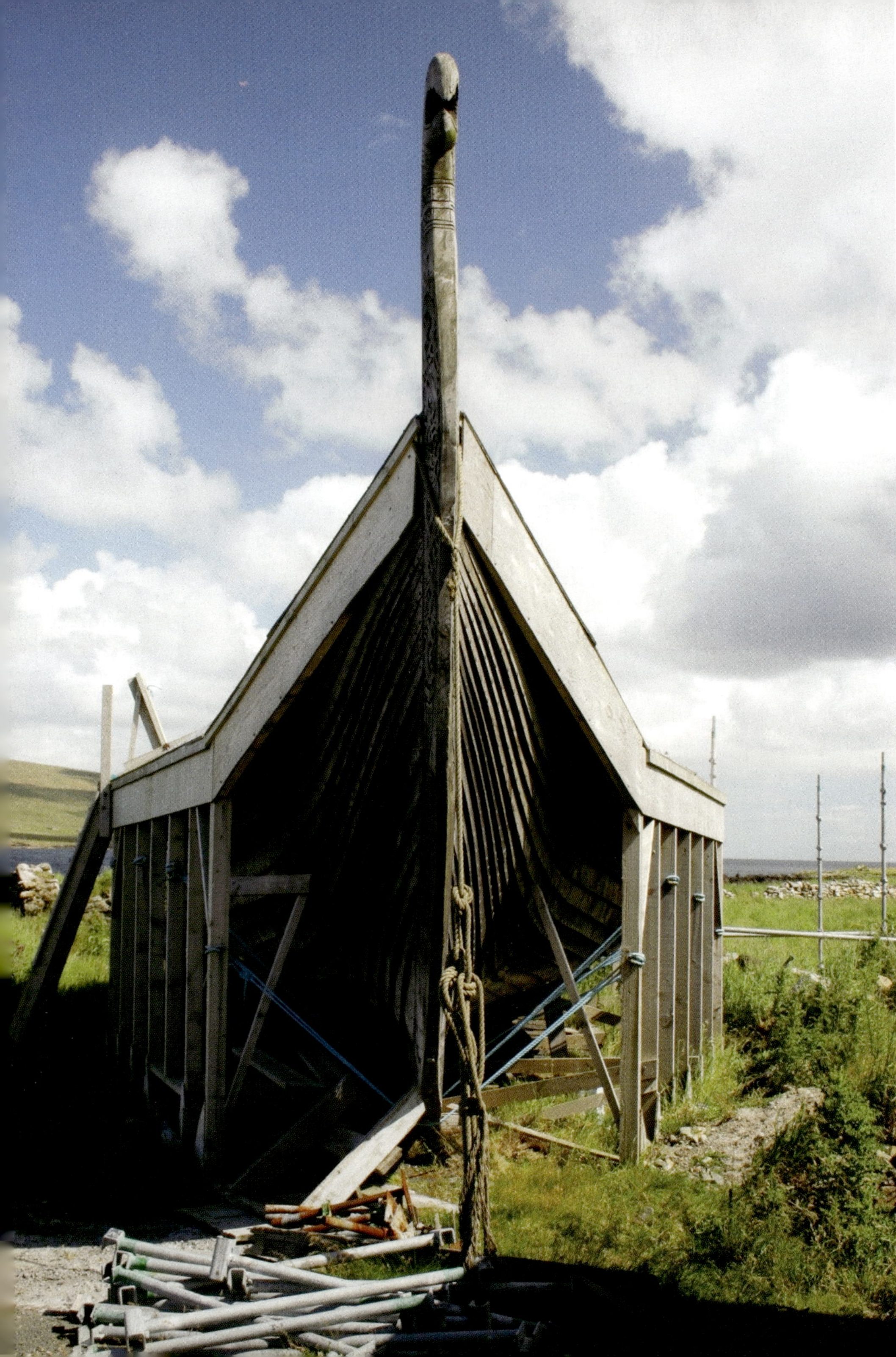

A traditional boat under construction at Haroldswick on the island of Unst. Nearby is the Unst Boat Haven, a superb museum to this ancient Shetland craft.

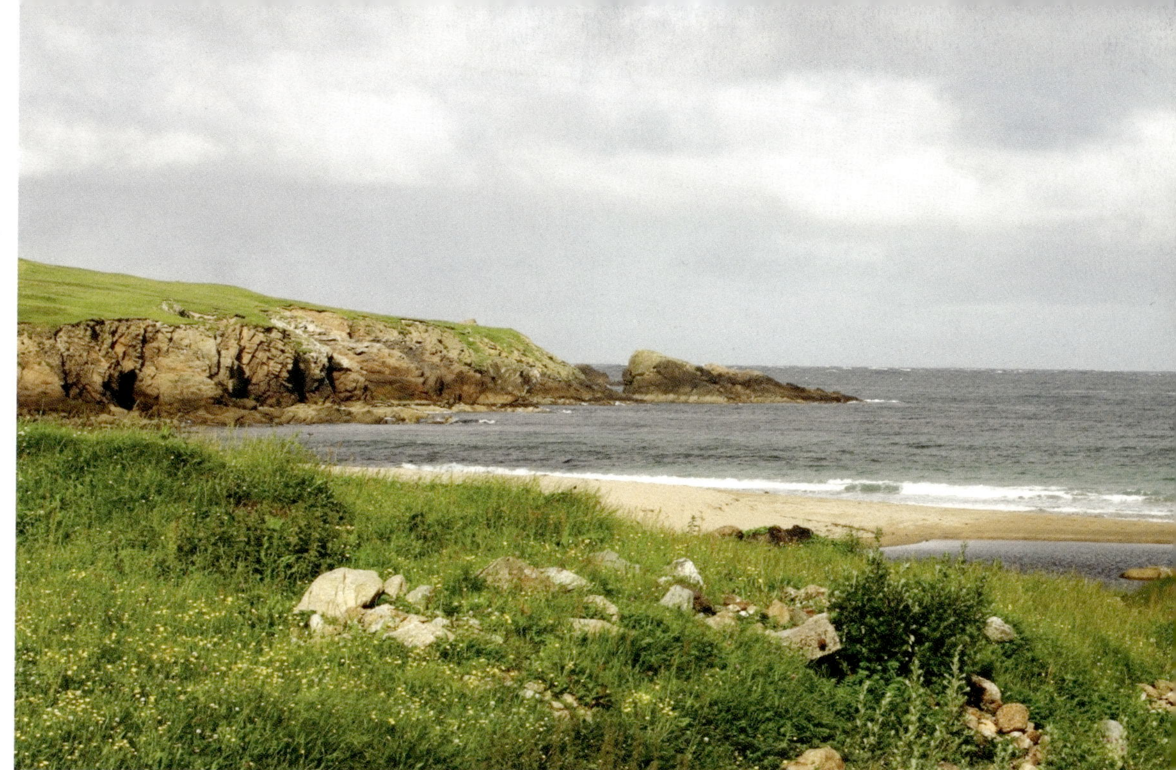

The lovely beach at Nor Wick on Unst.

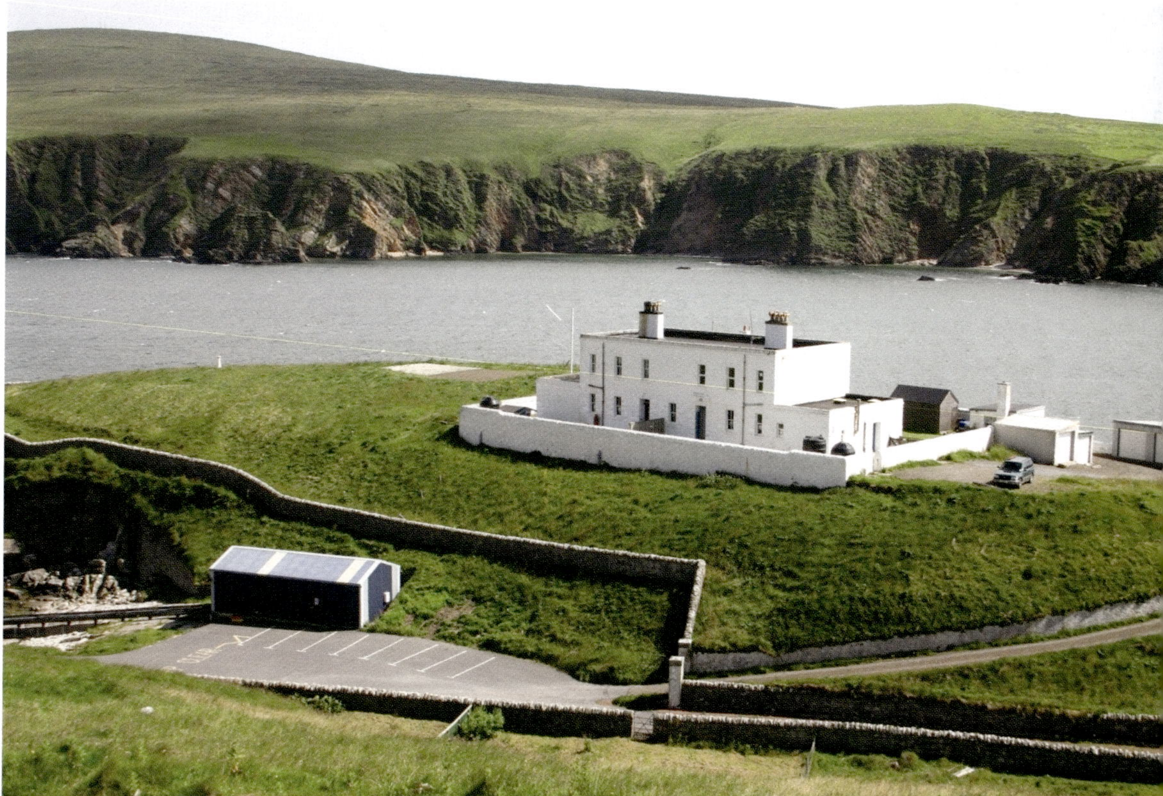

Near the most northerly tip of Unst, looking over Burra Firth to Saxa Vord, is the old Lighthouse Shore Station. It was built in 1855 as a service base for the lighthouse on Muckle Flugga. Today the Shore Station is a visitor centre for the Hermaness National Nature Reserve.

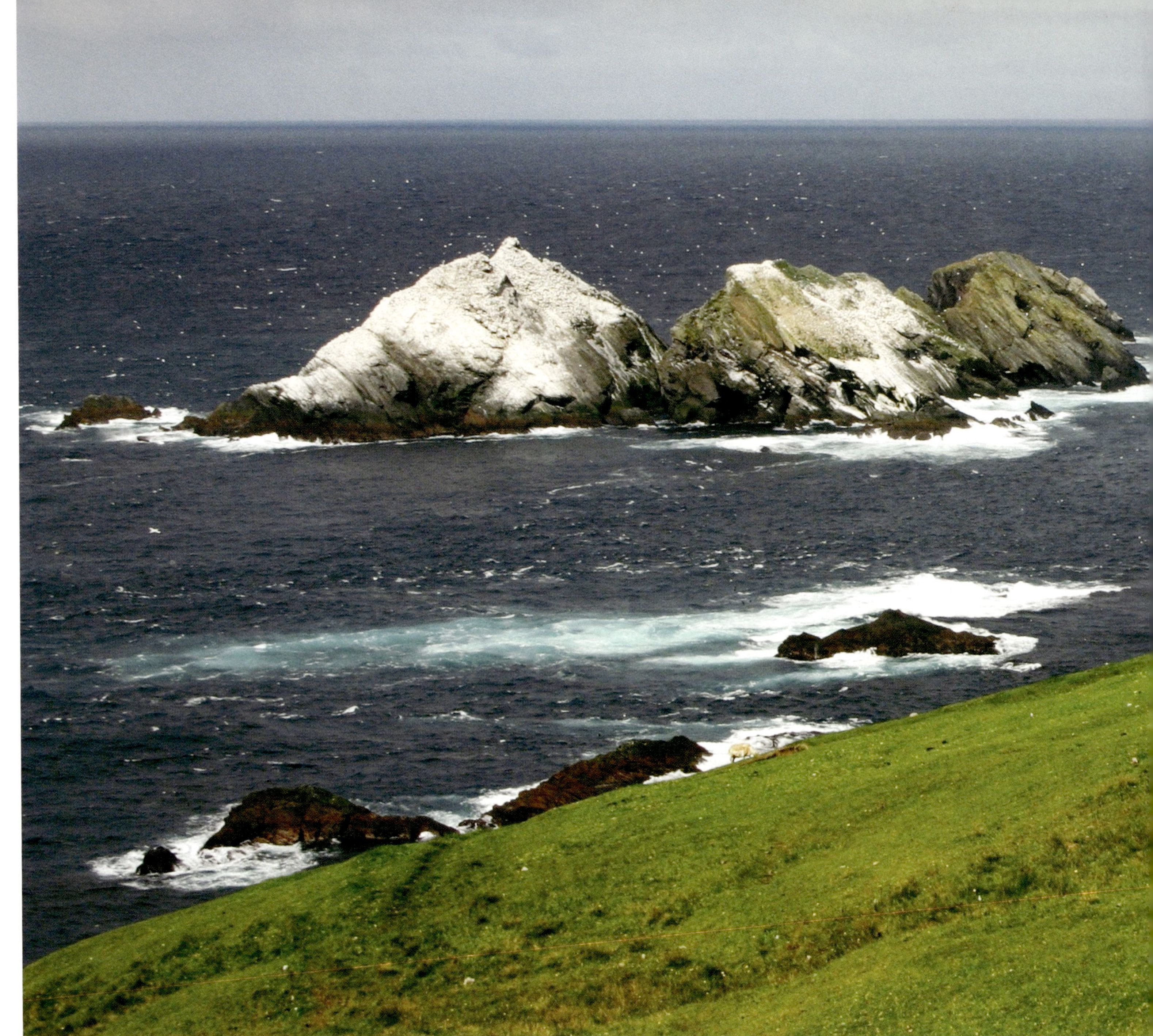

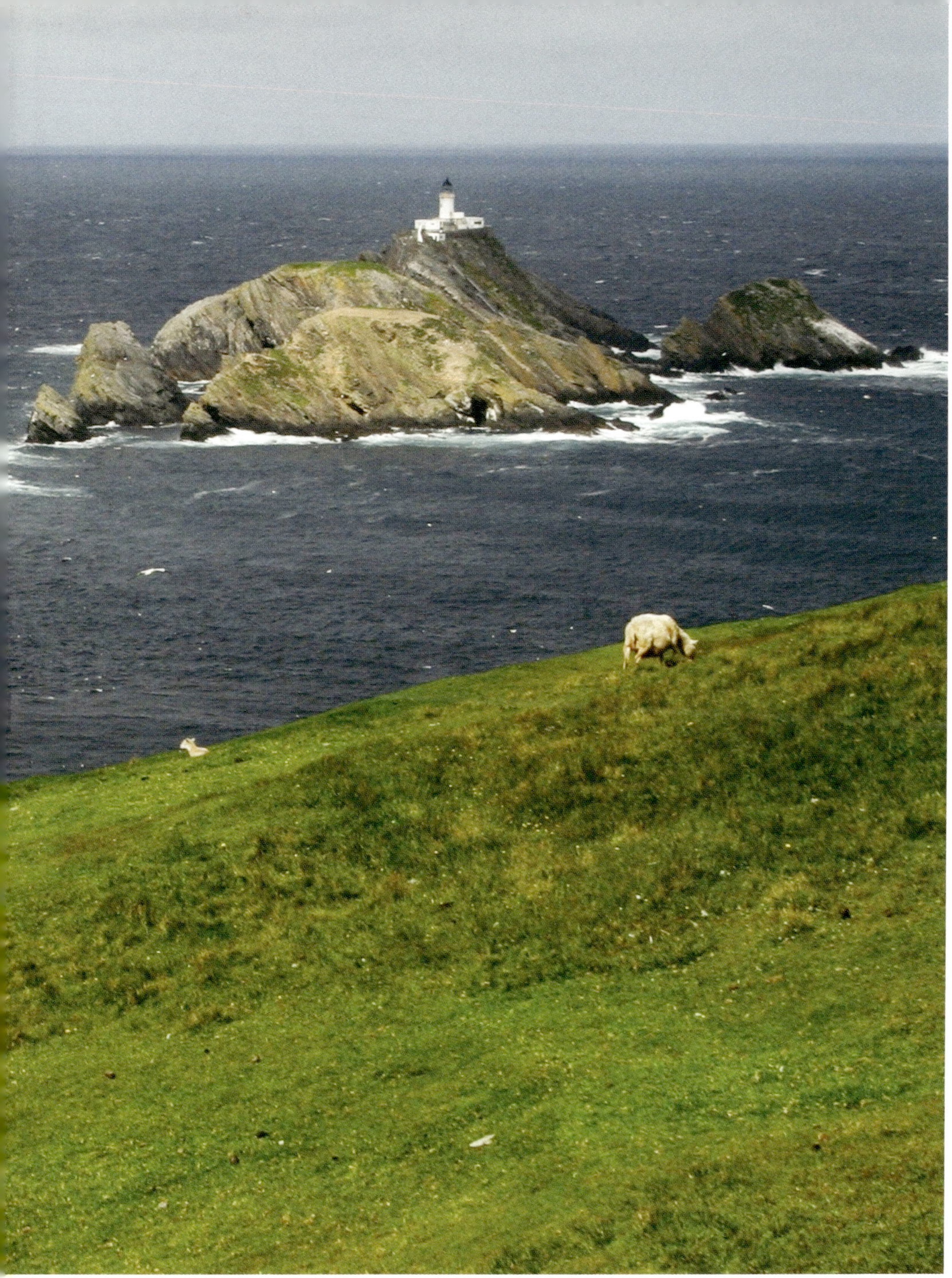

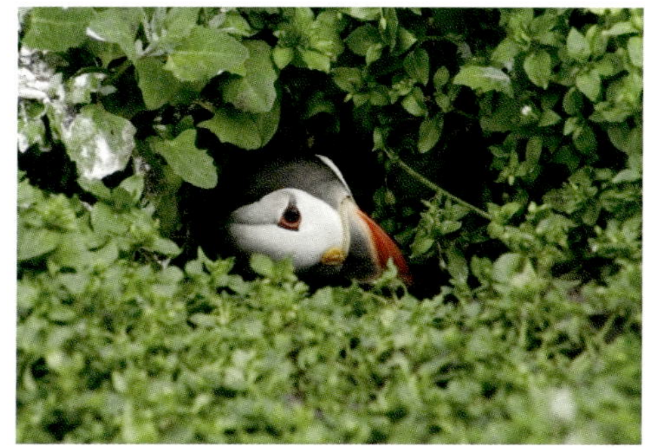

Hermaness National Nature Reserve is important as a nesting ground for seabirds. It is home during the summer months to 50,000 puffins and 32,000 gannets, as well as countless guillemots, razorbills, fulmars, kittiwakes, and shags. You walk across open moorland to get to the cliffs, and on these moors nest bonxies, Arctic skuas, red-throated divers, golden plover, and dunlin.

Off the northern tip of Hermaness lies the breathtaking fin of rock known as Muckle Flugga – the most northern point of Britain. The lighthouse on the right-hand skerry replaced the original lighthouse which was damaged by a huge winter storm. The first lighthouse was built in 1854, but its replacement, built by Thomas and David Stevenson was not lit until 1858. The white on the rocks on the left are nesting gannets and their copious guano!

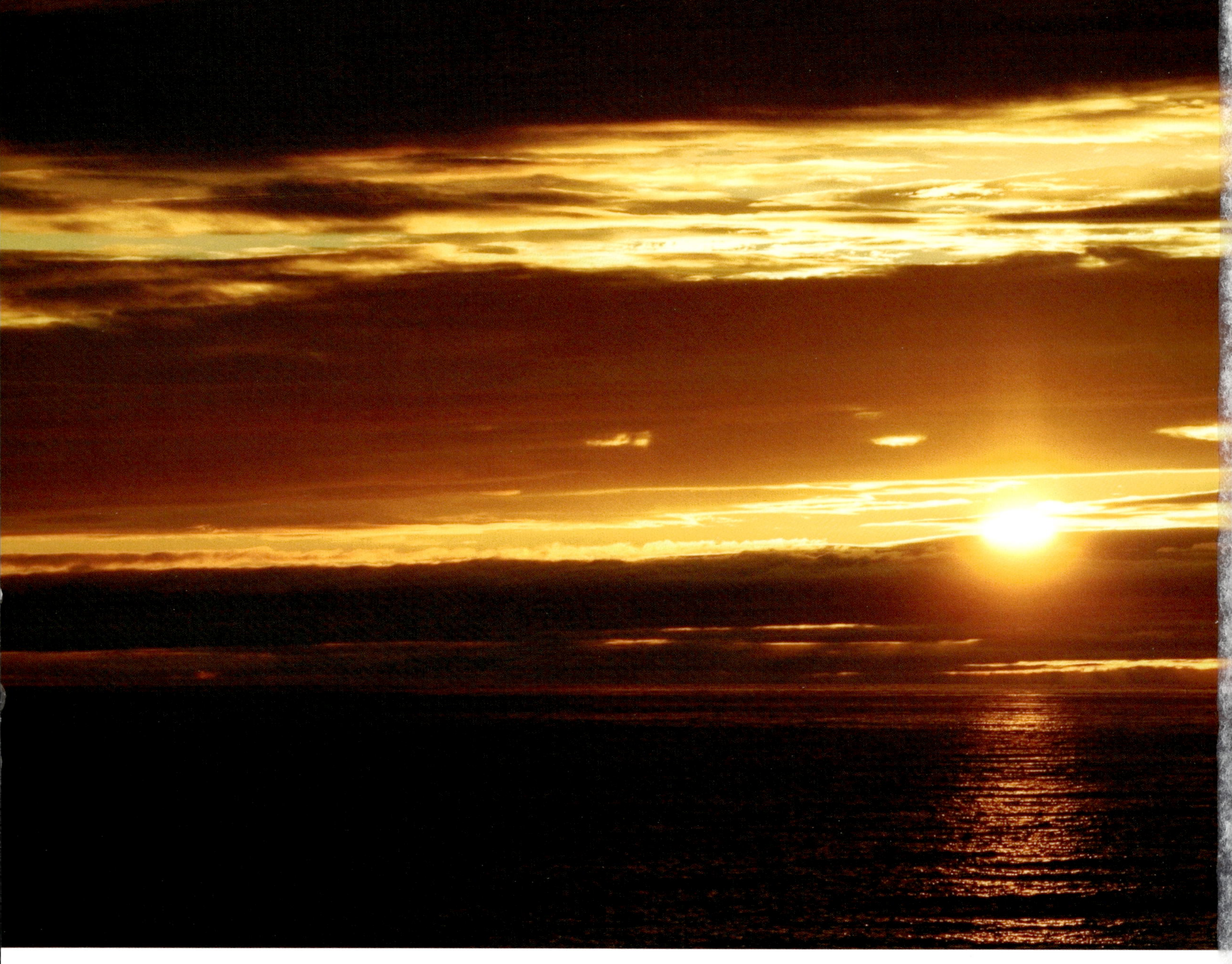

A moody, fiery sunset from the clifftops at Hermaness National Nature Reserve on Unst.